DENIZATIONS, NATURALIZATIONS,

AND OATHS OF ALLEGIANCE

IN COLONIAL

NEW YORK

By
KENNETH SCOTT
And
KENN STRYKER-RODDA

CLEARFIELD COMPANY

Reprinted for
Clearfield Company, Inc. by
Genealogical Publishing Co., Inc.
Baltimore, Maryland
1994

Library of Congress Catalogue Card Number 75-10680
International Standard Book Number 0-8063-0679-3

PUBLISHER'S NOTE

Special thanks are due Mrs. Dorothy Scutt
for typing the manuscript of this book.

Made in the United States of America

TABLE OF CONTENTS

INTRODUCTION

DENIZATION AND NATURALIZATION

An alien who took up residence in England or in one of its colonies was deeply concerned with the right to acquire real estate, to dispose of it, to bequeath it, or to inherit it. Likewise, he desired the liberty to trade and traffic, to own vessels, or to be a master of a ship.

According to English law, an alien could neither hold nor bequeath real property, and if he acquired such, it escheated to the Crown upon his demise. Prospective colonists who were aliens therefore frequently sought either denization by letters patent from the King, or naturalization by special act of Parliament. Denization was more quickly obtained than naturalization and was generally considered adequate, despite some disadvantages as compared with naturalization. An alien was careful to provide himself in England with a certificate from a notary to the effect that the notary had seen said alien's name on a list of persons granted letters of denization. Such certificate was carefully kept and the person endenized would have it recorded by the Secretary of the province in which he settled.

It soon became the practice of some governors to grant letters of denization to foreign Protestants in the belief that a governor or a deputy of the King had such powers. Denization in New York was a comparatively expensive procedure, for Governor Bellomont in 1699 charged twelve shillings, while Governor Fletcher had charged ten pounds for himself and five pounds for the Attorney General (CDNY 4:520).

In 1692 Chief Justice North in England gave the opinion that denization in a colony was purely local and did not extend to England or to other English colonies (Shaw I:xxviii). Indeed, denization in the colonies was terminated as a result of action taken in the case of a French alien, Arnold Nodine, to whom, in November 1677, Governor Fletcher of New York granted letters of denization. The letters specified that Nodine was enabled "to take and hold lands, tenements, hereditaments, etc., to himself, his heirs and assigns in fee simple, with power to sue and be sued, and to enjoy all other rights and privileges as a natural born subject of that Province without any restriction or regard to the ... Act of Navigation or any other statute of England." The Attorney General in London studied the case and reported to the Privy Council as follows: "We do not find that the said Co. Fletcher had any express power by his Commission to grant any letters of denization" (Acts of the Privy Council, Colonial Series 2:348). His report led to an order in Council on 18 January 1700 that no governor was to grant letters of denization unless expressly authorized to do so in his commission. The order further specified: "No act of denization or naturalization in any colony will qualify any person to be master

of a ship within any of the statutes made in this Kingdom which re-
quire masters of ships to be Englishmen" (<u>Calendar</u> <u>of</u> <u>State</u> <u>Papers</u>:
<u>Colonial</u> <u>1700</u>:34).

Since by 1700 it was no longer possible to obtain letters of
denization from a governor, citizenship could be acquired in New
York by an alien not previously granted denization in England or
naturalized by act of Parliament, only by an act of naturalization
by the Provincial Assembly and the Legislative Council. Like other
acts, naturalization laws were subject to veto by the governor or
the Crown. Moreover, an act could only authorize naturalization;
each person had to complete the process by taking an oath of allegiance within a specified time. Some dilatory persons had to start
the process over again.

Naturalization was granted in New York on various occasions:
(1) In 1664, by the terms of the surrender of New Netherland to
England; (2) by a proclamation made 9 November 1694 by Governor
Edmond Andross confirming all grants, privileges, concessions, or
estates legally possessed in the time of the late Dutch government;
(3) by an act of the General Assembly assented to in 1683 by Governor Thomas Dongan and a proclamation of 13 June 1687; (4) by an
act passed 5 July 1715 declaring that "all Persons of Forreign Birth
heretofore Inhabiting within this Colony and dying Seized of any
Lands, Tenements, or Hereditaments shall be forever hereafter Deemed,
Taken, and Esteemed to have been Naturalized, and for Naturalizing
all Protestants of Forreign Birth now Inhabiting within this Colony
(Laws, ch. 293).

The next general naturalization in New York was by an act of
13 George II, c.7 in 1740, for "naturalizing such foriegn Protestants as are or shall settle in any of his Majesty's colonies in
America." It provided that such foreigners living for seven years
in a colony, on taking the oaths and the Sacrament (Quakers and Jews
exempted), were to be deemed natives of the Kingdom provided they
did not absent themselves from the colony more than two months at a
time. A certificate of naturalization was to be given, and the
Secretary of the colony was to send to the Office of Trade and Plan-
tation in London an annual list of persons naturalized under the act.
No person so naturalized was entitled to be of the Privy Council of
Parliament or to hold office of trust or receive grants of land from
the Crown.

Such remained naturalization law up to the American Revolution,
save for three changes: by an act of 20 George II,c.44 an affirma-
tion of fidelity and abjuration was allowed in place of the naturalization oaths to extend the benefits of the act to the Moravian
brethren; an act of 2 George III, c. 25 naturalized such foreign
Protestants as well, as officers or soldiers who had served or should
serve in the Royal American Regiment or as engineers in America for
two years, upon their taking the oath and subscribing to declaration
as in 1 George I, c. 13, and taking the Sacrament.

Fees charged varied greatly. In 1708 Domine Kocherthal and
the members of his group paid no fee. By the act of 5 July 1715
(Laws, ch. 293), six shillings were to be paid to the judge and

three to the clerk when taking the test and abjuration oath, and
one shilling six pence to each of them for a certificate. Under the
act of 3 July 1718 (Laws, ch. 356), the fees were the same except
that judge and clerk each received three shillings for the certificate. The same scale of fees was authorized by the act of 27 July
1721 (Laws, ch. 418). By the act of 8 November 1735 (Laws, ch. 634),
ten shillings was to be paid to the Speaker of the General Assembly,
six shillings to the judge of court, and three shillings to the clerk
of court.

Some bills authorizing naturalizations seem never to have been
passed. From the Journal of the Votes and Proceedings of the General Assembly of the Colony of New-York (New-York: Hugh Gaine, 1764,
1766) and the Journal of the Legislative Council of the Colony of
New-York (Albany: Weed, Parson & Co., 1861) it appears that there
were at least six: (1) "At a Councill held at ffort James Thursday
ye 18th of August 1687...Petition of Daniel Duchemin and othr
ffrenchmen praying to be naturalized. Read. Ordered, yt it be
referred and yt the Attorny General Draw a Bill for Naturalizeing
the Petitioners." No more is heard of it. The names of the other
petitioners appear in CEM 167. The names of these and all other
unsuccessful petitioners are included in the naturalization list
that follows.
(2) On 28 August 1731 Huro Ellis petitioned for leave to present a
bill for naturalization, which was done on the 30th. On 1 September
Theunis Visser requested his name to be added, on 4 September Anna
D'Harriette, wife of Benjamin, made the same request, and on 10 September Phillipus Langerbeen's name was added. The bill, with several amendments (not specified), was ordered engrossed on 16 September and sent to the Council the next day. There the bill was read
on 20 and 21 September "and committed to the Gentlemen of the Council or any five of them." Ellis's name appears in Laws, Chapter 586
(14 December 1732); none of the others' names appears in a naturalization act.
(3) On 31 October 1739 Johan William Smith, Nicholas Mispagh,
Johannis Crist, Adam Neuppennye, Hendrick Weaver, Andries Wyse, Johan
Tennis Sensebach, Johan Crist Sensebach, Philip Miller, Paul Francis
Cebe, Mariane Cebe, Johannis Miller, and Christian Bording petitioned to be naturalized. The bill was read twice on 1 November and
"committed to the Members of New-York, and County of Westchester,
or the major part of them." On 3 November Henry Heder, John Meintzer, and Lawrence Meintzer petitioned to be included, and on 13 November Jacob Ferro, Jr. and Levy Sammuel made the same request. The
amended bill was passed on third reading 13 November and sent to the
Council. There it was twice read on 15 November, and passed with
further amendment on the 16th. However, the Assembly refused to ac-
cept the Council amendment, and, the Council being adamant, the bill
died. Nine were subsequently naturalized in 1740/1.
(4) On 11 November 1748 the Assembly received notice that the bill
to naturalize Hendrick Van Denham, Adrian Houtvat, and Haeman Levy
had been amended in committee, and on the following day approved
adding thereto the names of Louis DuBois, James Harpain, Elias Bonnain, Isaac Van Haeren, Casper Engelbert Kemmena, Jacob Stinebranner,
John Ute, Godfrey Miller, John Smith, Jacob Metger, Charles Shults,

Hendrick Snyder, and John Frederick Neithe. On 12 November, after a first reading in the Council, a second reading was ordered, but no further action is recorded. Some of the persons listed were authorized naturalized on 24 November (Chapter 902), where the names were spelled somewhat differently, Metger being Matcher, for instance.
(5) According to the printed journals, an act for naturalizing John Will, Gottlieb Wohlhaupter, Hayman David, Manuel Josephson, Gershom Moses Levy, Benjamin Lyon, Jonas Solomon, Levy Hart, Johan Casper Zincke, Johannes Kleyn, Myer Levy, Jacob Graf, John Anderson, and John Brooks was passed by the Assembly on 27 November 1756; it was read for the first time in the Council on 26 November and a second reading ordered. There is no further entry.
(6) "An Act for Naturalizing the Several Persons therein named" was passed by the Assembly 23 March 1775, read in the Council on 23 March, given a second reading the next day, and committed. Because of the unsettled times, no colonial laws were passed after 3 April 1775, and this bill did not become a law. Neither the Assembly nor the Council journal lists the names of the persons for whom the bill was presented.

The lists that comprise the body of this book are presented in three groups. In one alphabetical list appear the names of persons granted letters of denization who removed to or resided in New York. If denization was granted in London, it is so indicated; otherwise, it was by grant of the colonial governor. Similarly, the list of persons naturalized or authorized naturalized - with occasional added notation as to some individuals - has been arranged alphabetically. These names have been found chiefly in the Laws of the Province of New York, in naturalizations by the acts of 1715 and 1740, and occasionally by act of Parliament when the alien so naturalized had the fact officially recorded in New York. Because of the alphabetical arrangement of the first two lists, only the names of those mentioned incidentally are to be found in the index. However, because of the number of lists involved and the fact that most of them are not arranged alphabetically, all names appearing in the section on oaths of allegiance have been indexed.

We gratefully acknowledge assistance from the Staffs of the Manuscript Division of the New York State Library, the Office of the Secretary of State in Albany, the New-York Historical Society, the New York Genealogical and Biographical Society, the Manuscript Division of the New York Public Library and the Office of the County Clerk of New York.

SOURCE REFERENCES

Alb. CCM   Albany Common Council Minutes in Manuscript Division,
New York State Library.

CDM   _Calendar of Historical Manuscripts in the Office of the
Secretary of State, Albany, N.Y., Part I, Dutch Manuscripts,
1630-1664_, ed. by E. B. O'Callaghan (Albany: Weed, Parsons &
Co., 1865).

CDNY   _Documents Relative to the Colonial History of the State
of New York_. vols. 1-11 ed. by E. B. O'Callaghan; vols. 12-15
ed. by Berthold Fernow (Albany: Weed, Parsons & Co., 1856-
1887).

CEM   _Calendar of Historical Manuscripts in the Office of the
Secretary of State, Albany, N.Y., Part II, English Manuscripts,
1664-1776_, ed. by E. B. O'Callagahn (Albany: Weed, Parsons &
Co., 1866).

Cert. Min.   Minister who certified the applicant had taken commun-
ion in a Protestant church.

CLNY   _Colonial Laws of New York_, 1664-1775. 5 vols. (Albany:
James B. Lyon, 1894).

CNYHS 1885 _Collections of the New-York Historical Society for the
Year 1885_ (New York, 1886).

C.O.   Colonial Office. Records are designated by number and
by double letters (Gg, Oo, Ss, etc.)

Deed Bk BB   Original in the office of the Clerk of Ulster County,
Kingston, N.Y. (See also Rec. 103:85-88.)

Deeds   Manuscript in the Office of the Secretary of State as
of 1974.

Den.   Denization or endenized

DHNY   _The Documentary History of the State of New York_, ed.
by E. B. O'Callaghan, 4 vols. (Albany: Weed, Parsons & Co.,
1849-51).

ECM   _Minutes of the Executive Council of the Province of New
York, 1668-1673_, ed. by Victor Hugo Paltsits. 2 vols. (Albany:
State of New York 1910).

EP   Andrew Elliot papers in the Manuscript Division, New
York State Library.

Gen. Ent.   _General Entries Vol. I, 1664-65. State Library Bulletin - History No. 2_ (Albany, 1899).

Gottesman   Rita A. Gottesman, _The Arts and Crafts in New York,
1762-1776_. (N.Y.: New-York Historical Society, 1938).

HHN   _History of New Netherland_, by E. B. O'Callaghan, 2 vols.
(N.Y.: D. Appleton & Co., 1846,1848).

Huhner   Leon Huhner, "Naturalization of Jews in New York under
the Act of 1740," _Publications of the American Jewish Historical Society XIII_, 1905: 1-6.

Laws ch.   Laws of the colony of New York, chapter (as printed in
CLNY).

Laws and Ordinances of New Netherland, 1638-1675, comp. & tr. by
E. B. O'Callaghan (Albany: Weed, Parsons & Co., 1868).

lic.   License

MCC   Minutes of the Common Council of the City of New York, 1675-1776. 8 vols. 1905.

MCM   Mayor's Court Minutes, manuscript in the Hall of Records, New York City.

MCRM   Rough Minutes of the Mayor's Court, manuscript in the Hall of Records, New York City.

NYC   New York City.

NY Col Mss New York Colonial Manuscripts in the Manuscript Division, New York State Library.

NYHMD   New York Historical Manuscripts: Dutch, translated and annotated by Arnold J. F. van Laer, edited and indexed by Kenneth Scott and Kenn Stryker-Rodda (Baltimore: Genealogical Publishing Co., 1974).

NYHS Oath Roll   Manuscript at the New-York Historical Society.

NYM   New York Marriages Previous to 1784 (Names of Persons for Whom Marriage Licenses Were Issued by the Secretary of the Province of New York, Previous to 1784, with 3 supplements, Baltimore: Genealogical Publishing Co., 1968).

NYPL   New York City Public Library manuscript.

Patents   Manuscripts in the Manuscript Division, New York State Library.

Rec.   New York Genealogical and Biographical Record, 1870.

RNA   The Records of New Amsterdam from 1653 to 1674, ed. by Berthold Fernow. 7 vols. (N.Y.: Knickerbocker Press, 1897).

Samuel   Wilfred S. Samuel, "A List of Jewish Persons Endenized and Naturalized 1609-1799," Miscellanies of the Jewish Histori-cal Society of England, Part VII, (London, 1970): 111-44.

SCJ   Supreme Court Journals. Manuscript in the Hall of Records, New York City.

Scott, Adm. Bonds   Kenneth Scott, Genealogical Data from New York Administration Bonds (N.Y.: The New York Genealogical and Biographical Society, 1969).

Scott, Adm. Papers   Kenneth Scott, Genealogical Data from Adminis-tration Papers from the New York State Court of Appeals in Albany (N.Y.: The National Society of Colonial Dames in the State of New York, 1972).

Shaw I   William A. Shaw, Letters of Denization and Acts of Natu-ralization for Aliens in England and Ireland, 1603-1700 (Lymington, The Hugenot Society of London, Publications Vol. XVIII, 1911).

Shaw II   William A. Shaw, Letters of Denization and Acts of Natu-ralization for Aliens in England and Ireland, 1701-1800 (Man-chester: The Hugenot Society of London, Publications Vol. XXVII, 1923).

T.R.   Town Records.

WNYHS   Abstracts of Wills, 17 vols. Collections of the New-York Historical Society, Vols. XXV-XLI, 1892-1908.

Additional Sources

L. F. Bellinger, "Our Early Citizens. Names of Those Taking the oath of Allegiance from 1715 to 1773" in The Book of Names ed. by Lou D. MacWeathy (St. Johnsville, N.Y.: The Enterprise and News, 1933): 1-7.

Montague S. Guiseppi, Naturalizations of Foreign Protestants in the American and West Indian Colonies (The Hugenot Society of London, Publications Vol. XXIV, 1921. Reprint: Baltimore: Genealogical Publishing Co., 1964).

Harlem Records: among James Riker papers in Manuscript Division, New York Public Library.

Letters of Denization: manuscript in the New-York Historical Society.

"The Oath of Abjuration, 1715-1716," Quarterly Bulletin of the New-York Historical Society III (1919), pp. 35-40.

Cora Start, Naturalization in the English Colonies in America," American Historical Association, Annual Report for the Year 1893: 317-28.

Kenn Stryker-Rodda, "Ulster County Naturalizations, 1715," New York Genealogical and Biographical Record 103 (1972): 85-88.

Van Rensselaer Bowier Manuscripts, ed. by A. J. F. van Laer, Albany, 1910.

Richard J. Wolfe, "The Colonial Naturalization Act of 1740 with a List of Persons Naturalized in New York Colony, 1740-1729," New York Genealogical and Biographical Record 94 (1963): 132-47.

DENIZATIONS and LICENSES

ABELAIN, John - den. London 24 June 1703 (Shaw II:35) and cert.
3 July 1703 (Deeds 10:17-18)

ABELAIN, John (son of John) - den. London 24 June 1703 (Shaw II:35)
and cert. 3 July 1703 (Deeds 10:17-18)

ABOAB, Moses, of New York - lic. 25 June 1684 to trade and traffic
within the city (CEM:130); possibly Moses Aboab Furtado, as
Ishack Aboab of London was also known as Ishac Aboab Furtado
(Shaw I:239)

AERTSE, William - den. oaths 8 Nov. 1698 (Pat. 7:215)

ALLAIRE, Alexander - den. 6 Feb. 1695/6 (Pat. 1696-1712:10)

ANTHONY, Allard - den. 16 Jan. 1664/5; "has taken oath of allegiance; is free denizen of New York, permitted freely to trade
or traffic" (Gen. Ent.: 183-4)

APELL, Hendryck - pet. 3 Sept. 1694 for letters of den. (CEM:242);
den. 3 Sept. 1694 and oaths administered 4 Sept. 1694 (Pat.
6:467)

AUPVIN, Isaac Zacharias - den. 12 Dec. 1695 and oaths administered
31 Jan. 1695/6 (Pat. 6:553)

BALCK, Jacob - pet. 21 Mar. 1702 for letters of den., with cert.
from Rev. Du Bois, and cert. of the Lt.-Gov. and Council recom-
mending Balck be endenized (CEM:291)

BARAND, Lazare - took den. oaths 22 Oct. 1697 (Pat. 7:161)

BARBARIE, John - den. London 16 Dec. 1687 (Shaw I:193) and cert.
by Nicholas Hayward, notary, in London 17 Jan. 1687/8
(Deeds 8:257-8)

BARBARIE, John Peter (son of John) - den. London 16 Dec. 1687
(Shaw I:193) and cert. by Nicholas Hayward, notary, in London
17 Jan. 1687/8 (Deeds 8:257-8)

BARBARIE, Peter (son of John) - den. London 16 Dec. 1687 (Shaw I:
193) and cert. by Nicholas Hayward, notary, in London 17 Jan.
1687-8 (Deeds 8:257-8)

BARGE, Jean - pet. 28 Sept. 1695 for letters of den. granted
(CEM:247)

BARREAU, Lazare - pet. 14 Oct. 1697 of Peter Perret for letters of
den. for Barreau and other French Protestants taken in a prize
ship on the Banks of Newfoundland (NY Col Mss 41:120)

BAYARD, Nicholas - den. 12 Oct. 1668 (ECM I:62, note 4)

BEIGNEN, Henry - den. 6 Feb. 1695/6 (Pat. 1696-1712:10)

BERTRAND, Peter - den. London 11 Mar. 1699/1700 (Shaw I:313) and
cert. by Thomas Lawrence, notary, in London 18 Mar. 1699/1700
(Deeds 10:67)

BOISBILLAND/BOISBELLAUD, John - den. 2 Sept. 1685 (CEM:140); John
Boisbilland, of Gravesend, in country 2 years, took oath of al-
legiance and "had Letters of Denisatie" 26-30 Sept. 1687
(DHNY I:432)

BONNEFOY, David - den. 6 Feb. 1695/6 (Pat. 1696-1712:10)

BOSMON, Francois - den. 16 Aug. 1686, with liberty to trade or
traffic (CEM:146)

BOURDET, Pierre - den. 10 Mar. 1686, with liberty to trade or
traffic (CEM:143)

BOURDET, Samuel - den. London 5 Jan. 1686/7 and cert. 18 Jan.
1686/7 by Thomas Lawrence, notary, in London, recorded 11 May
1703 (Deeds 10:46)

BOUTINEAU, Stephen - den. London 24 June 1703 (Shaw II:35); cert.
by Thomas Lawrence, notary, in London 3 July 1703 (Deeds 10:46)

BOUYER, John - den. 2 Oct. 1695; oaths administered 23 Oct. 1695
(Pat. 6:551); a Jean Bouyer was a clothmaker (NY Col Mss 40:74)

BOWYER, Etienne - den. 29 July 1686, with liberty to trade or
traffic (CEM:145)

BRANT, Albertus - den. 14 July 1686, with liberty to trade or
traffic (CEM:145)

BROUSSARD, Saviott, alias DESCHAMPS - pet. 12 Mar. 1695/6 for letters of den. (CEM:250); took oaths 17 Mar. 1695/6 (Pat. 7:9)

BROWN, Joseph - den. 12 May 1686, with liberty to trade or traffic
(CEM:144); a Joseph Browne on 9 Oct. 1686 was granted license to
peddle in Ulster Co. (CEM:147)

BUENO, Joseph - granted license 8 Feb. 1683 to trade and traffic
in New York City (CEM:154); den. London 2 Oct. 1662 to a Joseph
Bueno (Shaw I:89)

BURETELL, Pierre - den. 18 Aug. 1686, with liberty to trade or
traffic (CEM:146); a Peter Burtel was granted den. London 9 Apr.
1687 (Shaw I:183) and a Peter Buretell was granted den. London
29 Sept. 1698 (Shaw I:291)

CAILLARD, Isaaq - den. 6 Feb. 1695/6 (Pat. 1696-1712:10)

CANCHE, Ayme - den. 10 Sept. 1686 (CEM:146)

CANON, Andre/Andreas - den. London 3 July 1701 (Shaw II:10); original cert. 15 July 1701 by Thomas Lawrence, notary, in London
(document now in N-Y Hist. Soc.); his son, Abraham Canon den.
3 July 1701 in London (Shaw II:10)

CARTIER, John, of New Rochelle - pet. 6 June 1695 for letters of
den. (CEM:245); his wife ("who is with child") and their two
children dwelt in New Rochelle about 9 years (NY Col Mss 40:26)

CHINTRIER, Marie ("now wife of Saviott Broussard, alias Deschamps")
- den. 12 Mar. 1695/6 and oaths taken 19 Mar. 1695/6 (Pat. 7:
9-11)

CHRISTIANSE, David - den. and oaths taken 29 Jan. 1693/4 (Pat. 6:448)

COCK, John - den. 12 Dec. and oaths taken 17 Dec. 1695 (Pat. 6:551)

COESAART, John - den. oaths taken 4 Nov. 1692 (Pat. 6:397)

COLLINEAU, Mathew - pet. 12 July 1694 for letters of den. (CEM:241);
den. and oaths taken 12 July 1694 (Pat. 6:452); made freeman of
NYC 14 June 1698 as merchant (CNYHS 1885:61); a Mathew Collineau,
born at Paris, France, (son of Mathew Collineau by Jane his wife)
was naturalized in England 11 Apr. 1700 (Shaw I:303)

CONSTANT, Jean - den. 6 Feb. 1695/6 (Pat. 1696-1712:10)

CORNIFLEAU, Laurens - pet. 1691 to be made burgher and citizen
(CEM:206)

COTHONNEAU, Guilleaume (son of Marie) - den. 6 Feb. 1695/6 (Pat.
1696-1712:10) (See CEM:240 - 21 May 1694 Guillaume was at New
Rochelle)

COTHONNEAU, Marie - den. 6 Feb. 1695/6 (Pat. 1696-1712:10)

COUSTURIER, Hendrick - den. 8 July 1672 (ECM I:130, note 6)

COUTY, Rabba – den. before 1671 (Jacob R. Marcus, Early American
    Jewry:41)
CRUGER, John – den. and oaths taken 30 Mar. 1694/5 (Pat. 6:533)

DACOSTA/DECOSTA, Isaac – den. 29 July 1686, with liberty to trade
    or traffic (CEM:145,155)
DAS (or VAS?), Pierre – den. 6 Feb. 1695/6 (Pat. 1696-1712:10)
DAVENE, John – den. 17 Sept. 1685, with lic. to trade or traffic
    (CEM:140)
DE BONREPOS, David – den. 6 Feb. 1695/6 (Pat. 1696-1712:10)
DECOR (? LECOR), Pierre – den. 16 Aug. 1686, with liberty to trade
    or traffic (CEM:145)
DE FENNE, Francis – took den. oaths 1 June 1698 (Pat. 7:215)
DE HAART, Balthazer – den. 16 Jan. 1664/5 (Gen. Ent.:184)
DE KOCHERTHAL, see KOCHERTHAL
DE LA CHESNAYE, Charles Aubert – lic. 13 May 1684 to bring beavers,
    peltry and other goods in his vessel from Quebec to New York,
    and to trade and traffic in that city (CEM:128)
DE LANCEY, Stephen – den. London 5 Mar. 1685/6 (Shaw I:177) and re-
    corded 7 July 1686, with lic. to trade or traffic (CEM:145);
    made freeman of NYC 12 July 1686 as merchant (CNYHS 1885:53)
DE MEYER, Nicholas – den. 21 Mar. 1664/5 (ECM I:179, note 3)
DE PAUL, Asher Michells – den. 8 Feb. 1683 to trade or traffic
    within NYC (CEM:154)
DESBROSSES, James – den. London 24 June 1703 (Shaw II:30) and cert.
    by Thomas Lawrence, notary, in London (Deeds 10:218-9)
DES IMBRES, Rene Fesan – den. 18 Sept. 1686, with lic. to trade or
    traffic (CEM:147)
DESOSAMENDES, Abraham – lic. 8 Feb. 1683 to trade and traffic within
    NYC (CEM:154)
DE WILDE, John – took oaths 17 Feb. 1697/8 (Pat. 7:183)
DOUBLET, Jean – den. 23 Dec. 1695 and oaths taken 27 Jan. 1695/6
    (Pat. 6:553)
DOUSSINET, Etienne – den. 17 Sept. 1685, with lic. to trade or
    traffic (CEM:140)
DUPINE, Peter Chevalier – took den. oaths 7 Oct. 1698 (Pat. 7:214)
DUPUY, Andrew – den. London 29 Sept. 1698 (Shaw I:289); Henry Smith,
    notary, in London cert. 12 Oct. 1698 as to letters of den. per-
    mitting to Dupuy all privileges and to be a mariner or master
    of ships (Deeds 10:23); Andrew Dupuy, master of sloop Jacob,
    petitions 15 Oct. 1703 for redenization, having lost by ship-
    wreck his denization papers (CEM:317); made freeman of NYC 30
    Apr. 1706 as mariner (CNYHS 1885:87)

ENDRIVETT, John – took den. oaths 18 Apr. 1695 (Pat. 6:536)

FAGETT, John – took den. oaths 13 May 1699 (Pat. 7:215)
FEBER, Abraham (son of Isaac)– den. London 25 Aug. 1708 (Shaw II:
    68; Deeds 10:241)
FEBER, Catherine (wife of Isaac) – den. London 25 August. 1708
    (Shaw II:68; Deeds 10:241)
FEBER, Isaac – den. London 25 Aug. 1708 (Shaw II:68; Deeds 10:241)
FEWERT/FUERT, Bartholomew – pet. 17 June 1698 for letters of den.,
    with attorney general's report thereon (CEM:262); den. oaths
    taken 17 June 1698 (Pat. 7:414)

FIERE, Andrew (son of Daniel) - den. London 25 Aug. 1708 (Shaw II:
68; Deeds 10:241)

FIERE, Anne Maria (wife of Daniel) - den. London 25 Aug. 1708
(Shaw II: 68; Deeds 10:241)

FIERE, Daniel - den. London 25 Aug. 1708 (Shaw II:68; Deeds 10:241)

FIERE, Johannes (son of Daniel) - den. London 25 Aug. 1708 (Shaw
II:68; Deeds 10:241)

FISCHER, Johannes - den. London 25 Aug. 1708 (Shaw II:67; Deeds
10:241)

FISCHER, Maria Barbara (wife of Johannes) - den. London 25 Aug. 1708
(Shaw II:67; Deeds 10:241)

FLEURIAU, Daniel - den. 29 July 1686, with liberty to trade or
traffic (CEM:145). Den. London 16 Dec. 1687 to a Daniel
Fleuriau (Shaw I:197)

FLEURIAU, Pierre - den. 29 July 1686, with liberty to trade or
traffic (CEM:145). Den. London 9 Apr. 1687 to Peter Fleuriau
(Shaw I:186)

FOURRESTIER, Charles - den. 6 Feb. 1695/6 (Pat. 1696-1712:10)

FOURRESTIER, Theophile - den. 6 Feb. 1695/6 (Pat. 1696-1712:10)

GABAY, Isaac - den. 15 June 1686, with liberty to trade or traffic
(CEM:144); lic. 9 Oct. 1705 to peddle in Ulster Co. (CEM:147)
On 24 Aug. 1705 Solomon Gabay, age 16, with consent of his
father, Isaac Gabey, merchant, was apprenticed to Isaac Rodrigues Marques, merchant (CNYHS 1885:610)

GARNER, Jean - den. 23 Dec. 1695 and oaths taken 27 Jan. 1695/6
(Pat. 6:553)

GARROTT, Jacob - den. 17 Sept. 1685, with lic. to trade or traffic
(CEM:140)

GAUDINEAU, Ellena (dau. of Dr. Giles) - den. 26 Aug. 1686, with
liberty to trade or traffic (CEM:146)

GAUDINEAU, Gilles/Giles - den. 26 Aug. 1686 with liberty to trade
or traffic (CEM:146); made freeman of NYC 30 May 1702 as
chirurgeon (CNYHS 1885:83); see Kenneth Scott, "Giles Gaudineau
and his Medicines," Medical History 12 (1968):278-80

GAUDINEAU, Susanna (dau. of Dr. Giles) - den. 26 Aug. 1686, with
liberty to trade or traffic (CEM:146)

GELON, Louis - den. 23 Dec. 1695 and oaths taken 27 Jan. 1695/6
(Pat. 6:553)

GERBRANTS, Francis - den. London 24 June 1703 (Shaw II:33); cert.
5 July 1703 (Deeds 10:26)

GODIN, Pierre - den. 17 Sept. 1685, with lic. to trade or traffic
(NY Col Mss 33:180; CEM:140)

GOMEZ, Daniel, of New York, merchant - den. London 29 Dec. 1714
(Shaw II:122; Samuel:121)

GOMEZ, Jacob, of New York, merchant - den. London 29 Dec. 1714
(Shaw II:122; Samuel:121)

GOMEZ, Ludovico (Luis) - den. London 18 Apr. 1705 (Shaw II:47);
of New York according to Malcolm Stern

GOMEZ, Mordecay, of New York, merchant - den. London 29 Dec. 1714
(Shaw II:122; Samuel:121)

GRAVERAET, Isaac - den. NYC 9 Nov. 1670 "as being here at y^e
Surrend^r in 1664" (ECM I:159, note 3)

GUILLETT, Charles - den. London 29 Sept. 1698 (Shaw I:289; Deeds
9:654)

GUION/GOUIN, Abraham - pet. 14 Oct. 1697 of Peter Perret, Minister
of the French Church in NYC, for letters of den. for Abraham
Gouin and other French Protestants recently taken in a prize
captured on the Banks of Newfoundland (CEM:259; NY Col Mss
41:120); took den. oaths 22 Oct. 1697 (Pat. 7:161)
GUION, Louis - den. 6 Feb. 1695/6 (Pat. 1696-1712:10)
GUION, Louis (son of Louis) - den. 6 Feb. 1695/6 (Pat. 1696-1712:10)
GULCH , Anne Catharine (wife of Melchior) - den. London 25 Aug. 1708
(Shaw II:67; Deeds 10:241)
GULCH, Heinrich (son of Melchior) - den. London 25 Aug. 1708
(Shaw II:67; Deeds 10:241)
GULCH, Magdalene/Margaret (dau. of Melchior) - den. London 25 Aug.
1708 (Shaw II:67; Deeds 10:241)
GULCH, Melchior - den. London 25 Aug. 1708 (Shaw II:67; Deeds 10:
241)

HARRISON, Erasmus - den. 12 Sept. 1696 (NY Col Mss 40:201; CEM:253)
HART, Casper - den. 22 June 1686, with liberty to trade or traffic
(NY Col Mss 33:255; CEM:145)
HATIER, John - den. 30 May 1695; took oaths 11 June 1695 (Pat.
6:538)
HOWRIEAU, Daniel (brother of Pierre - den. 19 July 1686 (NY Col
Mss 34 Part I:11; CEM:155)
HOWRIEAU, Pierre - den. 19 July 1686 (NY Col Mss 34 Part I:11;
CEM:155)
HUBERTSON, Hubert - den. London 25 Aug. 1708 (Shaw II:68; Deeds
10:241)
HUBERTSON, Jacob (son of Hubert) - den. London 25 Aug. 1708 (Shaw II:
68; Deeds 10:241)

JAMAIN/JAMIN/JAMEINE, Elias - den. London 11 Mar. 1699/1700 (Shaw
I:315);Thomas Lawrence, notary, in London, attests 19 Mar.
1699/1700 that he saw the letters of den. (Deeds 10:200); recorded 25 June 1705 (Deeds 8:260, 10:200)
JOHNSON, Paulus - pet. 20 June 1686 for letters of den. (NY Col Mss
32:116; CEM:119); den. 22 June 1686, with liberty to trade or
traffic (NY col Mss 33:257; CEM:145)
JOLYNE/JOLAIN, Andrew - den. 6 Aug. 1686, with liberty to trade or
traffic (NY Col Mss 33:277, 281; CEM:145)

KOCHERTHAL/DE KOCHERTHAL, Benigna Sibylle (dau. of Rev. Joshua) -
den. London 25 Aug. 1708 (Shaw II:67; Deeds 10:241)
KOCHERTHAL/DE KOCHERTHAL, Christian Joshua (son of Rev. Joshua) -
den. London 25 Aug. 1708 (Shaw II:67; Deeds 10:241)
KOCHERTHAL/DE KOCHERTHAL, Rev. Joshua - den. London 25 Aug. 1708
(Shaw II:67; Deeds 10:241)
KOCHERTHAL/DE KOCHERTHAL, Sibylle Charlotte (wife of Rev. Joshua) -
den. London 25 Aug. 1708 (Shaw II:67; Deeds 10:241)
KOCHERTHAL/DE KOCHERTHAL, Susanne Sibylle (dau. of Rev. Joshua) -
den. London 25 Aug. 1708 (Shaw II:67; Deeds 10:241)

LAFORT, Marias - took den. oaths 27 Mar. 1693 (Pat. 6:398-9)
LANDRIN, Guilleaume - den. 6 Feb. 1695/6 (Pat. 1696-1712:10)
LA NORR, Isaac - den. 14 May 1696; oaths taken 13 June 1696
(Pat. 7:36)

LA TOURRETTE/LETOURRETT, Jean/John - pet. 28 Sept. 1695 for letters
   of den. (NY Col Mss 40:74; CEM:247): den. 2 Oct. 1695 and oaths
   taken 28 Oct. 1695 (Pat. 6:551)
LAURANS, John - den. London 24 June 1703 (Shaw II:33); Thomas
   Lawrence, notary, in London attests 5 July 1703 he saw letters
   of den. (Deeds 10:179-80)
LAURANS, Mary (wife of John) - den. London 24 June 1703 (Shaw II:
   33); Thomas Lawrence, notary, in London attests 5 July he saw
   letters of den. (Deeds 10:179-80)
LAVIGNE, Estienne - den. 6 Feb. 1695/6 (Pat. 1696-1712:10)
LE BOYTEUX/LE BOYTEULX, Gabriel - den. London 16 Dec. 1687 (Shaw
   I:99); Nicholas Hayward, notary, in London attests 17 Jan.
   1687/8 he saw letters of den. (Deeds 8:193)
LE CHEVALIER, Jean - pet. 28 Sept. 1695 for letters of den. (CEM:
   247); den. 2 Oct. 1695 and oaths taken 28 Oct. 1695 (Pat. 6:
   551); he was a joiner (CEM:318)
LE CONTE, Francis - took den. oaths 17 Apr. 1695 (Pat. 6:535)
LECONTE, John - den. 29 July 1686, with liberty to trade or traffic
   (CEM:145)
LECOR, see DECOR
LEGRAND, Pierre - den. 12 Apr. 1685, with liberty to trade or
   traffic (NY Col Mss 33:230; CEM:143); made freeman of NYC
   30 Aug. 1698 as tobacconist (CNYHS 1885:67)
LE ROUX, John - den. London 20 Mar. 2 James II according to Nicholas
   Hayward, notary, in London, who attests 29 Apr. 1686 he has seen
   letters of den. (Deeds 8:239)
LEVI, Moses - den. 30 May 1695 and oaths taken 4 June 1695 (Pat.
   6:538)
LEVY, Asser - den. 21 Mar. 1664/5 (ECM I:179, note 3)
L'HOMMEDIEU, Benjamin - den. 10 Mar. 1686, with liberty to trade
   or traffic (NY Col Mss 33:221; CEM:143)
LIBOSCHAIN, Marie Johanna - den. London 25 Aug. 1708 (Shaw II:67;
   Deeds 10:241)
LIBOSCHAIN, Susanna - den. London 25 Aug. 1708 (Shaw II:67; Deeds
   10:241)
LOOKERMANS, Govert - memorandum 19 Dec. 1664 that a cert. of den.
   was granted him (Gen. Ent.:65)
LOTTONNEAU, Guillaume - den. 6 Feb. 1695/6 (Pat. 1696-1712:10)
LYRON, Leuwis, French Protestant - took den. oaths 28 Oct. 1696
   (Pat. 7:46)

MAHAULT, Estienne - den. 10 Mar. 1686, with liberty to trade or
   traffic (NY Col Mss 33:222; CEM:143)
MAIN/MANY, Jeremiah - den. London 22 June 1694 (Shaw I:235);
   Nicholas Hayward, notary, in London attests 11 July 1694 he
   has seen the letters of den. and on 16 Aug. 1694 William Water-
   son testifies that there is no clause to prevent Main from
   owning a vessel or being a master or mariner (Deeds 10:237-8)
MANHOUT, Jean - den. 2 Apr. 1686, with liberty to trade or traffic
   (NY Col Mss 33:229; CEM:143)
MARQUES, Isaque Rodrigues, merchant - den. 16 Oct. 1695 and oaths
   taken 17 Oct. 1695 (Pat. 6:549-50)
MASSONNEAU, Jacob - took den. oaths 12 Sept. 1698 (Pat. 7:214);
   probably the Jacob Massonneau, born at Lion (son of Peter and
   Lewize Massonneau) who is named in the naturalization bill read

first in the House of Lords on 21 Jan. 1689-90 and a second time
on 27 Jan. 1689/90 but which did not become an act (Shaw I: 216,
218)

MAURITTS, Jacob - claimed in 1677 to have been a denizen of New York
for 8 years (Shaw I:xxvii-xxviii); his wife was Margaret (CEM:
218)

MELYN, Isaac - den. 13 Jan. 1671/2 (Gen. Ent. 4:86, 93: ECM I:103,
note 1)

MENERRAN, Daniel - den. 23 Dec. 1695 and oaths taken 27 Jan. 1695/6
(Pat. 6:553)

MENFRULLE, Jean - den. 6 Feb. 1695/6 (Pat. 1696-1712:10)

MERCEREAU, Daniel - pet. 20 June 1695 for letters of den. (NY Col
Mss 40:31; CEM:245); he left his own country for religious
reason; there is an indenture dated 9 July 1697 of Stephen
Susso (son of Gabriell Susso) to a Daniel Mersereau, tailor
(CNYHS 1885:573-4)

MERCIER, Bartholomew - den. 17 Oct. 1685, with liberty to trade
or traffic (NY Col Mss 33:188; CEM:141)

MERCIER, Catharine - den. 17 Oct. 1685, with liberty to trade or
traffic (NY Col Mss 33:188; CEM:141)

MERCIER, Henry - den. 17 Oct. 1685, with liberty to trade or traffic
(NY Col Mss 33:188; CEM:141)

MERCIER, Isaac - den. 3 Sept. 1686 (NY Col Mss 33:290; CEM:146)

MEYNART, Samuel - den. 29 July 1686 (NY Col Mss 33:272; CEM:145)

MILLER, Paul - den. 29 Mar. 1693 and oaths taken 2 Apr. 1693
(Pat. 6:400-401)

MILLETT, John Peterson - den.oaths taken 20 Apr. 1695 (Pat. 6:536)

MINVIELLE, Gabriel - den. London 19 Aug. 1688 (Shaw I:213); Nicholas
Hayward, notary, in London attests 26 Oct. 1688 that he saw the
letters of den. granted to Gabriel Minvielle, merchant, and on
22 May 1691 Minvielle swore before the Mayor of New York that he
was the person mentioned in the letters of den. (Deeds 8:257).
Gabriel's will was proved 1 Oct. 1702 (NYHS Abst. Wills I:339-
341). Presumably Gabriel was born at Montauban, France, as were
his brother Peter and his niece Isabeau (Deeds 10:144-7).
In 1706 David Minvielle, a brother of Isabeau, was a merchant
in London.

MORILLE, Jaques - den. 10 Mar. 1686, with liberty to trade or
traffic (NY Col Mss 33:223; CEM:143)

MORRISSET, Alexander - pet. 1691 to be made burgher and citizen
(CEM:206); apparently pet. was not granted in New York but letters of den. were granted in London 29 Sept. 1698 to an Alexander Morisset (Shaw I:292)

MOYON, William - den. London 15 Apr. 1693 (Shaw I:231); Nicholas
Hayward, notary, in London attests 25 Apr. 1693 that he saw said
letters of den. and that thereby Moyon was permitted to purchase,
buy, sell and dispose of real estate; the letters of den. were
recorded in Jamaica 23 Feb. 1703/4 (Deeds 10:24)

NAPTHALI, Isaac - pet. 29 Aug. 1695 of Simon Bonan for letters of
den. for Isaac Naphtali (NY Col Mss 40:65; CEM:247); den. oaths
taken 29 Aug. 1695 (Pat. 6:547)

NAUDIN, Andrew - den. 6 Feb. 1695/6 (Pat. 1696-1712:10)

NAUDIN, Andrew (son of Andrew) - den. 6 Feb. 1695/6 (Pat. 1696-1712:10)

NAUDIN, Louis (son of Andrew) - den. 6 Feb. 1695/6 (Pat. 1696-1712:10)

NEAU, James - den. London 11 Mar. 1699/1700 (Shaw I:317); Thomas Lawrence, notary, in London cert. 10 Mar. 1705 that he has seen said letters and that there is a clause inserted permitting persons then granted den. to be masters of ships (Deeds 10:243-4)

NODINE, Arnold - on 27 Oct. 1698 Council of Trade declared void the letters of den. granted Nodine in Nov. 1697 by Gov. Fletcher of New York (CEM:264). The Privy Council on 18 Jan. 1700 stated that Fletcher's commission gave him no express power to grant letters of den. (Acts of the Privy Council, Colonial Series II:348)

NORBERY, John - took den. oaths 17 June 1698 (Pat. 7:214)

NUNES, Joseph, "now resident in New York" - den. London 30 May 1704 (Shaw II:43; Samuel:120)

ODERE, Isac - den. 23 Dec. 1695 and oaths taken 27 Jan. 1695/6 (Pat. 6:553)

PACHECO, Rodrigo, of New York, merchant - den. London 12 Dec. 1711 (Shaw II:71; Samuel:121)

PALTOT, Pierre - den. 6 Feb. 1695/6 (Pat. 1696-1712:10)

PARLNER, John - den. 25 Nov. 1695; den. oaths taken 6 Dec. 1695 (Pat. 6:551)

PELTRAU, Jean - den. 17 Sept. 1685, with lic. to trade or traffic (CEM:140)

PERODEAU, Guillaume - den. 2 Sept. 1685, with lic. to trade or traffic (CEM:140)

PEROT, James - den. London 24 June 1703 (Shaw II:31); Thomas Lawrence, notary, in London 5 July attests he has seen said letters of den. (Deeds 10:288-9)

PHANNET, Andrew - den. 6 Feb. 1695/6 (Pat. 1696-1712:10)

PINTARD, Anthony, "of France" - pet. 1691 for letters of den. (CEM: 206); apparently they were not granted in New York; an Anthony Pintard, however, was granted den. in London 10 July 1696 (Shaw I:244)

PLETTEL, Anne (dau. of Johannes Jacob) - den. London 25 Aug. 1708 (Shaw II:67; Deeds 10:241)

PLETTEL, Catharine (dau. of Johannes Jacob) - den. London 25 Aug. 1708 (Shaw II:67; Deeds 10:241)

PLETTEL, Johannes Jacob - den. London 25 Aug. 1708 (Shaw II:67; Deeds 10:241)

PLETTEL, Margaret (dau. of Johannes Jacob) - den. London 25 Aug. 1708 (Shaw II:67; Deeds 10:241)

PLETTEL, Sarah (dau. of Johannes Jacob) - den. London 25 Aug. 1708 (Shaw II:67; Deeds 10:241)

QUINTARD, Isaac - den. London 24 June 1703 (Shaw II:33); Thomas Lawrence, notary, in London 5 July 1703 attests he has seen letters of den. granted to Quintard (Deeds 10:201)

RENAU/RENAND, Jean - pet. 14 Oct. 1697 of Peter Perret for letters
of den. for Renau and other French Protestants taken in a prize
ship on the Banks of Newfoundland (NY Col Mss 41:120); on 22 Oct.
1697 Jean (by mark) took den. oaths (Pat. 7:161)

RENNAU, Heinrich - den. London 25 Aug. 1708 (Shaw II:67; Deeds
10:241)

RENNAU, Heinrich (son of Heinrich) - den. London 25 Aug. 1708
(Shaw II:67; Deeds 10:241)

RENNAU, Joanna (wife of Heinrich, Sr.) - den. London 25 Aug. 1708
(Shaw II:67; Deeds 10:241)

RENNAU, Lourentz (son of Heinrich, Sr.) - den. London 25 Aug. 1708
(Shaw II:67; Deeds 10:241)

RIBOT, Charles - den. 10 Dec. 1694 - oaths 11 Dec. 1694 (Pat. 1686-
1696:504)

RIORTEAN, Jean (by mark) - took den. oaths 22 Oct. 1697 (Pat.7:161)

ROBERT, Daniel - den. London 3 July 1701 (Shaw II:10,11); Thomas
Lawrence, notary, in London cert. 9 Aug. 1701 he saw name of
Daniel Robert on list of persons granted letters of den. 3 July
1701 (Deeds 10:45-6)

ROLLAND, John Abraham - den. London 29 Sept. 1698 (Shaw I:291);
Thomas Lawrence, notary, in London attests 7 May 1702 that name
of John Abraham Rolland was on list of persons granted den. in
time of William III (Deeds 10:111)

ROLLAND, Peter - den. London 29 Sept. 1698 (Shaw I:291); Thomas
Lawrence, notary, in London attests 7 May 1702 that he saw
name of Peter Rolland on den. list (Deeds 10:111)

ROSE, Johanna (wife of Peter) - den. London 25 Aug. 1708 (Shaw II:
68; Deeds 10:241)

ROSE, Peter - den. London 25 Aug. 1708 (Shaw II:68; Deeds 10:241)

SCHUNEMAN, Herman - den. London 25 Aug. 1708 (Shaw II:68; Deeds
10:241)

SCHWISSER, Anne Catherine (wife of Lorentz) - den. London 25 Aug.
1708 (Shaw II:67; Deeds 10:241)

SCHWISSER, Johannes (son of Lorentz) - den. London 25 Aug. 1708
(Shaw II:67; Deeds 10:241)

SCHWISSER, Lorentz - den. London 25 Aug. 1708 (Shaw II:69; Deeds
10:241)

SIMAILLEAU/SIRMAILLAUS, Jean - pet. 14 Oct. 1697 of Peter Perret for
letters of den. for Simailleau and other French Protestants
taken in a prize ship on the Banks of Newfoundland (NY Col Mss
41:120; CEM:259); Jean took den. oaths 22 Oct. 1697 (Pat. 7:161)

SOUMAIN, Simeon - took den. oaths 18 Apr. 1695 (Pat. 6:536)

SWEETEN, Ouzeel - took den. oaths 4 Nov. 1692 (Pat. 6:397)

SYCARD, Ambroise - den. 6 Feb. 1695/6 (Pat. 1696-1712:10)

SYCARD, Ambroise (son of Ambroise) - den. 6 Feb. 1695/6 (Pat. 1696-
1712:10)

SYCARD, Daniel (son of Ambroise) - den. 6 Feb. 1695/6 (Pat. 1696-
1712:10)

SYCARD, Jacques (son of Ambroise) - den. 6 Feb. 1695/6 (Pat. 1696-
1712:10)

TELLIEUR, Jacob, of New York - den. 15 Sept. 1685 (CEM:140)

THOROULDE, Dorotia - den. 14 June 1686, with liberty to trade or
traffic (CEM:144)

THOROULDE, Jacob - den. 14 June 1686, with liberty to trade or traffic (CEM:144)

THOROULDE, Marianne - den. 14 June 1686, with liberty to trade or traffic (CEM:144)

TILLOU, Peter - pet. 1691 to be made burgher and citizen (CEM:206)

TONNEAU, Abraham - pet. 1691 to be made burgher and citizen (CEM:206)

TRAVERRIE/TRAVERREI, Peter - den. 22 July 1695 and oaths taken 26 July 1695 (Pat. 6:543)

TREMBLE/TRAMBLE, Jean - pet. 14 Oct. 1697 of Peter Perret for letters of den. for Tremble and other French Protestants taken in a prize ship on the Banks of Newfoundland (NY Col Mss 41:120; CEM:259); Jean took (by mark) den. oaths 22 Oct. 1697 (Pat. 7:161)

TURCK/ZURCK, Isaac - den. London 25 Aug. 1708 (Shaw II:68; Deeds 10:241)

VANDERWATER, Abraham - den. 17 Oct. 1685, with liberty to trade or traffic (CEM:141)

VAN HOVEN, Hendryck - took den. oaths 9 June 1698 (Pat. 6:404)

VAN SEVENHOVE, John - den. 19 Apr. 1693 and oaths taken 20 Apr. 1693 (Pat. 6:404)

VARICK, Rudolphus - den. 29 July 1686, with liberty to trade or traffic (CEM:145)

VAS, see DAS

VEERMAN, Harman - took den. oaths 4 Oct. 1698 (Pat. 7:187)

VOLCK, Andreas - den. London 25 Aug. 1708 (Shaw II:67; Deeds 10:241)

VOLCK, Anna Catharine (wife of Andreas) - den. London 25 Aug. 1708 (Shaw II:67; Deeds 10:241)

VOLCK, Anne Gertrude (dau. of Andreas) - den. London 25 Aug. 1708 (Shaw II:67; Deeds 10:241)

VOLCK, Hieronemus (son of Andreas) - den. London 25 Aug. 1708 (Shaw II:67; Deeds 10:241)

VOLCK, Maria Barbara (dau. of Andreas) - den. London 25 Aug. 1708 (Shaw II:67; Deeds 10:241)

VONCK, Bartholomew - den. 6 Apr. 1697 and oaths taken 7 Aug. 1697 (Pat. 7:138)

WEBER, Anne Elizabeth (wife of Jacob) - den. London 25 Aug. 1708 (Shaw II:67; Deeds 10:241)

WEBER, Eve Elizabeth (dau. of Jacob) - den. London 25 Aug. 1708 (Shaw II:67; Deeds 10:241)

WEBER, Eve Maria (dau. of Jacob) - den. London 25 Aug. 1708 (Shaw II:67; Deeds 10:241)

WEBER, Jacob - den. London 25 Aug. 1708 (Shaw II:67; Deeds 10:241)

WEIGAND, Anne Catherine (wife of Michael) - den. London 25 Aug. 1708 (Shaw II:67; Deeds 10:241)

WEIGAND, Anne Maria (dau. of Michael) - den. London 25 Aug. 1708 (Shaw II:67; Deeds 10:241)

WEIGAND, George (son of Michael) - den. London 25 Aug. 1708 (Shaw II:67; Deeds 10:241)

WEIGAND, Michael - den. London 25 Aug. 1708 (Shaw II:67; Deeds 10:241

WEIGAND, Tobias (son of Michael) – den. London 25 Aug. 1708 (Shaw
    II:67; Deeds 10:241)
WEIMARIN/WEMARIN, Catharine (dau. of Marie) – den. London 25 Aug.
    1708 (Shaw II:68; Deeds 10:241)
WEIMARIN/WEMARIN, Marie – den. London 25 Aug. 1708 (Shaw II:68;
    Deeds 10:241)

ZURCK, Isaac, see TURCK

NATURALIZATIONS

AADIG, Ernest – 24 Mar. 1772 (Laws, ch. 1564)

ABBOT, John James – 23 Dec. 1765 (Laws, ch. 1295)

ABEL, Jacob – 3 May 1755 (Laws, ch. 975)

ABETTE (?), Jan Salomonse, of Albany Co. – 13 Mar. 1715/6 (Alb. CCM 6:119)

ABIGHT, Ernest Frederick, German Evangelical, of NYC, tanner – 22 Apr. 1772 (SCJ)

ABRAHAMS, Isaac – 21 Sept. 1744 (laws, ch. 787)
Made freeman of NYC as distiller 6 Nov. 1744 (CNYHS 1885:150). His house near the Kings Arms 8 Nov. 1758 (Gottesman:277). An Isaac Abrahams reported to have fallen overboard in 1792 from brig _Minerva_, Capt. Williams, on voyage to Faulkland Islands and to have been drowned (Scott, _Adm. Papers_: 1)

ABRAMS, Chapman – 3 May 1755 (Laws, ch. 975)

ADOLPHUS, Isaac, Jew, who resided in R.I., Conn. and New York, of NYC, trader – 27 July 1758 (Oo: 62; Huhner:4 & 6; SCJ)

AERTSE, Garret, of Ulster Co. – 8/9 Sept. 1715 (Deed Book BB:386)

AETTINGER, Casper – 3 July 1759 (Laws, ch. 1089)

AIMES, Georg – 3 July 1759 (Laws, ch. 1089)
A George Aim, of NYC, cordwainer, was a bondsman in Oct. 1744 (Scott, _Adm. Bonds_:112); George Aim, of NYC, cordwainer (whose wife was Catherine) was a bondsman in Oct. 1774 (_Ibid._:254)

AINUSHEFFER, Johan Willem, of Ulster Co. – 8/9 Sept. 1715 (Deed Book BB:387)

ALBRANDT, John – 11 Sept. 1761 (Laws, ch. 1154)

ALBRANT, Hannis – 27 Jan. 1770 (Laws, ch. 1462)

ALENDORPH, Henry – 3 May 1755 (Laws, ch. 975)

ALGAJER, Jacob – 3 July 1759 (Laws, ch. 1089)

ALL, Adam, German Evangelical, of NYC, yeoman – 19 Apr. 1769 (C.O. 1075, Tt:4; SCJ)

ALLAIRE, Alexander – Petition to be naturalized, 19 Aug. 1687 (CEM:167)

ALLEN, Elizabeth – 27 Jan. 1770 (Laws, ch. 1462)

ALSDORF, Lawrence, Dutch Reformed, of Ulster Co., farmer – 29 July (Ii:52) Cert. min. J. H. Goetschius; witnesses: Hans George Ranck, Hans George Neits (NYPL)

ALT, Hannis – 27 Jan. 1770 (Laws, ch. 1462)

ALT, John – 11 Sept. 1761 (Laws, ch. 1154)

AMENT, Pieter, of NYC, cooper – 23 Aug. 1715 (MCRM:94)

ANCKTEN, Peter – 16 Feb. 1771 (Laws, ch. 1508)

ANDERS, Patron, of Albany Co. – 17 Jan. 1715/6 (Alb. CCM 6:114)

ANDERSON, John – 24 Nov. 1750 (Laws, ch. 902)
A John Anderson was made freeman of NYC 4 Mar. 1760 as a joiner (CNYHS 1885:194); see introd.

ANDREWS, Abraham, a Jew, of NYC, shopkeeper – 22 Apr. 1762 (C.O. 5:1071)

ANGLE, Coenradt – 3 May 1755 (Laws, ch. 975)

ANNSBACH, Baltus, of Albany Co. – 3 Jan. 1715/6 (Alb. CCM 6:113)

ANTHONY, Joseph, French Protestant, of Westchester Co., merchant – 22 Apr. 1762 (C.O. 5:1071)

APPEL, Anton/Anston, German Reformed Congregation, of NYC, baker -
20 Apr. 1769 (C.O. 5:1075, Tt:4; SCJ)

APPEL, Hannes - 11 Sept. 1761 (Laws, ch. 1154)

APPLE, Anthony - 20 May 1769 (Laws, ch. 1404; Ss: 79)

APPLER, Adam - 3 May 1755 (Laws, ch. 975)

AREND/ARENTS, Hartwig/Hartwyck - 20 Mar. 1762 (Laws, ch. 1179)

ARMBRISTER, Christopher - 3 May 1755 (Laws, ch. 975)

ARMBRISTER, Johan Christoper - 11 Sept. 1761 (Laws, ch. 1154)

ARMPRIESTER, John Christopher, Reformed German Church, of NYC, inn-
holder - 21 Oct. 1761 (Oo:63); John Christophel, Reformed German
Church, cert. min. F. Rothenbuhler; witnesses: Johannes Myer,
Abraham Young - 21 Oct. 1761 (NYPL; SCJ)

ARNOLDI, John, of NYC, physician - 20 Mar. 1715/6 (MCRM:150)

ASH, William - 3 July 1759 (Laws, ch. 1089)
A William Ash, of NYC, Windsor chair-maker, was a bondsman in
July 1786 (Scott, Adm. Papers:228)

ASHER, Adam - 3 May 1755 (Laws, ch. 975)

AUBOYNEAU, John, Protestant - nat. between 1 June 1740 and 1 June
1741 (Gg:68; NYPL)

AUCH, Georg - 3 July 1759 (Laws, ch. 1089)

AUDIER, Moise - 6 Dec. 1746 (Laws, ch. 844)

AXON/AXSON, Elizabeth, Dutch Reformed, of NYC, widow; cert. min.
J. Ritzema; witnesses: Aeltye Binmer, Mary Wentworth - 18 Oct.
1750 (Hh:142; SCJ; Rec. 94:139)

AYRER, Fredrick - 8 Mar. 1773 (Laws, ch. 1638)

BAAL, Johan Peter, of Albany Co. - 13 Mar. 1715/6 (Alb. CCM 6:119)

BAAM, Philip - 11 Sept. 1761 (Laws, ch. 1154)

BACHER, Theobald - 8 Mar. 1773 (Laws, ch. 1638)

BACHUS, Johan Ernst. of Ulster Co. - 8/9 Sept. 1715 (Deed Book
BB:387)

BACHUS, Johanis, of Ulster Co. - 8/9 Sept. 1715 (Deed Book BB:387)

BACKUS, John - 3 May 1755 (Laws, ch. 975)

BALLAREAUX, Jean (wife of James Ballareaux/Bellareaux) - 17 June
1726 (Laws, ch. 476)
James Ballereau was made freeman of NYC 6 Dec. 1709 as a ship-
wright (CNYHS 1885:89)

BAMPER, Lodwyck - 24 Nov. 1750 (Laws, ch. 902)
Lodowick Bamper on 27 May 1751 at his house in Beekman St. offered for sale teakettles, piepans, candlesticks, etc. (Gottes-
man:221); Lodowick Bamper, of Brooklyn, gent., 3 June 1783 made
his will (Scott, Adm. Papers:13), which was proved 24 Mar. 1784
(WNYHS 12:224)

BAMPER, Margret - 24 Nov. 1750 (Laws, ch. 902)
Lodowick Bamper had a daughter Margaret, who married James Mc-
Kenny (WNYHS 12:224). Probably Bamper's wife was also named
Margaret.

BANGEL, Adam - 31 Dec. 1768 (Laws, ch. 1385)

BARBAULD, Ezekiel - 20 Sept. 1728 (Laws, ch. 520)
Ezekiel Barbauld was made freeman of NYC 19 Nov. 1728 as a merchant (CNYHS 1885:112)

BARENT, Hannes - 11 Sept. 1761 (Laws, ch. 1154)

BARES, Solomon, a Jew - between 1 June 1740 and 1 June 1741 (Gg:68)

BARNER, Hans Jury, of Albany Co. - 13 Mar. 1715/6 (Alb. CCM 6:119)

BARNES, Conradt, Lutheran, of NYC, hatter - 19 Oct. 1763 (C.O. 1071)
BARON, Anthony - 24 Mar. 1772 (Laws, ch. 1564)
BARRINGER, Coenraed, of Albany Co. - 17 Jan. 1715/6 (Alb. CCM 6:114)
BARTEL, Andries, of Albany Co. - 22 Nov. 1715 (Alb. CCM 6:109)
BARTEL, Philip, of Albany Co. - 22 Nov. 1715 (Alb. CCM 6:109)
BARTHOLOMEW, George - 8 Mar. 1773 (Laws, ch. 1638)
BARTHOLOMEW, John - 16 Feb. 1771 (Laws, ch. 1508)
BASTIANK, Hans Jacob - 11 Sept. 1761 (Laws, ch. 1154)
BASTIANSE, Johannis - 11 Sept. 1761 (Laws, ch. 1154)
BAUER, Casper - 11 Sept. 1761 (Laws, ch. 1154)
BAUSLEY, Peter - 3 July 1759 (Laws, ch. 1089)
BAYER, Jacob, of Albany Co. - 17 Jan. 1715/6 (Alb. CCM 6:114)
BAYEUX, Thomas, of NYC, merchant - 6 Mar. 1715/6 (MCRM:148)
BEAKER, John, Ancient Lutheran, of NYC, baker - 16 Jan. 1771 (SCJ)
BEAM, Gorg, of Ulster Co. - 8/9 Sept. 1715 (Deed Book BB:387)
BEAM, Johan Albert, of Ulster Co. - 8/9 Sept. 1715 (Deed Book BB:387)
BEAR, Jurry - 24 Mar. 1772 (Laws, ch. 1564)
BEAU, Daniel, of NYC, mariner - 16 Aug. 1715 (MCRM:92)
BEAUDOUIN, Jeremiah, French Protestant, of NYC, stay-maker;
   cert. the Mayor of NYC; witnesses: Daniel Mesnard, Francis Blan-
   chard - 17 Jan. 1754 (NYPL; Oo:62; SCJ)
BECKER, Frederick - 22 June 1734 (Laws, ch. 605)
   A Frederick Becker was made freeman of NYC 15 Oct. 1734 as a
   carman (CNYHS 1885:123); A Frederick Becker, jeweller, had a
   shop in Beekman St. on 18 Oct. 1736 (Gottesman:66)
BECKER, Henry - 8 Mar. 1773 (Laws, ch. 1638)
BECKER, Jacob - 27 Jan. 1770 (Laws, ch. 1462)
BECKER, Peter, of Ulster Co. - 8/9 Sept. 1715 (Deed Book BB:837)
BECKER, Zacharias, Dutch Reformed of Ulster Co., farmer; cert.
   min. Georgus Wilhelmus Mancius; witnesses: Matis Marckel,
   Conrd Myer - Oct. 1740 (NYPL; Gg:68)
BEEKMAN, Henr., of Ulster Co. - 8/9 Sept. 1715 (Deed Book BB:387)
BEEKMAN, Tedeus - 24 June 1719 (Laws, ch. 381)
BEENNER, Jurry, of Albany Co. - 11 Oct. 1715 (Alb. CCM 6:105)
BEERMAN, Johannis, of Albany Co. - 22 Nov. 1715 (Alb. CCM 6:109)
BEHM, Hans, Henrich, of Ulster Co. - 8/9 Sept. 1715 (Deed Book
   BB:387)
BELINGER, Peter, of Albany Co. - 31 Jan. 1715/6 (Alb. CCM 6:116)
BELL, Christopher, Reformed Protestant Dutch Church, of Orange Co.,
   farmer - 21 Apr. 1769 (C.O. 5:1075, Tt:4)
BELL, Henry - 3 May 1755 (Laws, ch. 975)
BELL, Johan Fredrick, of Albany Co. - 11 Oct. 1715 (Alb. CCM 6:105)
BELL, William, Sr., Dutch Reformed, of Orange Town, Orange Co.,
   cooper - 17 Oct. 1764 (C.O. 5:1072; Qq:63; SCJ)
BELLANGER, Philip - 8 Mar. 1773 (Laws, ch. 1638)
BELLINGER, Fredrick, of Albany Co. - 22 Nov. 1715 (Alb. CCM 6:109)
BENDER, Margaret - 29 Oct. 1730 (Laws, ch. 556)
BENDER, Philips, of Albany Co. - 31 Jan. 1715/6 (Alb. CCM 6:116)
BENDER, Valatin, of Ulster Co. - 8/9 Sept. 1715 (Deed Book BB:386)
BENDER, William - 8 Mar. 1773 (Laws, ch. 1638)
BENGLE, Adam - 8 Mar. 1773 (Laws, ch. 1638)
BENTER, Matthias, of NYC, cooper, age 14 - 14 Feb. 1715/6 (MCRM:142)
BENZEL, Adolphus - 20 Dec. 1763 (Laws, ch. 1236)
   Administrator of estate of Adolphus Benzell, Esq., of Crown Point,
   Charlotte Co., was appointed 31 Jan. 1775 (Scott, Adm. Papers:23)

BERCK, Christian, of Albany Co. - 31 Jan. 1715/6 (Alb. CCM 6:116)
BERK, Abraham, of Albany Co. - 17 Jan. 1715/6 (Alb. CCM 6:115)
BERLET, John Wolf - 3 July 1759 (Laws, ch. 1089)
BERRINGER, Michael - 24 Mar. 1772 (Laws, ch. 1564)
BERTAIN, Pierre, of New Rochell, cooper - 2 Aug. 1715 (MCRM:88)
BERTHON, Michel - 17 June 1726 (Laws, ch. 476)
    Michael Berthon 4 July 1727 was made freeman of NYC as a cook
    (CNYHS 1885:109)
BESHARN, Johan Jacob, of Albany Co. - 31 Jan. 1715/6 (Alb. CCM 6:
    116)
BESLEY, Nicholas - 20 Dec. 1763 (Laws, ch. 1236)
BESLEY, Oliver, of New Rochell, gent. - 10 Jan. 1715/6 (MCRM:135)
BESLY, Hester (wife of Thauvet Besly) - 25 Nov. 1727 (Laws, ch. 508)
    Thauvet Besly was made freeman of NYC 19 Dec. 1727 as a gold-
    smith (CNYHS 1885:110); his house in 1746 was on Golden Hill
    (Gottesman:30)
BEST, Jacob, of Albany Co. - 17 Jan. 1715/6 (Alb. CCM 6:115)
BEST, Jury, of Ulster Co. - 8/9 Sept. 1715 (Deed Book BB:387)
BETELLBRUNT, Anthony - 16 Feb. 1771 (Laws, ch. 1508)
BETSER, Adam, Lutheran; cert. min. G. W. Mancius; witnesses: Wilhelm
    Schneider, Teunis Schneider - 24 Oct. 1741 (NYPL)
BETSER, Marma, of Albany Co. - 17 Jan. 1715/6 (Alb. CCM 6:115)
BETSER, Peter, of Albany Co. - 17 Jan. 1715/6 (Alb. CCM 6:115)
BEVYER, Louys, of Ulster Co. - 8/9 Sept. 1715/6 (Deed Book BB:387)
BICKLE, Jacob - 16 Feb. 1771 (Laws, ch. 1508)
BINDER, George - 27 Jan. 1770 (Laws, ch. 1462)
BINDER, Hans Ulrich, Dutch Reformed, of Ulster Co., husbandman; cert.
    min. G. W. Mancius; witnesses: William Smith, Philip Sinseback -
    18 Oct. 1750 (NYPL; Hh:142; SCJ)
BIRD, Henry - 20 Dec. 1763 (Laws, ch. 1236)
BLANCHARD, Francois - 6 Dec. 1746 (Laws, ch. 844)
    A John Francis Blanchard, of NYC, carpenter, died before 29 Jan.
    1771 (Scott, Adm. Bonds:17)
BLANCHARD, James, French Protestant, of NYC, cooper; cert. min.
    J. Carle; witnesses: Peter Vallade, Jas. Desbrosses, Daniel
    Bonet - 22 Apr. 1761 (NYPL; Oo:63;SCJ)
BLANCK, Johan, of Ulster Co. - 8/9 Sept. 1715 (Deed Book BB:387)
BLANK, Frederick - 11 Sept. 1761 (Laws, ch. 1154)
BLARICK, --, of Ulster Co. - 8/9 Sept. 1715 (Deed Book BB:387)
BLATNER/BLATTNER, Jacob, Lutheran, of Manor of Livingston, Albany
    Co., miller and millwright; cert. min. J. A. Weygand; witnesses:
    Martin Shylr, Melcher Hoefnagel - 23 Apr. 1765 (Qq:63;
    Rec. 94:144; SCJ)
BLEEKER, Jan Janse, of Albany Co. - 11 Oct. 1715 (Alb. CCM 6:105)
BLEMSAN, Mattys, of Ulster Co. - 8/9 Sept. 1715 (Deed Book BB:386)
BLISS, Enrich, of Albany Co. - 17 Jan. 1715/6 (Alb. CCM 6:115)
BOBIN, James, of Bushwick, Kings Co., yeoman - 3 Apr. 1716
    (MCRM: 153-154)
BOECK, Martin, of Ulster Co. - 8/9 Sept. 1715 (Deed Book BB:387)
BOEL, Henricus - 3 July 1718 (Laws, ch. 356); subscribed 5 Aug.
    1718 (NYHS Oath Roll, 1718)
    Henricus Boel, Minister of the Gospel, was deceased by 23 Aug.
    1758, when Nicholas Roosevelt, goldsmith, and Henricus Boel,
    merchant, were bondsmen (Scott, Adm. Bonds:18)

BOEL, Tobias - 3 July 1718 (Laws, ch. 356); subscribed 5 Aug. 1718
(NYHS Oath Roll, 1718)
   Tobias Boel was made freeman of NYC as attorney-at-law 5 Aug.
   1718 (CNYHS 1885:98). Hendricus Boel of NYC, gent., brother of
   Tobias, was appointed 3 Nov. 1727 administrator of estate of
   Tobias, then deceased, and Hendricus Boel and Wynant Van Zandt,
   block-maker, were bondsmen (Scott, Adm. Papers:30)

BOELEN, Jacob, silversmith - 26 July 1715 (MCRM:88)

BOGAERT, William, of NYC, turner - 14 Feb. 1715/6 (MCRM:142)

BOGART, Hendrick, of Ulster Co. - 8/9 Sept. 1715 (Deed Book BB:386)

BOMPER, Jacob - 25 Nov. 1727 (Laws, ch. 508)
   Jacob Bomper was made freeman of NYC 19 Dec. 1727 as a brewer
   (CNYHS 1885:110)

BOMPER, Philip Jacob, Jr. - 12 July 1729 (Laws, ch. 538); took oath
   NYC Mayor's Court 9 Sept. 1729

BOMSER, Estienne - petition to be naturalized 19 Aug. 1687 (CEM:167)

BONNAIN, Elias - 24 Nov. 1750 (Laws, ch. 902)
   See introd.

BONNESTEEL, Niecolas, of Albany Co. - 17 Jan. 1715/6 (Alb. CCM 6:
   115)

BONNET, Daniel, of New Rochell, yeoman - 27 Sept. 1715 (MCRM:104)

BONTECOU, Daniel, cooper - 12 July 1715 (MCRM:85)

BONTECOU, Daniel, of French Church, of NYC, merchant; cert. min. L.
   Rou; witnesses: John Hastier, Alexander Allaire - 31 July 1741
   (NYPL; Gg:81)

BONTICOU, Marianne, wife of Daniel - 17 June 1726 (Laws, ch. 476)

BONWER, Pieter, of Ulster Co. - 8/9 Sept. 1715 (Deed Book BB:387)

BOOM, Hendrik - 11 Sept. 1761 (Laws, ch. 1154)

BOOS, Wendel, Lutheran, of NYC, baker; cert. min. J. A. Weygand;
   witnesses: William Mucklevain, Henry Ustick - 21 Apr. 1762
   (NYPL; C.O. 5:1071)

BORDING, Christian - pet. 16 Nov. 1739, see introd.

BORRELL, Matthias - 17 June 1726 (Laws, ch. 476)
   Matthias Borrell was made freeman of NYC 31 Aug. 1731 as merchant
   (CNYHS 1885:118)

BOSS/BOS, Peter, of Bergen Co., N.J., farmer - 16 Feb. 1771 (Laws,
   ch. 1508); took oath 22 Jan. 1772 (SCJ)

BOSHAER, Jorg, of Ulster Co. - 8/9 Sept. 1715 (Deed Book BB:387)

BOSHART, Jacob, Dutch Reformed, of NYC, stone-cutter; cert. min.
   Lambertus De Ronde; witnesses: Hans Zurigher, Casper Gester -
   21 Apr. 1752 (NYPL; Ii:52; SCJ)

BOSS, Jacob - 24 June 1734 (Laws, ch. 605)
   Jacob Boss was made freeman of NYC 15 Oct. 1734 as "gardiner"
   (CNYHS 1885:123)

BOUCH/BOUES, Elizabeth/Elisabet - 6 July 1723 (Laws, ch. 44; NYHS
   Oath Roll, 1723)

BOUGEAUD, Louis - petition to be naturalized 19 Aug. 1687 (CEM:167)

BOUTELLIER, Jean - petition to be naturalized 19 Aug. 1687 (CEM:167)

BOUWMAN, Abraham - 20 Mar. 1762 (Laws, ch. 1179)

BOUMAN, Golliep - 20 Mar. 1762 (Laws, ch. 1179)

BOWER, George - 8 Mar. 1773 (Laws, ch. 1638)
   A George Bower, private in Col. Van Schaick's Regt., dec'd; on
   7 Sept. 1784 Eve Margreth Keller, grandmother of the five orphan
   children of the deceased, was appointed administratrix of his
   estate (Scott, Adm. Papers:34)

BOWMAN, Mathew, Lutheran, of NYC, yeoman; cert. min. M. Christian Knoll; witnesses: Leendert Riegeler, John Michael Will - 28 July 1749 (NYPL; Hh:70)

BRAAMBOS, Willemina - 6 Dec. 1746 (Laws, ch. 844)

BRAAMBOS, William - 6 Dec. 1746 (Laws, ch. 844)

BRAAMBOS, William, Jr. - 6 Dec. 1746 (Laws, ch. 844)

BRACK, Hans Michall, of Albany Co. - 22 Nov. 1715 (Alb. CCM 6:109)

BRADER, John - 27 Jan. 1770 (Laws, ch. 1462)

BRADHOUR, Nicholas - 27 Jan. 1770 (Laws, ch. 1462)

BRAND, Paulus - 20 Mar. 1762 (Laws, ch. 1179)

BRANDAU, Nicolas, of Ulster Co. - 8/9 Sept. 1715 (Deed Book BB:387)

BRANDAU, Willheminus, of Ulster Co. - 8/9 Sept. 1715 (Deed Book BB:387)

BRATHOUWER, Nicholas - 20 Mar. 1762 (Laws, ch. 1179)

BRAUN, Simon - 20 Mar. 1762 (Laws, ch. 1179)

BREITENBEGER, Baltus - 8 Mar. 1773 (Laws, ch. 1638)

BREYTIGAM, Frederick, Lutheran, of NYC, baker - 26 July 1769 (C.O. 1075, Tt:4; SCJ)

BRICARD, Henry, of NYC, merchant - 10 Jan. 1715/6 (MCRM:135)

BRIDLIFE, Henrich - 20 Mar. 1762 (Laws, ch. 1179)

BRINGIER, Marie, French Church of NYC; cert. min. Lewis Rou; witnesses: James Faviere, Samuel Bourdet (NYPL; Gg:68)

BRITT, William, Reformed Protestant Dutch Church, of Manor of Philipsborough, Westchester Co., farmer - 24 Apr. 1767 (C.O. 5: 1073; Rr:30; SCJ)

BRONCE, George - 27 Jan. 1770 (Laws, ch. 1462)

BRONCK, Henrich, of Ulster Co. - 8/9 Sept. 1715 (Deed Book BB:387)

BROOKES, John - see introd.

BROOKS, John - 20 May 1769 (Laws, ch. 1404; Ss:79)

BROUGH, Matthew - 3 May 1755 (Laws, ch. 975)

BROWN, George - 8 Mar. 1773 (Laws, ch. 1638)

BROWN, John Hendrick/Johan Henrich, Dutch Reformed, of NYC, baker; cert. min. James Ritzema; witnesses: Marselus Gorbrants, Henry Swart - 25 July 1758 (NYPL; Oo:62; SCJ)

BROWN, William, Dutch Reformed, of Schohary, Albany Co., wheelwright; cert. min. Johannes Schuyler; witnesses: Johann Willem Dietz, Johann Jacob Werth - 25 July 1752 (NYPL; Ii:52)

BRUGMAN, Cornelius, of NYC, periwig-maker - 6 Apr. 1716 (MCRM: 153-154)

BRUGMAN/BURGMAN, Gotfried, Lutheran, of NYC, mason - 21 Oct. 1765 (C.O. 5:1072; Qq:63; SCJ)

BRUGMAN, George, of NYC, rope-maker - 18 Oct. 1715 (MCRM:110)

BRUNCKHORST, John, of NYC, sugar refiner - 20 May 1769 (Laws, ch. 1404; Ss:79; SCJ)
John Brunckhorst in Oct. 1766 was witness to renunciation of Eve Oosterman, widow (sister-in-law of Coenradt Oosterman, of NYC, sugar-boiler, dec'd) to administer on estate of said Coenradt (Scott, Adm. Papers:236); John Brunckhorst, of NYC, sugar baker, in 1782 was administrator of estate of John Norbergh, late commandant of Fort George (Scott, Adm. Bonds:103)

BRUNNER, Jacob - 3 July 1759 (Laws, ch. 1089)

BRYER, Francis - 11 Sept. 1761 (Laws, ch. 1154)

BRYN, Jacobus, of Ulster Co. - 8/9 Sept. 1715 (Deed Book BB:386)

BSHEERE, Jacob, of Albany Co. - 22 Nov. 1715 (Alb. CCM 6:109)

BUCH, Daniel, of Albany Co. - 17 Jan. 1715/6 (Alb. CCM 6:115)

BUCH, John Hend., of Albany Co. - 17 Jan. 1715/6 (Alb. CCM 6:115)
BURGER, Marten, of Ulster Co. - 8/9 Sept. 1715 (Deed Book BB:387)
BURGER, Peter, of Albany Co. - 17 Jan. 1715/6 (Alb. CCM 6:115)
BURY, John - 24 Nov. 1750 (Laws, ch. 902)
BUSCH/BUSH, Johann Henrich, Lutheran, of Ulster Co., blacksmith;
    cert. min. Wm. Chr. Berkenmeyer; witnesses: Charles Beekman;
    George Pettersson - 22 Oct. 1750 (NYPL; Hh:142;SCJ)
BUSH, Julius - 8 Mar. 1773 (Laws, ch. 1638)
BUSSARD, Hendrick - 11 Sept. 1761 (Laws, ch. 1154)
BUVELOT, James, French Church, of NYC, brasier; cert. min. L. Rou;
    witnesses: John Hastier, Alexander Allaire - 31 July 1741
    (NYPL; Gg:81)
BUVELOT, Jaques Gabriel - 20 Sept. 1728(Laws, ch. 520) and 12 July
    1729 (Laws, ch. 538)
    He took the oath in the NYC Mayor's Court on 9 Sept. 1729 and on
    16 Sept. 1729 was made freeman of NYC as a brazier (CNYHS
    1885:113)
BYDEMAN, Simon - 8 Mar. 1773 (Laws, ch. 1638)
BYRKEY, Jacob - 8 Mar. 1773 (Laws, ch. 1638)
BYRKEY, Jacob, Jr. - 8 Mar. 1773 (Laws, ch. 1638)
BYRKEY, Peter - 8 Mar. 1773 (Laws, ch. 1638)

CAAF, Christian - 11 Sept. 1761 (Laws, ch. 1154)
CALLMAN, Michael, of NYC, merchant - 28 Feb. 1715/6 (MCRM: 146)
CAMMERDINGER, Ludwig/Ludewig, Lutheran, of NYC, tailor - 21 Oct.
    1765 (C.O. 5:1072; Qq:63; SCJ)
CANTAIN, Moyse, of Ulster Co. - 8/9 Sept. 1715 (Deed Book BB:386)
CARCAS, Abraham - 17 June 1726 (Laws, ch. 476)
    Abraham Carcas was made freeman of NYC 19 July 1726 as snuff-
    maker (CNYHS 1885:108)
CARIO, Michael - 12 July 1729 (Laws, ch. 538)
    Michael Cario was made freeman of NYC 25 June 1728 as jeweller
    (CNYHS 1885:111) and took oath in NYC Mayor's Court 9 Sept.
    1729
CARLE, John, French Protestant, of NYC, clerk - 21 Apr. 1762 (C.O.
    5:1071)
CARON, Nicolas - 3 July 1718 (Laws, ch. 356); subscribed 5 Aug.
    1718 (NYHS Oath Roll, 1718)
    Nicolas "Carow" was made freeman of NYC 5 Aug. 1718 as jeweller
    (CNYHS 1885:98); will, dated 3 Oct. 1724, of Nicholas "Coron,"
    of NYC, jeweller, (son of Nicholas Coron) was proved 7 Nov. 1724
    (WNYHS 2:300-301)
CARSTENS, Johannes Lorents - 14 Oct. 1737 (Laws, ch. 646)
CARTWRIGHT, Mary, born in Amsterdam, daughter of Giles Silvester
    and Mary his wife, English parents - 29 Dec. 1660 (Shaw I; 79;
    Patents 1)
CASPARUS, Johannes Valentine - 11 Sept. 1761 (Laws, ch. 1154)
CASPEL, Isaac Van Haaren, of NYC, chirurgeon - 1 Aug. 1751 (SCJ)
CASPER, Casper - 24 Oct. 1755 (NYPL; Oo:62)
CASSELMAN, And. Lod'k, of Albany Co. - 17 Jan. 1715/6 (Alb. CCM 6:
    115)
CASSET, Joseph - 24 Nov. 1750 (Laws, ch. 902)
CASTANG, Gideon, of NYC, rope-maker - 16 Aug. 1715 (MCRM:92)
CATELMAN, Christian, of Ulster Co. - 8/9 Sept. 1715 (Deed Book
    BB:387)

CAUCHE, **Aime** - petition to be naturalized 19 Aug. 1687 (CEM:167)
CEBE, **Mariane** - pet. 16 Nov. 1739, see introd.
CEBE, **Paul Francis** - pet. 16 Nov. 1739, see introd.
CERMAN, **Jacob**, of Albany Co. - 14 Feb. 1715/6 (Alb. CCM 6:117)
CEYWIDS, **Frederick** - 11 Sept. 1761 (Laws, ch. 1154)
CHAPPELLE, **John Peter**, French Protestant, of NYC, labourer; cert.
    min. J. Carle; witnesses: Peter Vallade, Jas. Desbrosses,
    Daniel Bonet - 22 Apr. 1761 (NYPL; Oo:63; SCJ)
CHAPPELLE, **Peter**, Jr., French Protestant, of NYC, stocking-weaver -
    20 Apr. 1769 (C.O. 5:1075, Tt:4; SCJ)
CHARDAVEYNE, **Elias**, of NYC, victualler - 26 July 1715 (MCRM:88)
CHERBACHER, **John** - 20 May 1769 (Laws, ch. 1404; Ss:79)
CHIERTS, **David**, of Albany Co. - 22 Nov. 1715 (Alb. CCM 6:115)
CHRIST, **Hendrick** - 8 Nov. 1735 (Laws, ch. 634)
    Julian Christ (widow of a Henry Christ) and Jacob Christ (only
    son of a Henry Christ) on 16 Feb. 1768 were appointed adminis-
    trators on estate of a Henry Christ, of Ulster Co., farmer,
    dec'd; bond was signed by Julian Christ, Jacob Christ, yeoman,
    and James Barkley, yeoman, all of Ulster Co.; witnesses were
    John McClean and Arthur Parkes (Scott, Adm. Papers:56)
CHRIST/CHRISTEE, **Johannes**, Protestant - between 1 June 1740 and
    1 June 1741 (NYPL; Gg:68); petition 16 Nov. 1739, see introd.
CHRIST, **Lawrence** - 8 Nov. 1735 (Laws, ch. 634)
CHRIST, **Stephanus/Stephanes** - 8 Nov. 1735 (Laws, ch. 634)
    A Stephanus Christ on 17 Jan. 1732 held a commission as ensign
    for Orange Co. (CEM:516)
CHRISTIANSE, **Peter**, of NYC, boatman - 6 Mar. 1715/6 (MCRM:148)
CHRISTMAN, **Johans**, of Albany Co. - 17 Jan. 1715/6 (Alb. CCM 6:115)
CHRYSELAR, **Gorg**, of Ulster Co. - 8/9 Sept. 1715 (Deed Book BB:387)
CHRYSELAR, **Johan Phillip**, of Ulster Co. - 8/9 Sept. 1715 (Deed
    Book BB:387)
CLAJONT, **William**, French Protestant, of NYC - 27 Oct. 1775 (SCJ)
CLARCK, **Ellick**, of NYC, mariner - 27 Mar. 1716 (MCRM:152)
CLAUDI, **Jean** - 24 July 1724 (Laws, ch. 461)
    Jean Claudi was made freeman of NYC 24 Oct. 1724 as a tailor
    (CNYHS 1885:105)
CLAUSER, **Jacob** - 3 July 1759 (Laws, ch. 1089)
CLEAR, **John** - 19 Dec. 1766 (Laws, ch. 1319)
CLEMENS, **Matthias** - 8 Mar. 1773 (Laws, ch. 1638)
CLEMENS, **Philip** - 8 Mar. 1773 (Laws, ch. 1638)
CLEMENT, **Moses**, Church of England, of NYC, cabinetmaker; cert. min.
    H. Barclay; witnesses: Joseph Hildreth, Thos. Grigg, Jr. - 16
    Apr. 1755 (NYPL; Oo:62; SCJ)
CLEREMBAULT, **Francis** - 24 July 1724 (Laws, ch. 461)
    Francis Clerembault was made freeman of NYC 27 Oct. 1724 as a
    joiner (CNYHS 1885:105)
CLINE, **William** - 20 May 1769 (Laws, ch. 1404)
CLING, **George** - 11 Sept. 1761 (Laws, ch. 1154)
CLOCK, **Casper** - 3 July 1759 (Laws, ch. 1089)
CLOCK, **Hans Hendrick**, of Albany Co. - 3 Jan. 1715/6 (Alb. CCM 6:113)
CLOM, **Philip**, of Albany Co. - 31 Jan. 1715/6 (Alb. CCM 6:116)
CLOP, **Peter**, of Albany Co. - 17 Jan. 1715/6 (Alb. CCM 6:115)
CLOPPER, **Hendrick**, of Ulster Co. - 8/9 Sept. 1715 (Deed Book BB:387)
CLOSS, **Heinrich** - 3 July 1759 (Laws, ch. 1089)
CLUMP, **Peter** - 23 Dec. 1765 (Laws, ch. 1295)

COCK, Rev. Gerhard Daniel, minister German Reformed at Rhinebeck –
29 July 1773 (SCJ)

CODWISE, John Conrad, schoolmaster – 12 July 1715 (MCRM:85)

COELIE, Henry, of NYC, tailor – 27 Apr. 1715 (MCRM:104)

COENRAAD, Frederick – 11 Sept. 1761 (Laws, ch. 1154)

COENRAATS, Octavo, merchant – 19 July 1715 (MCRM:87)

COENRAET, Hendrick, of Albany Co. – 17 Jan. 1715/6 (Alb. CCM 6:115)

COENS, Jacob, of Albany Co. – 14 Feb. 1715/6 (Alb. CCM 6:117)

COENS, Johannis, of Albany Co. – 31 Jan. 1715/6 (Alb. CCM 6:116)

COENS, Mathys, of Albany Co. – 17 Jan. 1715/6 (Alb. CCM 6:115)

COENS, Philip, of Albany Co. – 14 Feb. 1715/6 (Alb. CCM 6:117)

COEYEMANS, Geertruyd (wife of Andries Coeymans, Esq.) – 6 July 1723
(Laws, ch. 445)

COGHNOT, John Everhart – 27 Jan. 1770 (Laws, ch. 1462)

COHEN, Abraham Meyers – 16 Dec. 1737 (Laws, ch. 662)
Took oath NYC in Mayor's Court 10 Jan. 1737/8 and was made freeman of NYC as shopkeeper (MCRM:135)

COHEN, Abraham Myers, Jew, of NYC, merchant – between 1 June 1740
and 1 June 1741 (NYPL; Gg:68; Huhner:6; NYHS Oath Roll, 1741)

COHEN, Samuel Myers, Jew, of NYC, merchant – between 1 June 1740
and 1 June 1741 (NYPL; Gg:68; Huhner:6)

COLECK, Jonas N., of NYC, baker; cert. min. M.C. Knoll; witnesses:
Hans Pfefter, Henrick Behr – 23 Apr. 1744 (NYPL)

COLLIN, Daniel – 3 Feb. 1768 (Laws, ch. 1350)

COLON, George – 27 Jan. 1770 (Laws, ch. 1462)

COLON, James – 27 Jan. 1770 (Laws, ch. 1462)
James Colon, of NYC, chair-maker, was cited 11 July 1786 as
executor of estate of Peter Colon (Scott, Adm. Papers:65)

COLON, Jean, of Schenectady, Albany Co., feltmaker, – 17 Apr. 1750
(SCJ)

COLON, John – 24 Nov. 1750 (Laws, ch. 902)

COLON, Jonas – 27 Jan. 1770 (Laws, ch. 1462)

COLONGE, Mary Elizabeth (widow of Disleau) – 25 Nov. 1751 (Laws,
ch. 921)

CONJES, Jacob – 24 Mar. 1772 (Laws, ch. 1564)

CONTERMAN, Johan Coenrart, of Ulster Co. – 8/9 Sept. 1715 (Deed
Book BB:387)

CONTERMAN, Johan Fredrich, of Ulster Co. – 8/9 Sept. 1715 (Deed
Book BB:387)

CONTERMAN, Johan Gorg, of Ulster Co. – 8/9 Sept. 1715 (Deed Book
BB:387)

COOK, Henry Mickael – 6 July 1723 (Laws, ch. 444)

COOK, John – 16 Feb. 1771 (Laws, ch. 1508) A John Cook, of NYC,
baker, was a bondsman in Mar. 1767 (Scott, Adm. Bonds:53)

COOK, John George – 6 Dec. 1746 (Laws, ch. 844)
John George Cook was made freeman of NYC 26 Sept. 1748 as a
stocking-weaver (CNYHS 1885:164). In Jan. 1744 he was living
at the house of John Peter Zenger in Stone St. (Gottesman:257)

COOKE, Peter, German Reformed, of NYC – 27 July 1774 (SCJ)

COOKENHAM, Johan Jury – 11 Sept. 1761 (Laws, ch. 1154)

COOKENHEIM, Daniel – 3 July 1766 (Laws, ch. 1299)

COOL, Cornelis, of Ulster Co. – 8/9 Sept. 1715 (Deed Book BB:386)

COOL, Philip – 8 Mar. 1773 (Laws, ch. 1638)

COONS, Joost – 24 Mar. 1772 (Laws, ch. 1564)

COOPER, Christian – 11 Sept. 1761 (Laws, ch. 1154)

CORCILIUS, Peter - 8 Nov. 1735 (Laws, ch. 634)
CORCILIUS, William - 8 Nov. 1735 (Laws, ch. 634)
CORDT, Marchand - 24 Nov. 1750 (Laws, ch. 902)
CORNEE, Peter - 29 Oct. 1730 (Laws, ch. 556)
   Peter Corne, merchant, was a bondsman in Dec. 1757 (Scott, Adm.
   Bonds:113)
CORNELIS, John - 26 Aug. 1696 (CEM:146)
CORNELISSEN, Gerrit - 17 June 1726 (Laws, ch. 476)
CORNING, Johan Lodolph, of Albany Co. - 31 Jan. 1715/6 (Alb. CCM
   6:116)
COSSMAN, Johannis - 25 Nov. 1751 (Laws, ch. 921)
COTTIN, Jean, of Kingston, took oath of allegiance 2 Dec. 1687
   before Thomas Chambers, of Foxhall, Ulster Co. (Deeds 10:231-232)
COTTIN, Jean, of Ulster Co. - 8/9 Sept. 1715 (Deed Book BB:387)
COUNS, George Necol - 29 Oct. 1730 (Laws, ch. 556)
COUNTRYMAN, Andries, of Ulster Co. - 8/9 Sept. 1715 (Deed Book
   BB:387)
COUSALMET (?), Johan, of Ulster Co. - 8/9 Sept. 1715 (Deed Book
   BB:387)
COVERT, Johannes - 11 Sept. 1761 (Laws, ch. 1154)
CRALLER, Peter - 22 June 1734 (Laws, ch. 605)
CRAMER, Anthony, of Ulster Co. - 8/9 Sept. 1715 (Deed Book BB:386)
CRAMER, Christopher - 3 May 1755 (Laws, ch. 975)
CRAMER, George - 31 Dec. 1761 (Laws, ch. 1170)
CRAMER, George - 24 Mar. 1772 (Laws, ch. 1564)
CRAMER, Michael, of NYC, boatman - 22 Nov. 1715 (MCRM:121)
CRANE, Josiah, Church of England, of NYC, tobacconist merchant;
   cert. min. Samuel Auchmuty; witnesses: Peter Ewetse, James
   Wells - 21 Apr. 1752 (NYPL; Ii:52; SCJ)
CRAPSER, Casper - 3 May 1755 (Laws, ch. 975); took oath 24 Oct.
   1755 (SCJ)
CRAPSER, Isaac - 3 May 1755 (Laws, ch. 975)
CRAPSER, John - 3 May 1755 (Laws, ch. 975)
CRAPSER, Uldrick - 3 May 1755 (Laws, ch. 975)
CRATSER, Leanhart - 31 Dec. 1768 (Laws, ch. 1385)
CRATZINBERGER, Coenraedt - 3 July 1759 (Laws, ch. 1089)
CREIGHOOF, Jacob - 16 Feb. 1771 (Laws, ch. 1508)
CREITZ, Han Ury - 27 Jan. 1770 (Laws ch. 1462)
CREITZ, Hans Georg - 3 July 1759 (Laws, ch. 1089)
CREMER, Johan N. - 24 Mar. 1772 (Laws, ch. 1564)
CREPPER, Karrel - 11 Sept. 1761 (Laws, ch. 1154)
CREUTZ, Christopher Godlieb, Lutheran, of NYC, baker; cert. min.
   M.C. Knoll; witnesses: Henricus Schrifter, Casparus Hertz -
   1 Aug. 1748 (NYPL; Hh:22)
CROCHERON, Jean/John, of Staten Island, yeoman - 23 Aug. 1715
   (MCRM:94)
CROCK, Coenradt - 24 Mar. 1772 (Laws, ch. 1564)
CROLGES, William - 17 June 1726 (Laws, ch. 476)
   William Crolyas was made freeman of NYC 18 Mar. 1729 as a
   potter (CNYHS 1885:112 - as Crolius)
CROOB, Nicholas, Lutheran, of NYC, cordwainer; cert. min. J. M.
   Kurts; witnesses: Philip Lydig, John Ebert - 21 Apr. 1762
   (NYPL; C.O. 5:1071)
CROSSKOP, John George, Lutheran, of NYC, baker - 20 Apr. 1763
   (C.O. 5:1071; SCJ)

CRUGER, John, of NYC, merchant - 20 Mar. 1715/6 (MCRM:150)

CRUYSELAR, Johannis, of Ulster Co. - 8/9 Sept. 1715 (Deed Book BB:387)

CYFFER, William, Dutch Reformed, of Dutchess Co., farmer ; cert. min. Benjamin Meynerd; witnesses: John Brinckerhoff, Johannes Schurri - 18 Oct. 1750 (NYPL; Hh:142; SCJ)

DA COSTA, Daniel Nunes - 25 Nov. 1727 (Laws, ch. 508)

DAET, Hans Bernhard, of Albany Co. - 14 Feb. 1715/6 (Alb. CCM 6:117)

DAET, Johannis, of Albany Co. - 14 Feb. 1715/6 (Alb. CCM 6:117)

DALIS, Johan Willem, of Albany Co. - 17 Jan. 1715/6 (Alb. CCM 6:115)

DANDLER, Uldrich, of Albany Co. - 31 Jan. 1715/6 (Alb. CCM 6:116)

DATS, Peter, of New Rochell, yeoman - 16 Aug. 1715 (MCRM:92)

DAVID, Hayman, see introd.

DEALING, John, Unitas Fratrum, of NYC, shopkeeper - 20 Apr. 1768 (C.O. 5:1074, Ss:59)

DEBELE, John George, Lutheran, of NYC, gardener; cert. min. M. C. Knoll; witnesses: Jacob Boss, Jacob Foerster, Jeronimus Riegler - 31 Oct. 1745 (NYPL; Gg:213)

DE CASSEREZ/DE CASERES, Abraham - 3 July 1718 (Laws, ch. 356); subscribed 5 Aug. 1718 (NYHS Oath Roll, 1718)
    Abraham De Casarez was made freeman of NYC 5 Aug. 1718 as a tallow chandler (CNYHS 1885:98)

DECKER, Harmanus, of Ulster Co. - 8/9 Sept. 1715 (Deed Book BB:386)

DECKER, Jacob, of Ulster Co. - 8/9 Sept. 1715 (Deed Book BB:387)

DEDERICH, Christ., of Albany Co. - 17 Jan. 1715/6 (Alb. CCM 6:115)

DEDRICH, Fredrich, of Ulster Co. - 8/9 Sept. 1715 (Deed Book BB:387)

DEDRICH, Johan Wilhelm, of Ulster Co. - 8/9 Sept. 1715 (Deed Book BB:387)

DEDRICK, Christian, of Ulster Co. - 8/9 Sept. 1715 (Deed Book BB:387)

DEDRICK, Johan Christian, of Ulster Co. - 8/9 Sept. 1715 (Deed Book BB:387)

DEETS, Adam - 11 Sept. 1761 (Laws, ch. 1154)

DEETS, Hendrick - 20 Mar. 1762 (Laws, ch. 1179)

DEETS, William - 11 Sept. 1761 (Laws, ch. 1154)

DEETZ, Frederick, Lutheran, of NYC, tailor - 29 July 1762 (C.O. 5:1071)

DE FREIDENBERGH, Charles - 3 July 1766 (Laws, ch. 1299)

DEG, Andreas - 3 July 1759 (Laws, ch. 1089)

DEGE, Hendrick - 11 Sept. 1761 (Laws, ch. 1154)

DE GRAAF, Johannis - 23 Dec. 1765 (Laws, ch. 1295)

DE JONCOURT, Jane, Church of England, of NYC, widow - 20 Jan. 1768 (C.O. 5:1073; Rr:30; SCJ)

DE KLERCK, Daniel, of Tappan, yeoman - 23 Aug. 1715 (MCRM:94)

DE KLERCK, Jacobus, of Tappan, yeoman - 23 Aug. 1715 (MCRM:94)

DE KLEYN, Leendert Huygen, of NYC, merchant - 13 Dec. 1715 (MCRM:129)

DE LAGE, Peter - 17 June 1726 (Laws, ch. 476)
    Peter De Lage was made freeman of NYC 2 Nov. 1731 as a merchant (CNYHS 1885:119)

DE LA GRANGIE, Omy, of Albany Co. - 3 Jan. 1715/6 (Alb. CCM 6:113)

DE LEAS, Abraham, Jew - nat. 27 Apr. 1742 by Act of 1740 (NYPL; Huhner:6)

DE LANCEY, Stephen, Church of England, of NYC, merchant; cert.
min. William Vesey; witnesses: Richard Charlton, Anthony Duane -
between 1 June 1740 and 1 June 1741 (NYPL; Gg:68)

DE LISLE, John - 11 Sept. 1761 (Laws, ch. 1154)

DEMETZ, Benjamin, of Ulster Co. - 8/9 Sept. 1715 (Deed Book BB:387)

DENCKER, Hendrick - 11 Sept. 1761 (Laws, ch. 1154)

DE NEUFVILLE, Jean - petition to be naturalized 19 Aug. 1687
(CEM:167)

DE NOYELLES, John, Church of England, of Orange Co., gentleman -
18 Jan. 1769 (C.O. 5:1074; Ss:59; SCJ)

DE PEYSTER, Catherine (wife of Abraham De Peyster) - 6 July 1723
(Laws, ch. 445) Report of committee of Council on Act for
naturalizing her 4 July 1723 (CEM:479)

DE RIVERA/DE RIVERES, Abraham Rodrigues, Jew - between 1 June 1740
and 1 June 1741 (NYPL; Gg:68; Huhner:6)

DERNIE, Philip, mariner - 12 July 1715 (MCRM:85)

DERONDE, Adrian - 20 May 1769 (Laws, ch. 1404; Ss:79)

DeRONDE, Mattheus/Matheus - 20 May 1769 (Laws, ch. 1404; Ss:79)

DeRONDE, Nicholas - 3 July 1759 (Laws, ch. 1089)

DE SCER, Paulus - 17 June 1726 (Laws, ch. 476)

DESCH, John Baltus - 3 July 1759 (Laws, ch. 1089)
John Balthus Dash, tinman, from Germany, in 1765 was living near
the Oswego Market in NYC (Gottesman:204)

DES MAIZEAUX, Peter (son of Lewis and Magdaline Des Maizeaux), born
at Paillat, Auvergne, France - 6 Ann (8 Mar. 1707 - 7 Mar. 1708)
(Deeds 10:326-8)

DETLOFF, Henry, Lutheran, of NYC, cartman - 24 Apr. 1767 (C.O. 5:
1073; Rr:30; SCJ)

DEVAUX, Frederik, of Westchester, husbandman - 2 Aug. 1715 (MCRM:90)

DE WEISSENFELS, Fredrick - 20 Dec. 1763 (Laws, ch. 1236)

DE WINT, John - 29 Oct. 1730 (Laws, ch. 556) - 14 Oct. 1732 (Laws,
ch. 586)
A John De Wint of NYC, was a baker; his wife was Elizabeth
Collins (Scott, Adm. Papers:64)

DE WINT, Pieter - 21 Sept. 1744 (Laws, ch. 787)
Peter De Wint was made freeman of NYC 28 May 1745 as a labourer
(CNYHS 1885:152)

DE WITT, Jacob, of Ulster Co. - 8/9 Sept. 1715 (Deed Book BB:387)

DE WULFFEN, Johanis, of Ulster Co. - 8/9 Sept. 1715 (Deed Book
BB:387)

DE WULFSEN, Godfrid, of Ulster Co.-8/9 Sept. 1715 (Deed Book
BB:387)

DEYBERTSYER, George, German Evangelical, of NYC, chimney-sweeper -
20 Apr. 1769 (C.O. 5:1075; Tt:4; SCJ)

DEYGERT, Sefreen, of Albany Co. - 31 Jan. 1715/6 (Alb. CCM 6:116)

DEYGERT, Warnaer, of Albany Co. - 11 Oct. 1715 (Alb. CCM 6:105)

DE YOUNG, Aaron - 3 Feb. 1768 (Laws, ch. 1350)

D'HARRIETTE, Anna, see introd.

DIARCE, Alexander - 3 July 1766 (Laws, ch. 1299) - 3 Feb. 1768
(Laws, ch. 1350) Took oath in Mayor's Court 1 Mar. 1768 (MCM)

DICK, Dederick - 16 Dec. 1737 (Laws, ch. 662)

DICK, Paul - 16 Dec. 1737 (Laws, ch. 662)

DIEDER, Lourens, of Ulster Co. - 8/9 Sept. 1715 (Deed Book BB:387)

DIEDERIGH, Christiaen, of Albany Co. - 17 Jan. 1715/6 (Alb. CCM
6:115)

DIEFFENDORF, Hendrick - 11 Sept. 1761 (Laws, ch. 1154)

DIEFFENDORF, Hannes - 11 Sept. 1761 (Laws, ch. 1154)

DIEFFERDORF, Jorg - 11 Sept. 1761 (Laws, ch. 1154)

DIEGERT, Johan Pieter, of Albany Co. - 31 Jan. 1715/6 (Alb. CCM 6:116)

DIEL, Adolf, of Ulster Co. - 8/9 Sept. 1715 (Deed Book BB:387)

DIEL, Laurentz, Lutheran, of Dutchess Co., yeoman; cert. min. M.C. Knoll; witnesses: E. Christian Hoyer, Hendrick Beringer - 19 Oct. 1743 (NYPL; Gg:97)

DIETER, Hendrick, Lutheran, of Dutchess Co., farmer; cert. min. G. M. Weiss; witnesses; Johannis Snue, Frederick Beringer - 17 Oct. 1744 (NYPL; Gg:118)

DIETRICH, Jacob - 20 Mar. 1762 (Laws, ch. 1179)

DIETZ, John, German Lutheran, of NYC, yeoman - 28 July 1773 (SCJ)

DING, Adam, of Albany Co. - 17 Jan. 1715/6 (Alb. CCM 6:115)

DINGMAN, Adam, of Albany Co. - 27 Apr. 1716 (Alb. CCM 6:123)

DINGS, Johan Jacob, of Ulster Co. - 8/9 Sept. 1715 (Deed Book BB: 387)

DINSER, Paul, of Albany Co. - 11 Oct. 1715 (Alb. CCM 6:105)

DIPEL, Johan Pieter, of Ulster Co. - 8/9 Sept. 1715 (Deed Book BB:387)

DISCH, Johan Baltus (see also DESCH) - 3 May 1755 (Laws, ch. 975) John Baltus Dash was made freeman of NYC 24 July 1759 as a tinman (CNYHS 1885:193)

DITZ, Johan Wilhelm - 3 Feb. 1768 (Laws, ch. 1350)

DITZ, Johan Willem, Dutch Reformed, of Schohary, Albany Co., shoemaker; cert. min. J. Schuyler; witnesses: Johan Jacob Werth, William Brown - 29 July 1752 (NYPL; Ii:52)

DOBB, Johannes, of Ulster Co. - 8/9 Sept. 1715 (Deed Book BB:387)

DODINE, Anthony - 20 May 1769 (Laws, ch. 1404; Ss:79) Anthony Dodine advertised in Sept. 1769 that he made chimneypieces, tombstones and headstones (Gottesman:229)

DOHER, Georg, of Ulster Co. - 8/9 Sept. 1715 (Deed Book BB:386)

DOMPSBACK, Franz, of Albany Co. - 17 Jan. 1715/6 (Alb. CCM 6:115)

DOMPSBACK, Jost Hend., of Albany Co. - 17 Jan. 1715/6 (Alb. CCM 6:115)

DOOLHAGEN, Denys/Dennis, of NYC, victualler - 23 Aug. 1715 (MCRM: 94)

DOPP, Johan Peter, of Ulster Co. - 8/9 Sept. 1715 (Deed Book BB:387)

DOPP, Johannes Peter, Jr., of Ulster Co. - 8/9 Sept. 1715 (Deed Book BB:387)

DRAGAUD, John - 17 June 1726 (Laws, ch. 476)

DREHER, Sebastian, of Ulster Co. - 8/9 Sept. 1715 (Deed Book BB:387)

DREWID, John Christian, Lutheran Trinity Church, of NYC - 20 Jan. 1776 (SCJ)

DROM, Johan Andries, of Albany Co. - 22 Nov. 1715 (Alb. CCM 6:109)

DU BOIS, Gualtherus, minister of the Dutch Church - 19 July 1715 (MCRM:87)

DU BOIS, Jacob, of Ulster Co. - 8/9 Sept. 1715 (Deed Book BB:386)

DUBOIS, John - 29 Dec. 1763 (Laws, ch. 1236) A John Dubois, of Rumbout Precinct, Dutchess Co., yeoman, was a bondsman in June 1782 (Scott, Adm. Papers: 130)

DU BOIS, Louis, see introd.

DUCHEMIN, Daniel - petition to be naturalized 19 Aug. 1687 (CEM:167)
DUCHEMIN, Daniel - 20 May 1769 (Laws, ch. 1404; Ss:79)
DUMM, Adam - 8 Mar. 1773 (Laws, ch. 1638)
DUMM, Melicher - 8 Mar. 1773 (Laws, ch. 1638)
DUMM, Nicholas - 8 Mar. 1773 (Laws, ch. 1638)
DUNCKEL, John Ludwig - 3 July 1759 (Laws, ch. 1089)
DUNSHMAN, Johannes Gerardus - 3 July 1759 (Laws, ch. 1089)
DUPONNER, Ferdinand - 3 July 1759 (Laws, ch. 1089)
DUPONT, Pierre - 3 July 1759 (Laws, ch. 1089)
DUPUY, Jubatiste, of NYC, merchant - 20 May 1769 (Laws, ch. 1404;
    Ss:79); took oath 28 July 1769 (SCJ)
DUPUY, Mosyse, of Ulster Co. - 8/9 Sept. 1715 (Deed Book BB:386)
DURAND, Peter, French Protestant, of NYC, tailor - 29 July 1762
    (C.O. 5:1071)
DUROT, George David - 11 Sept. 1761 (Laws, ch. 1154)
DU SIMITIERE, Pierre Eugene - 20 May 1769 (Laws, ch. 1404; Ss:79)
    Du Simitiere, a miniature painter, who boarded at the house of
    Mrs. Ferrara in Maiden Lane, advertised 31 July 1769 that he
    intended shortly to leave NYC (Gottesman:3)
DUSLAR, Jacob - 8 Mar. 1773 (Laws, ch. 1638)
DUSLER, Andreas - 11 Sept. 1761 (Laws, ch. 1154)
DUTEN, Charles John - 24 Nov. 1750 (Laws, ch. 902)
    Charles Dutens, jeweller, in 1751 was in business at the house
    of Mrs. Eastham, near the Long Bridge, in Broad St.; he offered
    to teach children the French language (Gottesman:69-70)
DUYCKINCK, Evert, painter - 12 July 1715; he took oaths 12 July
    1715 (MCRM:85)

EASY, Godfrid - 16 Feb. 1771 (Laws, ch. 1508)
EBBERT, John, tailor - 12 July 1715 (MCRM:85)
EBERT, Adam - 6 Dec. 1746 (Laws, ch. 844)
ECKART, Jonathan, German Lutheran, of NYC, trader - 18 Oct. 1769
    (C.O. 5:1075; Tt:4; SCJ)
ECKER, Abraham - 11 Sept. 1761 (Laws, ch. 1154)
    Abraham and William Ecker were executors of the estate of Sibert
    Ecker, of Phillipsburgh, Westchester Co., who died 25 July 1771
    (Scott, Adm. Papers:103)
ECKER, George - 11 Sept. 1761 (Laws, ch. 1154)
ECKER, George - 27 Jan. 1770 (Laws, ch. 1462)
ECKERT, Adam, of Ulster Co. - 8/9 Sept. 1715 (Deed Book BB:387)
ECKERT, John George, of Ulster Co. - 8/9 Sept. 1715 (Deed Book
    BB:387)
ECKERT/EKERT, Philip, Lutheran, of NYC, carpenter - 21 Oct. 1765
    (C.O. 5:1072; Qq:63; SCJ)
ECKHAR, Niccolas, of Albany Co. - 31 Jan. 1715/6 (Alb. CCM 6:116)
ECKLER, Augustus - 11 Sept. 1761 (Laws, ch. 1154)
ECKLER, Hendrick - 11 Sept. 1761 (Laws, ch. 1154)
ECKMAN, Lawrens - 3 July 1759 (Laws, ch. 1089)
EDICH, Hans Michiel, of Albany Co. - 14 Feb. 1715/6 (Alb. CCM 6:117)
EDICH, Hans Michiel, Jr., of Albany Co. - 14 Feb. 1715/6 (Alb. CCM
    6:117)
EELL, Hermanus - 3 July 1759 (Laws, ch. 1089)
EEMAN, Laurens - 3 July 1759 (Laws, ch. 1089)
    Lawrence Eman, of NYC, shopkeeper, was a bondsman on 24 June 1766
    (Scott, Adm. Bonds:86)

EEN, see UIN

EGLE, Martin, Lutheran, of NYC, carpenter - 23 Oct. 1765 (C.O. 5:
1072; Qq:63; SCJ)

EHL, Johannes - 11 Sept. 1761 (Laws, ch. 1154)

EHLICH, Hans Gorg, of Ulster Co. - 8/9 Sept. 1715 (Deed Book BB:387)

EHNY, David - 31 Dec. 1761 (Laws, ch. 1170)

EHNY, Joachin George - 31 Dec. 1761 (Laws, ch. 1170)

EHRING, Christian, Evangelical Lutheran, of NYC, weaver - 29 July
1772 (SCJ)

EIGENBRODE, Peter - 8 Mar. 1773 (Laws, ch. 1638)

EIGENBROOD, Johannes - 3 July 1759 (Laws, ch. 1089)

EIGENBROODT, Hannes - 11 Sept. 1761 (Laws, ch. 1154)

EIKLER, Augustus - 27 Jan. 1770 (Laws, ch. 1462)

EISENLORD, John - 20 Mar. 1762 (Laws, ch. 1179)

EISENLORD, John - 8 Mar. 1773 (Laws, ch. 1638)

ELESEN, Tunis, of Ulster Co. - 8/9 Sept. 1715 (Deed Book BB:386)

ELIAS, David - 6 July 1723 (Laws, ch. 444)

ELICH, Andris, of Ulster Co. - 8/9 Sept. 1715 (Deed Book BB:387)

ELIZER, Isaac, Jew, of Rhode Island, formerly of NYC, merchant -
23 July 1763 (C.O. 5:1071; Huhner:4,6); 28 July 1763 (SCJ)

ELL, Johan Jacob - 14 Oct. 1732 (Laws, ch. 586)

ELLIS, Hero - 14 Oct. 1732 (Laws, ch. 586)
See introd.

ELSHEVER, Ludwick - 11 Sept. 1761 (Laws, ch. 1154)

EMAR/EMAU, Jean, French Church, of NYC, yeoman; cert. min. Lewis
Rou; witnesses: Peter Vergereau, Jeremiah Latouch - Oct. 1740
(NYPL: Gg:68)

EMEGIN, Johan Earnest, of Albany Co. - 13 Mar. 1715/6 (Alb. CCM
6:119)

EMEGIN, Johannis, of Albany Co. - 13 Mar. 1715/6 (Alb. CCM 6:119)

EMICH, Niclas, of Ulster Co. - 8/9 Sept. 1715 (Deed Book BB:387)

EMRICH, Johanis, of Ulster Co. - 8/9 Sept. 1715 (Deed Book BB:387)

ENTERS, John, Reformed Protestant Dutch Church of Manor of Philipsborough, Westchester Co., farmer - 24 Apr. 1767 (C.O. 5:1073;
Rr:30; SCJ)

EPPLY, Jacob, Lutheran, of NYC, carman; cert. min. J. A. Weygand;
witnesses: John Baltus Dasch - 22 Apr. 1761 (NYPL: Oo:63; SCJ)

ERGETSINGER, Baltus - 3 July 1759 (Laws, ch. 1089)

ERNEST, Mathias - 16 Dec.1737 (Laws, ch. 662)
Matthew Ernest, in partnership with Nicholas Bayard, about 1758
opened a glass manufactory within 4 miles of NYC; they offered
the glasshouse for sale in 1762; in 1773 Ernest was living
near the Coenties Market (Gottesman:92, 93, 280)

ESTHARN (?), Jacob, of Ulster Co. - 8/9 Sept. 1715 (Deed Book BB:387)

ESWINE, Jacob, of Albany Co. - 31 Jan. 1715/6 (Alb. CCM 6:116)

ETZ, Christian - 20 Mar. 1762 (Laws, ch. 1179)

EVERTHERT, Johanis, of Ulster Co. - 8/9 Sept. 1715 (Deed Book BB:387)

EVERTSON, Nicholas, of NYC, mariner - 22 Nov. 1715 (MCRM; 121)
Cert. of naturalization 24 Jan. 1702 (CEM:290); made freeman of
NYC 17 Dec. 1700 as a mariner (CNYHS 1885:75)

EYGENAAR, Peter, of Ulster Co. - 8/9 Sept. 1715 (Deed Book BB:387)

FACH/FACK, George - 20 Dec. 1763 (Laws, ch. 1236)
   George Fach, Lutheran, of NYC, baker - 15 Oct. 1765 (C.O. 5:1072;
   Qq:63). George Fack was made freeman of NYC 7 Feb. 1769 as a
   baker (CNYHS 1885:223; SCJ)
FACH, Henry, German Lutheran, of NYC, shoemaker - 18 Oct. 1765 (C.O.
   5:1072; Qq:63, SCJ)
FAGH, John, Lutheran, German Evangelical Congregation, of NYC, cart-
   man - 20 Apr. 1769 (C.O. 5:1075; Tt:4; SCJ)
FAIL, Lodewich - 20 Mar. 1762 (Laws, ch. 1179)
FAIRDAY, Adam, of NYC, mariner - 15 Nov. 1715 (MCRM:119)
FAIRLEY, David - 3 July 1759 (Laws, ch. 1089)
FALCK, Arnoldt, of Ulster Co. - 8/9 Sept. 1715 (Deed Book BB:387)
FALCK, Johanis, of Ulster Co. - 8/9 Sept. 1715 (Deed Book BB:387)
FALCKNER, Rev. Justus, minister of the Lutheran Church - 25 Oct.
   1715 (MCRM:114)
FALK, Nicholas - 20 Oct. 1764 (Laws, ch. 1272)
FALKENHAM, Samuel - 3 July 1759 (Laws, ch. 1089)
   A Samuel Falkenham was made freeman of NYC 2 Aug. 1768 as a
   leather-dresser (CNYHS 1885:215). On 4 Feb. 1782 Magdalen
   Falkingham (widow of Samuel Falkingham, of NYC, leather-breeches-
   maker) was appointed administratrix of her late husband's estate
   (Scott, Adm. Papers:107)
FARLINGER, John - 27 Jan. 1770 (Laws, ch. 1462)
FAUGERES, Louis, of NYC, physician - 20 May 1769 (Laws, ch. 1404;
   Ss:79); took oath 28 July 1769 (SCJ)
   A Louis/Lewis Faugeres, of NYC, physician, was a bondsman in
   Oct. 1774 and Oct. 1775 (Scott, Adm. Bonds: 31,41)
FAUIERE, Charlotte (wife of James) - 25 Nov. 1727 (Laws, ch. 508)
FAUIERE, James, French Church, of NYC, merchant; cert. min. Lewis
   Rou; witnesses: Jeremiah Lattouch, Peter Vergereau (NYPL) - 25
   Nov. 1727 (Laws, ch. 508)
   James Faviers was made freeman of NYC 19 Dec. 1727 as a merchant
   (CNYHS 1885:110). His widow, Charlotte, renounced administration
   on his estate on 15 Sept. 1774 (Scott, Adm. Papers:108)
FAVIERE, James, Protestant - between 1 June 1740 and 1 June 1741
   (Gg:68)
FAVIERS, Charlotte Bouyer, French Church, of NYC, married woman;
   cert. min. L. Rou; witnesses: Moise Gombauld, Samuel Bourdett -
   27 Apr. 1742 (NYPL; Gg:81)
FEDER, Johann - 20 Mar. 1762 (Laws, ch. 1179)
FEECK, Jacob, of Albany Co. - 11 Oct. 1715 (Alb. CCM 6:105)
FEECK, Johannis, of Albany Co. - 11 Oct. 1715 (Alb. CCM 6:105)
FEECK, Peter, of Albany Co. - 11 Oct. 1715 (Alb. CCM 6:105)
FEES, Henrich, of Ulster Co. - 8/9 Sept. 1715 (Deed Book BB:387)
FEICK, Daniel - 16 Feb. 1771 (Laws, ch. 1508)
FEINNAUER, Andreas - 20 Mar. 1762 (Laws, ch. 1179)
FEIX, Peter - 3 July 1759 (Laws, ch. 1089)
FELINCK, Peter - 24 July 1724 (Laws, ch. 461)
FELTA, Johannes - 31 Dec. 1768 (Laws, ch. 1385)
FELTHUYSEN, Christopher - 3 May 1755 (Laws, ch. 975)
FELTHUYSEN, John Georg - 3 May 1755 (Laws, ch. 975)
FELTON, Girronimus - 1740 (Rec. 94:135)
FERRO, Jacob, Jr., Jew, of NYC, merchant - nat. by Act of 1740
   (NYPL; Huhner:6; NYHS Oath Roll, 1741); see introd.

FIEGENHEIM, Christopher, deacon of Reformed German Church, of NYC -
18 Oct. 1774 (SCJ)

FINK, Alexander, Jr., Lutheran, of NYC, butcher - 18 Oct. 1765
(C.O. 5:1072; Qq:63; SCJ)

FISCHER, Leonhard, Reformed German Congregation, of NYC - 27 July
1774 (SCJ)

FISHER, John, Lutheran, of NYC, tanner - 21 Oct. 1765 (C.O. 5:1072;
Qq:63; SCJ)
A John Fisher was made freeman of NYC 11 Sept. 1770 as a tanner
(CNYHS 1885:234)

FISHER, John - 8 Mar. 1773 (Laws, ch. 1638)

FLAAKE, Arendt - 24 Nov. 1750 (Laws, ch. 902)

FLAMIN, Cornelius, of NYC, baker - 18 Oct. 1715 (MCRM:110)

FLANDER, Jacob - 31 Dec. 1768 (Laws, ch. 1385)

FLANDER, Jacob - 8 Mar. 1773 (Laws, ch. 1638)

FLANDREAU, James, of New Rochell, yeoman - 27 Mar. 1716 (MCRM:152)

FLUNEAN, George - 27 Jan. 1770 (Laws, ch. 1462)

FOESHAY, John Luca - 24 Mar. 1772 (Laws, ch. 1564)
John Foshay (son of William and Jane Foshay), of Phillips Manor,
yeoman, on 26 Apr. 1784 was appointed administrator of his
father's estate (Scott, Adm. Papers: 116)

FOEX, Johan Willem, of Albany Co. - 31 Jan. 1715/6 (Alb. CCM 6:116)

FOLK, Nicholas, of NYC, chirurgeon - 26 Oct. 1764 (SCJ)

FOLLAND, Johan Phillip, of Ulster Co. - 8/9 Sept. 1715 (Deed Book
BB:387)

FOLMER, Johannes, Protestant Evangelical Church, of Rheinbeck -
26 Apr. 1773 (SCJ)

FORMER, Christian, of Albany Co. - 3 Jan. 1715/6 (Alb. CCM 6:113)

FORNER (TORNER?), John, German Reformed Congregation, of Albany Co.,
farmer - 29 July 1773 (SCJ)

FORNEYEE, John - 8 Mar. 1773 (Laws, ch. 1638)

FORSTER/FOSTER, Jacob Christopher - 6 Dec. 1746 (Laws, ch. 844)
A Jacob Christopher Foster was made freeman of NYC 13 Jan. 1746/7
as a tallow chandler (CNYHS 1885:157)

FORSTER, Peter - 27 Jan. 1770 (Laws, ch. 1462)

FORT, Andreas - 16 Feb. 1771 (Laws, ch. 1508)

FOURESTIER, Charles, of New Rochell, yeoman - 16 Aug. 1715 (MCRM:92)

FOX, Peter - 20 Mar. 1762 (Laws, ch. 1179)

FRANCE, Jacob - 24 Mar. 1772 (Laws, ch. 1564)

FRANCK, Conrad - 16 Dec. 1737 (Laws, ch. 662)

FRANCK, Frederick - 3 July 1759 (Laws, ch. 1089)
A Frederick Franck, soldier under the command of Capt. Briant
Hammel of the Indian Rangers, was deceased by 8 Aug. 1780 (Scott,
Adm. Bonds:54)

FRANCK, Johanis, of Ulster Co. - 8/9 Sept. 1715 (Deed Book BB:387)

FRANCKEN, Henry Andrew - 3 Feb. 1768 (Laws, ch. 1350)

FRANK, Andries - 20 Mar. 1762 (Laws, ch. 1179)

FRANK, Christophel - 20 Mar. 1762 (Laws, ch. 1179)

FRANK, Frederick - 11 Sept. 1761 (Laws, ch. 1154)

FRANK, Johan Adam - 16 Feb. 1771 (Laws, ch. 1508)

FRANK, Stephanus - 11 Sept. 1761 (Laws, ch. 1154)

FRANKLIN, Christian - 31 Dec. 1761 (Laws, ch. 1170)

FRANKS, Moses Benjamin, Jew, of NYC - 18 Oct. 1748 (NYPL; Hh:22;
Huhner:6)

FREDERICK, Andrew, Lutheran, of NYC, baker; cert. min. J. A. Weygand; witnesses: John Balthus Daesch, Joh. Matth. Rudolph -
17 Apr. 1760 (NYPL; Oo:63)

FREDERICK, Phillip - 11 Sept. 1761 (Laws, ch. 1154)

FREDERICKS, Hans - 11 Sept. 1761 (Laws, ch. 1154)

FREIDENBERGH, Charles - 20 May 1769 (Laws, ch. 1404)

FREIDRICK, Peter - 3 July 1759 (Laws, ch. 1089)

FRERE, Hugo, of Ulster Co. - 8/9 Sept. 1715 (Deed Book BB:387)

FRETCHER, John - 8 Mar. 1773 (Laws, ch. 1638)
Fanna Fritcher, of Nessethaw (widow of a John Fritcher, of
Albany Co., a soldier) was appointed 26 Feb. 1781 administratrix
of her late husband's estate (Scott, Adm. Papers:119)

FRETZ, Ernst - 31 Dec. 1761 (Laws, ch. 1170)

FRETZ, Jacob - 31 Dec. 1761 (Laws, ch. 1170)

FRIEHOUT, Abraham - 20 Dec. 1763 (Laws, ch. 1236)

FRIERICH, Johan Adam, of Ulster Co. - 8/9 Sept. 1715 (Deed Book
BB:387)

FRILICH, Stephen, of Ulster Co. - 8/9 Sept. 1715 (Deed Book BB:387)

FRITZ, Christopher, Lutheran, of Dutchess Co., farmer; cert. min.
G. M. Weiss; witnesses: Johannis Snue, Teunis Snyder (NYPL;
Gg:118)

FRITZ, Elias, Lutheran, of NYC, yeoman; cert. min. J. A. Weygand;
witnesses: Charles Luyfferditz, Lodwick Roose - 21 Apr. 1757
(NYPL; Oo:62; SCJ)

FRITZ, Hendrick - 3 May 1755 (Laws, ch. 975)

FRIWA, Frans - 11 Sept. 1761 (Laws, ch. 1154)

FROLICK, Christian, Unitas Fratrum, of NYC, sugar baker - 21 Apr.
1763 (C.O. 5:1071; SCJ)

FROLLIG, Henrich, of Ulster Co. - 8/9 Sept. 1715 (Deed Book BB:387)

FROLLIG, Vallindin, of Ulster Co. - 8/9 Sept. 1715 (Deed Book
BB:387)

FRY, Francis - 16 Feb. 1771 (Laws, ch. 1508)

FRY, Francis - 8 Mar. 1773 (Laws, ch. 1638)

FRY, Jacob, Church of England, of New Rochell, Westchester Co.,
yeoman; cert. min. P. Stouppe; witnesses: John Durham, William
Baldwin, Isaac Guion - 24 Oct. 1757 (NYPL; Oo:62; SCJ)

FRY, Jacob - 20 Mar. 1762 (Laws, ch. 1179)

FRY, Jurry - 20 Mar. 1762 (Laws, ch. 1179)

FRYDAY, John George, Evangelical German Reformed, of NYC, schoolmaster - 19 Jan. 1774 (SCJ)

FRYENMOET, Rev. John Caspar, Dutch Reformed of Manor of Livingston,
Albany Co. - 15 Oct. 1765 (C.O. 5:1072; Qq:63; SCJ)

FRYMEYER, Michiel, of Albany Co. - 13 Mar. 1715/6 (Alb. CCM 6:119)

FUETER, Daniel Christian - 3 July 1759 (Laws, ch. 1089)
Daniel Fueter, goldsmith and silversmith, on 27 May 1754 advertised that he had lately arrived from London and was living
near the brewery of the late Harmanus Rutgers (Gottesman:41);
in 1769 he was in business with his son Lewis (Gottesman:43).
Daniel Fueter, Unitas Fratrum of NYC, silversmith, was naturalized 31 July 1765 (C.O. 5:1072; Qq:63; SCJ)

FUETER, Lewis, of NYC, silversmith - 16 Feb. 1771 (Laws, ch. 1508;
SCJ); took oath 27 Apr. 1771
Lewis Fueter was made freeman of NYC 28 Mar. 1775 as a gold-
smith (CNYHS 1885:238). He was a bondsman in Oct. 1781 (Scott,
Adm. Bonds: 66)

FUHRER, Johann, of Ulster Co. - 8/9 Sept. 1715 (Deed Book BB:387)
FUHRER, Valedien, of Ulster Co. - 8/9 Sept. 1715 (Deed Book BB:387)
FUNCK, Jacob, Lutheran, of NYC, baker; cert. min. Philippus Sten-
    rious; witnesses: John Debele, John George Cook - 17 Oct. 1753
    (NYPL; Oo:62;SCJ)

GALLAUDET, Pierre Elizee - 17 June 1726 (Laws, ch. 476)
GALLER, Martin - 3 May 1755 (Laws, ch. 975)
GALLINGER, Michael - 3 July 1759 (Laws, ch. 1089)
GANIAR, Francis, of New Rochell, yeoman - 27 Sept. 1715 (MCRM:104)
GANS, Bernard, Reformed German Church, of NYC, vintner; cert. min.
    Frederick Rothenbuhler; witnesses: Johannes Myer, Abraham Young-
    29 July 1761 (NYPL; Oo:63; SCJ)
GARDE, John - 6 Dec. 1746 (Laws, ch. 844)
GARDNER, Peter - 8 Mar. 1773 (Laws, ch. 1638)
GARLOF, Elias - 11 Sept. 1761 (Laws, ch. 1154)
GARLOUGH, Adam - 27 Jan. 1770 (Laws, ch. 1462)
GARNER/GARNIER, Isaac, cordwainer - 26 July 1715 (MCRM:88)
GARREAU, Jean, chirurgeon - 12 July 1715 (MCRM:85)
GARRISON, Isaac (son of Isaac Garrison by Catherine De Romagnac his
    wife), born at Montauban, France - 19 Mar. 1705/6 (Shaw II:50;
    Deeds 10: 151-7)
GARRIT, Nicholas (son of Garret Garrit by Baring/Barinque his wife),
    born at Rarenshing/Ravensting in Germany - 12 June 1689 (Shaw
    II:3; Deeds 9:703)
GARTNER, David, Reformed German Church, of NYC, tailor - 15 Oct.
    1765 (C.O. 5:1072; Qq:63; SCJ)
GASNER, John, Lutheran of NYC, glazier - 29 July 1762 (C.O. 5:1071)
GASSMAN, Rudolph - 20 Mar. 1762 (Laws, ch. 1179)
GEHLER, Fredrik - 20 Mar. 1762 (Laws, ch. 1179)
GEIGER, John Frederick - 3 July 1759 (Laws, ch. 1089)
GENTER, John Heinrich - 3 July 1759 (Laws, ch. 1089)
    A John Genter, brasier, in 1750 was in business in Duke St.
    (Gottesman:194). Mary Magdalen Genter was the daughter of a
    John Genter, of NYC, who died before 30 June 1788 (Scott, Adm.
    Papers:125)
GEORGE, John, Dutch Reformed, of Kakyat, Orange Co., farmer - 31
    July 1764 (C.O. 5:1072; Qq:63; SCJ)
GERBEAUX, Elias - 23 Dec. 1765 (Laws, ch. 1295)
GERBEAUX, Henry - 20 Mar. 1762 (Laws, ch. 1179)
GERLACH, William - 3 July 1759 (Laws, ch. 1089)
GERMAN, Jost, German Reformed Congregation in Hanover, of Hanover,
    Ulster Co. - 18 Oct. 1774 (SCJ)
GERNREICH, Johan Peter. Lutheran, of Dutchess Co., yeoman; cert.
    min. M. C. Knoll; witnesses: Johan Valentine Scheffer, Andrios
    Widerwax - 24 Oct. 1743 (NYPL; Gg:97)
GEROME, Charles of NYC, confectioner - 20 Dec. 1763 (Laws, ch. 1236)
    Took oath 26 Oct. 1764 (SCJ)
GERRETSEN, Arien, of Ulster Co. - 8/9 Sept. 1715 (Deed Book BB:837)
GERUREAU/JERVEREAU, Jacob, of NYC, currier - 2 Aug. 1715 (MCRM:90)
GESSINER, Hendrick, of Westchester Co., yeoman - 10 Jan. 1715/6
    (MCRM:135)
GEYGER, Frederick - 11 Sept. 1761 (Laws, ch. 1154)

GILLOT, Samuel, French Reformed, of Westchester Co., merchant; cert.
min. L. Rou; witnesses: James Buvelot, Alexander Alaire - 21 Oct.
1741 (NYPL; Gg:81)

GIRARD, Abraham, sail-maker - 19 July 1715 (MCRM:87)

GISELBREECHT, Gottfried, Lutheran, of Dutchess Co., physician; cert.
min. M. Christian Knoll; witnesses: Casper Hertz, Henricus
Schefter (or Schleffer?) - 24 Apr. 1749 (NYPL; Hh:70)

GLOUDISZ, Johanes Van Beverhoudt - 24 Nov. 1750 (Laws, ch. 902)

GLUNDORFF, Johannes - 24 July 1724 (Laws, ch. 461)
A Johannes Glundorff was made freeman of NYC 7 May 1728 as a
schoolmaster (CNYHS 1885:111)

GOBEL, David, Lutheran, of NYC, baker - 21 Oct. 1765 (C.O. 5:1072;
Qq:63; SCJ)

GODINEOU, Gilles - petition to be naturalized 19 Aug. 1687 (CEM:167)

GOEBEL, Maurits - 3 July 1759 (Laws, ch. 1089)
A Mawritz Goubel was made freeman of NYC July 1759 as a baker
(CNYHS 1885:193)

GOELET, Jacobus, of NYC, bricklayer - 27 Sept. 1715 (MCRM:104)

GOETSCHIUS, John Henry, Dutch Reformed, of Hackensack, N.J.,
Minister of the Gospel; conf. min. U. Van Sinderen, witnesses:
Abraham Lott, Barent Vandewater - 19 Jan. 1748/9 (NYPL; Hh:70)

GOETSCHIUS, John Mauritzius, Dutch Reformed of Hackensack, N.J.,
chirurgeon; conf. min. Jno. Henricus Goetschius; witnesses:
Abraham Lott, Berent Vandewater - 19 Jan. 1748/9 (NYPL; Hh:70)

GOLNECK, Constyn - 11 Sept. 1761 (Laws, ch. 1154)

GOMBAULD, Daniel - petition to be naturalized 19 Aug. 1687 (CEM:167)

GOMBAULD, Moise - 29 Oct. 1730 (Laws, ch. 556)
Moses Gombauld was made freeman of NYC 10 June 1735 as a mariner
(CNYHS 1885:120). Moses Gombeaux, commander of the sloop St.
Bertram of Martinico, petitioned 8 June 1726 for permission to
wood, water, provision and repair his sloop and on 14 June 1726
for permission to sell casks of sugar (CEM:495)

GOMBAULD, Moses, French Church, of NYC, merchant; cert. min. L. Rou;
witnesses: James Faviere, Jeremiah Latouch - 28 July 1741 (Rec.
94:136)

GOMEZ, Daniel, Jew, of NYC, merchant - 1740 (Huhner: 6; NYHS Oath
Roll, 1741)

GOMEZ, David, Jew, of NYC, merchant - between 1 June 1740 and 1
June 1741 (NYPL; Gg:68) - 24 Jan. 1740/1 (Huhner:66; NYHS Oath
Roll, 1741)

GOMEZ, Mordecai, Jew, of NYC, merchant - between 1 June 1740 and
1 June 1741 (NYPL; Gg:68; Huhner:6)

GOODBARDLY, John - 3 July 1759 (Laws, ch. 1089)

GOODBRODE, William - 8 Mar. 1773 (Laws, ch. 1638)

GOODPERLET, John, Lutheran, of NYC, tailor; cert. min. J. A. Weygand; witnesses: Henry Ritter, Alexander Augspurger - 19 Apr.
1759 (NYPL; Oo:63; SCJ)
A John Goodberlet was made freeman of NYC 29 Oct. 1765 as a
tailor (CNYHS 1885:211)

GOUVERNEUR, Abraham, gent. - 19 July 1715 (MCRM:87)

GOUVERNEUR, Isaac, merchant - 19 July 1715 (MCRM:87)

GOUVERNEUR, Sarah (wife of Isaac Gouverneur, merchant) - 6 July 1723
(Laws, ch. 445).
Isaac Gouverneur was made freeman of NYC 13 Dec. 1698 as a
merchant (CNYHS 1885:71)

GRAAF, Johannes Jacob, Dutch Reformed, of Kings Co., farmer; cert.
   min. L. DeRonde; witnesses: Willem Crelius, Willem Lawrence -
   29 July 1752 (NYPL; Ii:52)
GRAAF/GRAF, Jacob - 3 July 1759 (Laws, ch. 1089)
GRAAF, Jacob - 16 Feb. 1771 (Laws, ch. 1508)
GRAEFT, Johannes - 31 Dec. 1761 (Laws, ch. 1170)
GRAET, Johannis, of Albany Co. - 14 Feb. 1715/6 (Alb. CCM 6:117)
GRAF, Christian - 8 Mar. 1773 (Laws, ch. 1638)
GRESS,Michael, Lutheran, of NYC, sadler - 29 July 1762 (C.O.5:1071)
GRESSMAN, Ludwig - 3 July 1759 (Laws, ch. 1089)
   A Ludwig Gressman was made freeman of NYC 24 July 1759 as a
   tailor (CNYHS 1885:193)
GRIECHACH, Jacob - 20 Mar. 1762 (Laws, ch. 1179)
GRIM, David, German Evangelical Church, of NYC, vintner - 18 Apr.
   1769 (C.O. 5:1075; Tt:4; SCJ)
GRIM, Jacob, Lutheran, of NYC, felt-maker; cert. min. J. F. Ries;
   witnesses: Peter Grim, John Ebert - 1 Aug. 1750 (NYPL; Hh:142)
GRIM, Peter - 6 Dec. 1746 (Laws, ch. 844)
   Peter Grim was a tanner in NYC (Scott, Adm. Bonds:39,61,66,78,97)
   On 2 Sept. 1782 Peter Grim, of NYC, tanner, was appointed ad-
   ministrator of the estate of Sebastian Haller, chaplain to the
   staff of the troops of the Prince of Hesse Cassell (Scott, Adm.
   Papers:139)
GRIM, Philip - 6 Dec. 1746 (Laws, ch. 844)
GROEN, Jacob Marius, silversmith - 12 July 1715 (MCRM:85)
GRONCE, Peter - 27 Jan. 1770 (Laws, ch. 1462)
GRONDAIN, John - 22 June 1734 (Laws, ch. 605)
GROS, Johan Daniel - 8 Mar. 1773 (Laws, ch. 1638)
   On 26 Feb. 1787 Johan Daniel Gros and Catharine Paris, executors
   of the estate of Isaac Paris, late of Stone Arabia, Montgomery
   Co., petitioned for relief (Scott, Adm. Papers:240). On 29 July
   1793 Margaret Nestel, of Palatine District, Montgomery Co. (wid-
   ow of George Nestel, late of Sunbury, Ga., dec'd) renounced ad-
   ministration of her husband's estate in favor of Johan D. Gros,
   of NYC, D.D. (Scott, Adm. Papers:229)
GROTZINGER, Georg - 29 Mar. 1762 (Laws, ch. 1179)
GROUNDHART, John George - 8 Mar. 1773 (Laws, ch. 1638)
GUERINEAU, John - 20 Dec. 1763 (Laws, ch. 1236)
GUERPIN, Marie - petition to be naturalized 19 Aug. 1687 (CEM:167)
GUERRIN, Estienne, of New Rochell, yeoman - 16 Aug. 1715 (MCRM:92)
GUION, Lewis, of New Rochell, blacksmith - 6 Sept. 1715 (MCRM:99)
GUIONS, Lewis, of Eastchester, blacksmith - 16 Aug. 1715 (MCRM:92)
GUNTER, Johan Fredrick - 12 July 1729 (Laws, ch. 538)
   He took oath 9 Sept. 1729 in the NYC Mayor's Court (MCM) and the
   same afternoon was made freeman of NYC as a founder (CNYHS
   1885:113)
GYSELBREGHT, Godfreyd - 3 May 1755 (Laws, ch. 975)

HAAGHORT, Gerardus, Dutch Reformed, of Essex Co., N.J., clerk; cert.
   min. Gerardus Haaghort; witnesses: Francis Wouterse, Hendrick
   Bruyn, Jr. - 24 Oct. 1753 (NYPL; Oo:62; SCJ)
HAAN, Henry - 8 Mar. 1773 (Laws, ch. 1638)
HAAS, Hans, Jury - 16 Dec. 1737 (Laws, ch. 662)
HABENER, Andrew, Lutheran, of NYC, cordwainer - 29 July 1762 (C.O.
   5:1071)

HABER, Zacharias - 22 June 1734 (Laws, ch. 605)

HABERMAN, Hendrick - 11 Sept. 1761 (Laws, ch. 1154)

HABERMAN, Jacob - 11 Sept. 1761 (Laws, ch. 1154)

HAGEDORN, Christopel, of Albany Co. - 22 Nov. 1715 (Alb. CCM 6:109)

HAGEDORN, Willem, of Albany Co. - 14 Feb. 1715/6 (Alb. CCM 6:117)

HAGER, John Fredrick, Palatine minister - 4 Oct. 1715 (MCRM:107)

HAGNER, Hendrick - 8 Mar. 1773 (Laws, ch. 1638)

HAHN, Coenraad - 11 Sept. 1761 (Laws, ch. 1154)
    On 25 Jan. 1783 Jacob Dieffendorf, of Canajohary, nearest of kin
    to Conrad Hahn, late of Canajohary, Tryon Co., blacksmith, dec'd,
    was appointed administrator of the estate of the dec'd (Scott,
    Adm. Papers:137)

HAILENMANN, Mattheus - 3 July 1759 (Laws, ch. 1089)
    A Mathias Hadlenman was made freeman of NYC 7 Feb. 1769 as a
    labourer (CNYHS 1885:224)

HAINE, Peter - 20 Mar. 1762 (Laws, ch. 1179)

HALTH, John - 16 Feb. 1771 (Laws, ch. 1508)

HAM, Casper, of Albany Co. - 14 Feb. 1715/6 (Alb. CCM 6:117)

HAM, Coenraet, of Albany Co. - 17 Jan. 1715/6 (Alb. CCM 6:115)

HAM, Peter, of Albany Co. - 28 Feb. 1715/6 (Alb. CCM 6:118)

HAMBOUGH, Johan Wm., of Albany Co. - 17 Jan. 1715/6 (Alb. CCM 6:115)

HAMEL, Estienne - petition to be naturalized 19 Aug. 1687 (CEM:167)

HANN, Hendrick - 17 Jan. 1770 (Laws, ch. 1462)

HANSON, Godfrey/Godfried, of Rye, rope-maker - 28 Feb. 1715/6
    (MCRM:146)

HANSWURTH, Michael - 3 July 1759 (Laws, ch. 1089)

HARBERDINCK, Johannes, of NYC, shoemaker - 15 Nov. 1715 (MCRM:119)

HARDENBERGH, Johanis, of Ulster Co. - 8/9 Sept. 1715 (Deed Book
    BB:387)

HART, Levy, Jew, Colony of New York, merchant - 27 Oct. 1763 (C.O.
    5:1071; Huhner:4 & 6; SCJ; see introd.)

HART, Solomon, Jr., Jew, of NYC - 27 Apr. 1741 (NYPL; Gg:68;
    Huhner:6)

HARTEL, Hannis - 27 Jan. 1770 (Laws, ch. 1462)

HARTESTEIN, Michael, Lutheran, of NYC, labourer; cert. min. George
    Bager; witness: John Ebert - 15 Oct. 1765 (C.O. 5:1072; Qq:63;
    Rec. 94:144; SCJ)

HARTMAN, Adam - 8 Mar. 1773 (Laws, ch. 1638)

HARTMAN, Christian, of NYC, joiner - 23 Aug. 1715 (MCRM:94)

HASBROUCK, Abraham, of Ulster Co. - 8/9 Sept. 1715 (Deed Book BB:387)

HASIS, Georg - 3 July 1759 (Laws, ch. 1089)

HAUMAID, Jean - 8 Mar. 1773 (Laws, ch. 1638)

HAUSER, Joseph - 20 Dec. 1763 (Laws, ch. 1236)

HAUSZ, Johannus - 27 July 1721 (Laws, ch. 418)
    On 18 Apr. 1783 Anna House (widow of John House, late of Palatine
    District, Tryon Co., farmer) was appointed administratrix of her
    late husband's estate. The bond of administration was signed by
    her, Andrew Finck, Jr., and Jacob J. Cock, all of the Palatine
    District. It was witnessed by Christopher P. Yates (Scott, Adm.
    Papers:161)

HAVER, Christiaen, of Albany Co. - 17 Jan. 1715/6 (Alb. CCM 6:115)

HAWSE, Symon, of Albany Co. - 27 Apr. 1716 (Alb. CCM 6:123)

HAY, David, Jew - nat. by Act of 1740 (NYPL; Huhner:6; NYHS Oath
    Roll, 1741)

HAY/HAYES, Judah, Jew, of NYC, merchant - nat. by Act of 1740 (NYPL;
   Gg:68; Huhner:6; NYHS Oath Roll, 1741)
HAYS, David - 12 June 1729 (Laws, ch. 538). He took oath NYC
   Mayor's Court 8 Sept. 1729 (MCM)
   A David Hays was made freeman of NYC 16 Sept. 1735 as a merchant
   (CNYHS 1885:1238)
HAYS, Isaac, Jew, of NYC, tallow chandler - 26 Apr. 1748 (NYPL;
   Hh:22; Huhner: 4 & 6)
HAYS, Jacob - 6 July 1723 (Laws, ch. 444; NYHS Oath Roll, 1723)
   A Jacob Hays was made freeman of NYC 7 June 1726 as a merchant
   (CNYHS 1885:107)
HAYS, Judah - 12 July 1729 (Laws, ch. 538). He took oath NYC
   Mayor's Court 9 Sept. 1729 (MCM)
   A Judah Hays was made freeman of NYC 2 Dec. 1735 as a merchant.
   In 1762 his house was in Broad St. (Gottesman:51-52). In Aug.
   1762 Judah Hayes, of NYC, merchant, was a creditor of Samuel
   Levi, of Suffolk Co., merchant, dec'd (Scott, Adm. Papers:191)
HAZERMAN, Christopher - 11 Sept. 1761 (Laws, ch. 1154)
HEARING, Henry - 31 Dec. 1768 (Laws, ch. 1385)
HECHT/HEGHT, Frederick William, Church of England, of NYC, gentle-
   man - 1 Aug. 1766 (SCJ)
HEDDINGS, Lawrence - had a certificate of naturalization when on
   13 Dec. 1700 he was registered as a freeman of NYC (NY Col Mss
   45:64)
HEDER/HATER, Henrik, Dutch Reformed, of NYC, carman; cert. min.
   G. DuBois; witnesses: Abraham Lott, Johannes Lott - 7 Aug. 1744
   (NYPL; Gg:118, 161); see also introd.
HEEMMER, Juryh Herck, of Albany Co. 11 Oct. 1715 (Alb. CCM 6:105)
HEEN, Peter - 20 Mar. 1762 (Laws, ch. 1179)
HEERBENK, John, German Reformed Congregation, of NYC, tanner - 20
   Apr. 1769 (C.O. 5:1075; Tt:4)
HEERMANS, Jan, of Ulster Co. - 8/9 Sept. 1715 (Deed Book BB:387)
HEGER, Hendrick - 3 May 1755 (Laws, ch. 975)
HEIGLE, Michael - 16 Feb. 1771 (Laws, ch. 1508)
HEINER, Johannis, of Albany Co. - 3 Jan. 1715/6 (Alb. CCM 6:113)
HEINTZ, Andreas - 8 Mar. 1773 (Laws, ch. 1638)
HEITZ, Jacob, Lutheran, of NYC, carman; cert. min. J. A. Weygand;
   witnesses: David Fairley, Johan George Auch - 29 July 1761
   (NYPL; Oo:63)
HELM, Symon, of Ulster Co. - 8/9 Sept. 1715 (Deed Book BB:387)
HELMER, Leendert, of Albany Co. - 11 Oct. 1715 (Alb. CCM 6:105)
HELMER, Philips, of Albany Co. - 11 Oct. 1715 (Alb. CCM 6:105)
HELMS, Emus, Church of England, of NYC, mariner; cert. min. Richard
   Charlton; witnesses: Cornelis Tiebout, Christian Hertell - 4
   Aug. 1746 (NYPL; Gg:213)
HELMS, Michael, of Ulster Co. - 8/9 Sept. 1715 (Deed Book BB:387)
HENCKE, Christian, of Ulster Co. - 8/9 Sept. 1715 (Deed Book BB:386)
HENDERER, Jacob, Lutheran, of Manor of Livingston, Albany Co., cord-
   wainer - 23 Apr. 1765 (C.O. 5:1072; Qq:63; SCJ)
HENDRICK, Godfred - 16 Dec. 1737 (Laws, ch. 662)
HENNEGAR/HENNEGOR/HENNINGER, Michael, Lutheran, of NYC - 20 May 1769
   (Laws, ch. 1404; Ss:79; SCJ)
HENNINGER, Adam, Reformed German, of NYC - 27 July 1774 (SCJ)
HENNINGER, Christopher, Antient Lutheran Congregation, of NYC -
   27 July 1774 (SCJ)

HENRIAU, Daniel - petition to be naturalized 19 Aug. 1687 (CEM:167)
HENRIAU, Pierre - petition to be naturalized 19 Aug. 1687 (CEM:167)
HENRICH, Lourens, of Ulster Co. - 8/9 Sept. 1715 (Deed Book BB:386)
HENRIQUES, Isaac Nunes, Jew - 23 Oct. 1741 (NYPL: Gg:81; Huhner: 6;
    NYHS Oath Roll, 1741)
HERBERT, John, Lutheran, of NYC, butcher - 23 Oct. 1765 (C.O. 5:
    1072; Qq:63; SCJ)
HERCKHEMER, Hans Jury, of Albany Co. - 31 Jan. 1715/6 (Alb. CCM
    6:116)
HERDER, Lowrence, of Albany Co. - 28 Feb. 1715/6 (Alb. CCM 6:118)
HERDER, Michel, of Albany Co. 17 Jan. 1715/6 (Alb. CCM 6:115)
HEREINGER, Nicholas - 29 Oct. 1730 (Laws, ch. 556)
HERHARDT, Symon, of Albany Co. - 3 Jan 1715/6 (Alb. CCM 6:113)
HERING, John Andrew, Lutheran, of NYC, weaver; cert. min. M. C.
    Knoll; witnesses: Charles Beekman, Jr., John Michael Wille -
    25 Oct. 1748 (NYPL; Hh:22)
HERING, Karel - 3 May 1755 (Laws, ch. 975)
HEROY, Charles, Church of England, of New Rochel, Westchester Co.,
    weaver; cert. min. P. Stouppe; witnesses: Aman Guion, Elder,
    Isaac Coutant - 21 Jan. 1752 (NYPL; I1:52; SCJ)
HEROY, James, Church of England, of NYC, cartman; cert. min. P.
    Stouppe; witnesses: Aman Guion, Elder, Isaac Coutant - 21 Jan.
    1752 (NYPL; I1:52); of New Rochell (SCJ)
HERPAIN/HARPAIN, James - 22 Nov. 1750 (Laws, ch. 902); see introd.
HERRBENK, John, German Reformed, of NYC, tanner - 20 Apr. 1769 (SCJ)
HERRING, Henry - 8 Mar. 1773 (Laws, ch. 1638)
HERTTE, Peter, of Ulster Co. - 8/9 Sept. 1715 (Deed Book BB:387)
HERTZ, Casparus, Lutheran, of NYC, cartman; cert. min. M. C. Knoll;
    witnesses: Johan Frederick Harman, Jonas Melick - 17 Apr. 1746
    (NYPL; Gg:213)
HERTZ, Jacob, Lutheran, of NYC, carman - 29 July 1761 (SCJ)
HERWAGEN, Phillip - 11 Sept.1761 (Laws, ch. 1154)
HES, Johannis, of Albany Co. - 17 Jan. 1715/6 (Alb. CCM 6:115)
HES, Niccolas, of Albany Co. - 17 Jan. 1715/6 (Alb. CCM 6:115)
HESS, Johan - 3 May 1755 (Laws, ch. 975)
    A John Hess, of NYC, tallow chandler, was bondsman in Oct. 1763
    (Scott, Adm. Bonds:44)
HESS, John, Lutheran, of NYC, tallow chandler; cert. min. J. A.
    Weygand; witnesses: Jacob Reyslar, Daniel Wiedershyne - 21 Apr.
    1762 (NYPL; C.O. 5:1071)
HESZ, Hendrick - 11 Sept. 1761 (Laws, ch. 1154)
HEYDORN, Hendrick, of Albany Co. - 17 Jan. 1715/6 (Alb. CCM 6:114)
HEYER, Dietrick, Lutheran, of NYC, sugar boiler - 19 Apr. 1769
    (C.O. 5:1075; Tt:4; SCJ)
HEYN, Johannis Jury, of Albany Co. - 3 Jan. 1715/6 (Alb. CCM 6:113)
HEYNEY, Conrad - 31 Dec. 1768 (Laws, ch. 1385)
HEYNEY, Fredrick - 31 Dec. 1768 (Laws, ch. 1385)
HEYNS, William - 11 Sept. 1761 (Laws, ch. 1154)
HEYNTIE, Michial, of Albany Co. - 17 Jan. 1715/6 (Alb. CCM 6:115)
HEYPT, Philips, of Albany Co. - 17 Jan. 1715/6 (Alb. CCM 6:115)
HEYSER, Hans Pieter, of Albany Co. - 22 Nov. 1715 (Alb. CCM 6:109)
HEYSER, Hendrick - 3 July 1759 (Laws, ch. 1089)
    A Hendrick Heyser was made freeman of NYC 9 Dec. 1766 as a
    carpenter (CNYHS 1885:214)

HILDENBRANDT, Wendell - 20 Mar. 1762 (Laws, ch. 1179)
   A Wendell W. Hillebrant in Nov. 1813 was one of the bondsmen for
   Samuel Coley, of Bethlehem, Albany Co. (Scott, Adm. Papers:64)
HILL, Christian - 8 Mar. 1773 (Laws, ch. 1638)
HILL, John, German Reformed Congregation, of NYC, labourer - 20 Apr.
   1769 (C.O. 5:1075; Tt:4; SCJ)
HILL, John - 20 May 1769 (Laws, ch. 1404; Ss:79)
HILLECAS, Fredrick - 20 Dec. 1763 (Laws, ch. 1236)
HILLEGAS, John Pieter - 3 July 1759 (Laws, ch. 1089)
HILLMAN, Henry, German Reformed Congregation, of NYC - 22 Jan. 1772
HILSCHINER, Michel - 20 Mar. 1762 (Laws, ch. 1179)
HIP, George - 3 July 1759 (Laws, ch. 1089)
HIP, Stephen - 3 July 1759 (Laws, ch. 1089)
HOCK, Hans Hendrick, of Albany Co. - 17 Jan. 1715/6 (Alb. CCM 6:115)
HODLER, Peter - 24 Mar. 1772 (Laws, ch. 1564)
HOEFER, David, of Albany Co. - 22 Nov. 1715 (Alb. CCM 6:109)
HOEFLICH, Carl - 20 Mar. 1762 (Laws, ch. 1179)
HOERTSE, Jacob, Lutheran, of NYC, mason - 29 July 1762 (C.O. 5:1071)
HOFFGOET, Hans Jury - 3 May 1755 (Laws, ch. 975)
HOFFMAN, Carl - 3 July 1759 (Laws, ch. 1089)
   A Carl Hofman, of Poughkeepsie, yeoman, was a bondsman in May
   1775 (Scott, Adm. Papers:185)
HOFFMAN, Jury - 3 July 1759 (Laws, ch. 1089)
HOFFMAN, Michael - 3 May 1755 (Laws, ch. 975)
HOFFMAN, Michael - 3 July 1759 (Laws, ch. 1089)
HOFFMAN, Philip - 20 Mar. 1762 (Laws, ch. 1179)
HOFFSTEDER, Christian - 8 Mar. 1773 (Laws, ch. 1638)
HOFMAN, Coenrat, of Ulster Co. - 8/9 Sept. 1715 (Deed Book BB:387)
HOFMAN, Hendrick, of Ulster Co. - 8/9 Sept. 1715 (Deed Book BB:387)
HOFT, Adam, of Albany Co. - 31 Jan. 1715/6 (Alb. CCM 6:116)
HOFT, Andries, of Albany Co. 31 Jan. 1715/6 (Alb. CCM 6:116)
HOCHSTRASSER, Jacob - 16 Feb. 1771 (Laws, ch. 1508)
HOIN, Godfrey - 24 Nov. 1750 (Laws, ch. 902)
HOINING, Coenradt - 8 Mar. 1773 (Laws, ch. 1638)
HOLSAAERT, Anthony, of New Utrecht, shoemaker - 28 Feb. 1715/6
   (MCRM:146)
HOLZAPEL, William - 16 Dec. 1737 (Laws, ch. 662)
HOMAN, Peter - 11 Sept. 1761 (Laws, ch. 1154)
HOMMEL, Harmanus, of Ulster Co. - 8/9 Sept. 1715 (Deed Book BB:387)
HOOGSTRASSER, Paul - 11 Sept. 1761 (Laws, ch. 1154)
HOORENBEEK, Loudewyck, of Ulster Co. - 8/9 Sept. 1715 (Deed Book
   BB:386)
HORNEFFER, Henrich, Reformed German Church, of NYC, baker - 21 Oct.
   1765 (C.O. 5:1072; Qq:63; SCJ)
HORNING, Nicolas, of Albany Co. - 11 Oct. 1715 (Alb. CCM 6:105)
HORTEG, Johannes - 31 Dec. 1768 (Laws, ch. 1385)
HORTIGH, John - 8 Mar. 1773 (Laws, ch. 1638)
HORTILE, Adam, of Ulster Co. - 8/9 Sept. 1715 (Deed Book BB:387)
HOSMAN, Herman, of Ulster Co. - 8/9 Sept. 1715 (Deed Book BB:387)
HOSMAN, Johan Lowerns, of Ulster Co. 8/9 Sept 1715 (Deed Book
   BB:387)
HOSMAN, John Christian, of Ulster Co. - 8/9 Sept. 1715 (Deed Book
   BB:387)
HOUCH, George - 16 Feb. 1771 (Laws, ch. 1508)

HOUCK, Jury, of Albany Co. - 17 Jan. 1715/6 (Alb. CCM 6:115)
HOUS, Rynier, of Phillipsburgh, yeoman - 10 Jan. 1715/6 (MCRM:135)
HOUTSCHILT, Ernest - 25 Nov. 1751 (Laws, ch. 921)
HOUTVAT, Adrian - 24 Nov. 1750 (Laws, ch. 902)
    An Adrian Houswaet was made freeman of NYC 8 Jan. 1750/1 as a
    merchant (CNYHS 1885:171); see introd.
HOUYS, Christian, of Albany Co. - 11 Oct. 1715 (Alb. CCM 6:105)
HOYER, Erich Christian, Lutheran, of NYC, schoolmaster; cert. min.
    M. C. Knoll; witnesses: Johann David Wolf, Jacob Christopher
    Foerster - 29 July 1746 (NYPL; Gg:213)
HOYER, Mather/Matthew, Lutheran, of NYC, baker; cert. min. J. A.
    Weygand; witnesses: John Balthus Dalsen, Jan Godfrid Muller -
    28 Oct. 1760 (NYPL; Oo:63; SCJ)
HUBER, Casper - 3 July 1759 (Laws, ch. 1089)
HUBER, Hans Jacob, Dutch Reformed, of NYC, yeoman; cert. min. G.
    DuBois - 23 Apr. 1747 (NYPL)
HUBNER, Georg - 3 July 1759 (Laws ch. 1089)
    A George Hubner was made freeman of NYC 24 July 1759 as a
    labourer (CNYHS 1885:193)
HUBNER, Henry - 3 July 1759 (Laws, ch. 1089)
HUISMAN, Abraham - 22 June 1734 (Laws, ch. 605)
HUNTZIGER/HUNTZINGER, Johannes, Lutheran, of Dutchess Co., black-
    smith; cert. min. M. C. Knoll; witnesses: John Phafer, Laurens
    Van Boskerck - 25 Apr. 1743 (NYPL; Gg:97)
HUTH, Jacob - 3 July 1759 (Laws, ch. 1089)
HUY, David, Jew - nat. between 1 June 1740 and 1 June 1741 (Gg:68)
HYER, Johan Frederick, Evangelical German Lutheran, "orgin-builder"
    - 28 July 1773 (SCJ)

ISAACS, Aaron - 20 Oct. 1764 (Laws, ch. 1272)
    An Aaron Isaacs on 24 June 1773 witnessed the adm. bond of
    Ebenezer Hedges, of Suffolk Co., yeoman (Scott, Adm. Papers:149)
ISAACS, Abraham, Jew, of NYC, merchant - nat. between 1 June 1740
    and 1 June 1741 (NYPL; Gg:68; Huhner:6; NYHS Oath Roll, 1741)
ISAACS, Samuel - 27 Jan. 1770 (Laws, ch. 1462)
    A Samuel Isaacs, of Lower Salem, Westchester Co., was a bondsman
    in May 1768 (Scott, Adm. Papers: 41)
ISENHARDT, Christopher - 20 Mar. 1762 (Laws, ch. 1179)

JABOIEN, Nicholaus - 17 June 1726 (Laws, ch. 476)
JACOBI, Christopher, Lutheran, of Germantown, Pa., stocking-weaver;
    cert. min. J. F. Ries; witnesses: Peter Grim, John Eberts - 15
    Jan. 1750/I (NYPL; Ii:52)
JACOBI, Ulrigh, of Albany Co. - 17 Jan. 1715/6 (Alb. CCM 6:115)
JACOBS, David - 20 Mar. 1762 (Laws, ch. 1179)
JACOBS, Philip, Reformed German Church, of NYC, - 22 Apr. 1774 (SCJ)
JACOBSE, Cornelis, of NYC - certificate of naturalization 7 June
    1684 (CEM:128)
JACOBSE, Pieter, of NYC, bricklayer - 27 Sept. 1715 (MCRM:108)
JACOBSEN, Christopher - 3 May 1755 (Laws, ch. 975); affirmed 30 Sept.
    1755 NYC Mayor's Court by the people called Unitas Fratrum (MCM)
JAMAIN, Judith, of NYC, spinster - 6 Mar. 1715/6 (MCRM:148)
JANSE, Joseph, of Albany Co. - 6 Dec. 1715 (Alb. CCM 6:111)

JANSSEN/JANSEN, Joost/Just - 3 May 1755 (Laws, ch. 975); affirmed
    NYC Mayor's Court 30 Sept. 1755 by the people called Unitas
    Fratrum (MCM)
JANZE, Daniel, of Albany Co. - 17 Jan. 1715/6 (Alb. CCM 6:115)
JANZE, Evert, of Albany Co - 22 Nov. 1715 (Alb. CCM 6:109)
JEFBACK, Johan Coenraet, of Albany Co. - 31 Jan. 1715/6 (Alb.
    CCM 6:116)
JERVEREAU, see GERUREAU
JOHNSON, Christopher, Antient Lutheran Congregation, of NYC, tavern-
    keeper - 20 Apr. 1768 (C.O. 5:1074; Ss:59; SCJ)
JONG, Hendrick, of Albany Co. - 3 Jan. 1715/6 (Alb. CCM 6:113)
JONG BLOET, Johanes - 8 Nov. 1735 (Laws, ch. 634)
JORAN, Jacob - 8 Mar. 1773 (Laws, ch. 1638)
JORDAN, Casper, Jr. - 11 Sept. 1761 (Laws, ch. 1154)
JORDAN, Stephen - 20 Mar. 1762 (Laws, ch. 1179)
JORDON, Hannes, Jr. - 11 Sept. 1761 (Laws, ch. 1154)
JOSEPHSON, Manuel; see introd.
JOUCH, John, Antient Lutheran Congregation, of NYC, shingle-shaver
    - 18 Oct. 1768 (C.O. 5:1074; Ss:59; SCJ)
JOUNEAU, Pierre - petition to be naturalized 19 Aug. 1687 (CEM:167)
JUDAH, Baruch, of NYC, merchant - 10 Jan. 1715/6 (MCRM:135)
JULLIAN, Charle - 6 Dec. 1746 (Laws, ch. 844)
JUNCK, Johan Mattheis, of Ulster Co. - 8/9 Sept. 1715 (Deed Book
    BB:387)
JUNG, Abraham, German Reformed Congregation, of NYC, gardiner -
    22 Jan. 1772 (SCJ)
JUNY, Peter - 20 Mar. 1762 (Laws, ch. 1179)
JURIANSE, Johanes - 6 Dec. 1746 (Laws, ch. 844)
JURY, Hans - 11 Sept. 1761 (Laws, ch. 1154)

KAINE, John - 31 Dec. 1768 (Laws, ch. 1385)
    A John Kain was made freeman of NYC 20 June 1769 as a mariner
    (CNYHS 1885:226)
KAPOUCHE, Jacob, of Ulster Co. - 8/9 Sept. 1715 (Deed Book BB:386)
KAREL, Jurry - 24 Mar. 1772 (Laws, ch. 1564)
KARGER, Philip - 3 May 1755 (Laws, ch. 975)
KARNE, John - 27 Jan. 1770 (Laws, ch. 1462)
KASS, George - 3 July 1759 (Laws, ch. 1089)
KAST, Hans Jury, of Albany Co. - 11 Oct. 1715 (Alb. CCM 6:105)
KAUZER, Adam - 20 Mar. 1762 (Laws, ch. 1179)
KEILMAN,Philip - 3 July 1759 (Laws, ch. 1089)
KEKRIGH, Frederick - 3 July 1759 (Laws, ch. 1089)
KELDER, Frans, of Ulster Co. - 8/9 Sept. 1715 (Deed Book BB:386)
KELLAR, John, Jr. - 8 Mar. 1773 (Laws, ch. 1638)
KELLER, Andreas - 11 Sept. 1761 (Laws, ch. 1154)
KELLER, Felix - 3 July 1759 (Laws, ch. 1089)
KELLER, Henry - 3 July 1759 (Laws, ch. 1089)
KELLER, Jacob - 3 July 1759 (Laws, ch. 1089)
KELLER, Nicholas - 8 Mar. 1773 (Laws, ch. 1638)
KELLER, Rudolph - 3 July 1759 (Laws, ch. 1089)
KELMER, Jurich, of Albany Co. - 17 Jan. 1715/6 (Alb. CCM 6:115)
KELTHSH, Johannes - 8 Mar. 1773 (Laws, ch. 1638)

KEMMANE, Caspel Englebert - 24 Nov. 1750 (Laws, ch. 902); see introd.
   An Englebert Kemmena was made freeman of NYC 29 Oct. 1765 as a
   chirurgeon (CNYHS 1885:211)
KEMP, Thomas of Westchester Co., yeoman - 31 Dec. 1768 (Laws, ch.
   1385); took oath 18 Jan. 1769 (SCJ)
KERGER, Heinrick - 31 Dec. 1761 (Laws, ch. 1170)
KERMER, Michael, Jr. - 8 Mar. 1773 (Laws, ch. 1638)
KERN, Baltzer - 31 Dec. 1768 (Laws, ch. 1385)
KERN, Hans - 11 Sept. 1761 (Laws, ch. 1154)
KERN, Jacob - 20 Mar. 1762 (Laws, ch. 1179)
KERNER, Andries Lodewyck, of Ulster Co. - 8/9 Sept. 1715 (Deed
   Book BB:387)
KERNER, Nicolas, of Ulster Co. - 8/9 Sept. 1715 (Deed Book BB:387)
KERNWANER, George - 11 Sept. 1761 (Laws, ch. 1154)
KESMER, Michael, Jr. - 16 Feb. 1771 (Laws, ch. 1508)
KESSELAER, David, of Albany Co. - 17 Jan. 1715/6 (Alb. CCM 6:115)
KESSLER, Johannis, of Albany Co. - 3 Jan. 1715/6 (Alb. CCM 6:113)
KETTEL, Henrich, of Ulster Co. - 8/9 Sept. 1715 (Deed Book BB:387)
KETTEL, Nicolas, of Ulster Co. - 8/9 Sept. 1715 (Deed Book BB:387)
KETTLEMAN, John - 24 Nov. 1750 (Laws, ch. 902)
KEYSER, George Michael, Lutheran, of NYC, labourer; cert. min.
   J. A. Weygand; witnesses: John Balthus Dasch, Michael Nestil -
   21 Jan. 1761 (NYPL; Oo:63; SCJ)
KEYSER, Johannis, of Albany Co. - 11 Oct. 1715 (Alb. CCM 6:105)
KEYSERYCK, Bastiaen - 3 July 1759 (Laws, ch. 1089)
KIERMAN, Fredrick, of Albany Co. - 22 Nov. 1715 (Alb. CCM 6:109)
KIERS, Edward William, Reformed Protestant Dutch Church, of Orange
   Co., merchant - 25 July 1769 (C.O. 5:1075; Tt:4;SCJ)
KIESSLAR, Pieter, of Ulster Co. - 8/9 Sept. 1715 (Deed Book BB:387)
KILBRUNN/KILBURN, Lawrence, Unitas Fratrum, of NYC, merchant - 20
   Apr. 1768 (C.O. 5:1074; Ss:59;SCJ)
KILEMAN, Philip - 16 Feb. 1771 (Laws, ch. 1508)
KILMAN, Nicholas, Lutheran, of NYC, innholder - 2 Aug. 1763 (C.O.
   5:1072; Qq:63; SCJ)
KILTZ, Adam - 29 Mar. 1762 (Laws, ch. 1179)
KILTZ, Johan Nekel - 20 Mar. 1762 (Laws, ch. 1179)
KILTZ, Johannis - 20 Mar. 1762 (Laws, ch. 1179)
KILTZ, Peter - 20 Mar. 1762 (Laws, ch. 1179)
KING, Johann Marcus, of NYC, printer - 8 Nov. 1715 (MCRM:117)
KISELAR, Paulus, Dutch Reformed Church at Clarks Town, of Orange
   Co., farmer - 23 Oct. 1770 (SCJ)
KITTMAN, Johan - 3 May 1755 (Laws, ch. 975)
KITTS, Hans - 11 Sept. 1761 (Laws, ch. 1154)
KITTS, Jacob - 11 Sept. 1761 (Laws, ch. 1154)
KLEBSATEL, Andreas - 16 Dec. 1737 (Laws, ch. 662)
KLEIN, Frederick - 3 July 1759 (Laws, ch. 1089)
KLEIN, George, Lutheran, of NYC, baker - 21 Oct. 1765 (C. O. 5:1072;
   Qq:63; SCJ)
KLEIN, Hieronimus, of Ulster Co. - 8/9 Sept. 1715 (Deed Book BB:387)
KLEIN, Johan Jacob, of Ulster Co. - 8/9 Sept. 1715 (Deed Book BB:387)
KLEIN, John, Lutheran, of NYC, nailsmith - 21 Oct. 1765 (C. O. 5:
   1072: Qq:63; SCJ)
KLEYN, Adam, of Albany Co. - 31 Jan. 1715/6 (Alb. CCM 6:116)
KLEYN, Pieter - 3 May 1755 (Laws, ch. 975)

KLEYN/KLEYNE, Johannes - 8 Mar. 1773 (Laws, ch. 1638); see introd.

KLEYNE, Michael - 8 Mar. 1773 (Laws, ch. 1638)

KLEYNMAN, Thomas - 3 Feb. 1768 (Laws, ch. 1350)

KLIEN, Phillip Heinrich - 3 July 1759 (Laws, ch. 1089)

KLINCK, Jacob, Lutheran, of NYC, carman - 23 Apr. 1765 (C. O. 5: 1072; Qq:63; SCJ)

KLINE, John, Reformed German Church, of NYC, baker - 15 Oct. 1765 (C.O. 5:1072; Qq:63; SCJ)

KLOCK, Hendrick, of Albany Co. - 11 Oct. 1715 (Alb. CCM 6:105)

KLYN, Conradt - 31 Dec. 1768 (Laws, ch. 1385)

KLYN, Jacob - 31 Dec. 1768 (Laws, ch. 1385)

KLYN, Jacob, Jr. - 31 Dec. 1768 (Laws, ch. 1385)

KLYN, Johannis, of Ulster Co. 8/9 Sept. 1715 (Deed Book BB:387)

KLYN, Johannes Peter, Lutheran, of Dutchess Co., farmer; cert. min. G. M. Weiss; witnesses: Johannes Snue, Frederick Beringer (or Beringen?) - 17 Oct. 1744 (NYPL; Gg:118; Rec. 94:137)

KLYNE, Johannes - 31 Dec. 1761 (Laws, ch. 1170)

KNAFE, Jacob, Jr. - 11 Sept. 1761 (Laws, ch. 1154)

KNAFE, John - 11 Sept. 1761 (Laws, ch. 1154)

KNECHT, Mattys, Lutheran, of NYC, mason; cert. min. M. C. Knoll; witnesses: Johan Leonhard Weiland, Christoffer Meyer - 1 Aug. 1750 (NYPL; Hh:142)

KNESKERN, Peter, of Albany Co. - 11 Oct. 1715 (Alb. CCM 6:105)

KOAL, Georg Wilhelm, of Ulster Co. - 8/9 Sept. 1715 (Deed Book BB:387)

KOCK, Albertus - 31 Dec. 1761 (Laws, ch. 1170)

KOCK, Casparus - 31 Dec. 1761 (Laws, ch. 1170)

KOCK, Jan Joost - 3 July 1759 (Laws, ch. 1089)

KOCK, Rudolph - 31 Dec. 1761 (Laws, ch. 1170)

KOEFFER, Baltus, of Ulster Co. - 8/9 Sept. 1715 (Deed Book BB:387)

KOEFFOR. Wilhelm, of Ulster Co. - 8/9 Sept. 1715 (Deed Book BB:387)

KOGHNOT, John Everhardt - 11 Sept. 1761 (Laws, ch. 1154)

KOGHNOT, John Everhardt, Jr. - 11 Sept. 1761 (Laws, ch. 1154)

KOLE, Philip - 31 Dec. 1768 (Laws, ch. 1385)

KONIG, Michael - 20 Mar. 1762 (Laws, ch. 1179)

KOOL, Johannes, Dutch Reformed, of NYC, cordwainer; cert. min. G. D. Bois; witnesses: William Crelus, Christian Stouber - 23 Oct. 1747 (NYPL; Hh:22)

KOOSE, Frederick - 27 Jan. 1770 (Laws, ch. 1462)

KOP, Jacob, of Albany Co. - 11 Oct. 1715 (Alb. CCM 6:105)

KOPP, Michael, High German Reformed Church, of NYC, cooper - 21 Oct. 1765 (C.O. 5:1072; Qq:63; SCJ)

KORTREGHT, Hendrick, of Ulster Co. - 8/9 Sept. 1715 (Deed Book BB:387)

KOUGH, George - 8 Mar. 1773 (Laws, ch. 1638)

KOUGH, John - 8 Mar. 1773 (Laws, ch. 1638)

KOUGH, Jost - 8 Mar. 1773 (Laws, ch. 1638)

KOUGH, Matthias - 27 Jan. 1770 (Laws, ch. 1462)

KOUS, John Thys, Dutch Reformed, of Dutchess Co., farmer - 15 Oct. 1765 (C.O. 5:1072; Qq:63; SCJ)

KRAAN, Ludwick - 11 Sept. 1761 (Laws, ch. 1154)

KRAMER, Jan, carpenter - 12 July 1715 (MCRM:85)

KRATZER, Leonard - 8 Mar. 1773 (Laws, ch. 1638)

KRAUSKOP, Ludewyk, Antient Lutheran, of the Outward of NYC, farmer - 20 Apr. 1769 (C.O. 5:1075; Tt:4; SCJ)

KREMS, Johannis, of Albany Co. - 28 Feb. 1715/6 (Alb. CCM 6:118)
KROM, Gysbert, of Ulster Co. - 8/9 Sept. 1715 (Deed Book BB:387)
KROTZ, Johannis - 3 Feb. 1768 (Laws, ch. 1350)
KROUSH, Jacob, of Albany Co. - 14 Feb. 1715/6 (Alb. CCM 6:117)
KUGLER, Mattheus - 20 Mar. 1762 (Laws, ch. 1179)
KULTS, Conradt - 24 Nov. 1750 (Laws, ch. 902)
KURTS, Johannes, Lutheran, of Albany Co., shoemaker; cert. min.
    Michael Christian Knoll; witnesses: Jno. David Wolf, Custaph
    Martin Ruck - 20 Oct. 1741 (NYPL; Gg:81)
KURTZ, Johan Christopher, of Ulster Co. - 8/9 Sept. 1715 (Deed
    Book BB:387)
KUYPER, Cornelius, Unitas Fratrum, of NYC, house painter; cert.
    min. Thomas Yarrell; witnesses: Jacobus Montanye, Wm. Pearson -
    29 July 1761 (NYPL; Oo:63; SCJ)
KYNLANDER, Bernhard, of Westchester Co., tanner - 21 Apr. 1750
    (Hh:142)

LABAT, Ignace - 16 Feb. 1771 (Laws, ch. 1508)
LA CROIX, William - 3 July 1766 (Laws, ch. 1299)
LADNER, Andrew/Andreas, Lutheran, of NYC, baker; cert. min. J. A.
    Weygand; witnesses: John Balthus Dasch, Charles Beekman, George
    Gorgus - 22 Apr. 1761 (NYPL; Oo:63;SCJ)
LAGEAR, Pierre - 3 July 1759 (Laws, ch. 1089)
LAMBERTSEN, Huybert, of Ulster Co. - 8/9 Sept. 1715 (Deed Book BB:386)
LAMMERT, John, of Ulster Co. - 8/9 Sept. 1715 (Deed Book BB:387)
LAMPLIN, Jacob, Deacon of Reformed German Church, of NYC - 18 Oct.
    1774 (SCJ)
LANG, Christiaen, of Albany Co. - 17 Jan. 1715/6 (Alb. CCM 6:115)
LANGER, Abraham, of Albany Co. - 17 Jan. 1715/6 (Alb. CCM 6:115)
LANGERBEEN, Phillipus - see introd.
LANSINGH, Jan, of Albany Co. - 11 Oct. 1715 (Alb. CCM 6:105)
LASH, Daniel - 3 July 1759 (Laws, ch. 1089)
LASHIER, Johannes - 17 June 1726 (Laws, ch. 476)
    A John Lasher, Jr., was made freeman of NYC 7 Jan. 1745/6 as a
    cordwainer (CNYHS 1885:154)
LASLER, Martin - 16 Feb. 1771 (Laws, ch. 1508)
LAUTMAN, Peter, of Albany Co. - 17 Jan. 1715/6 (Alb. CCM 6:115)
LAWER, Johan Mathias (son of Johan Peter Lawer) - 1 Nov. 1715
    (MCRM:115)
LAWER, Johan Peter, of Dutchess Co., yeoman - 1 Nov. 1715 (MCRM:115)
LAWRENCE, Christopher - 6 July 1723 (Laws, ch. 444; NYHS Oath Roll,
    1723)
LAWRENCE, William, Dutch Reformed, of NYC, gardener; cert. min.
    Gualtherus DuBois; witnesses: Hermanus Rutgers, Jno. Roosevelt -
    25 Oct. 1742 (NYPL; Gg:81)
LAYDICK, Philip - 3 July 1759 (Laws, ch. 1089)
LEBER, Coenraad - 11 Sept. 1761 (Laws, ch. 1154)
LEBRIEUR, Jean Piere - 6 Dec. 1746 (Laws, ch. 844)
LE CONT, Moyse, of Ulster Co. - 8/9 Sept. 1715 (Deed Book BB:386)
LEEK, Johannis of Albany Co. - 17 Jan. 1715/6 (Alb. CCM 6:115)
LEER, Fredrick Willem, of Albany Co. - 31 Jan. 1715/6 (Alb. CCM
    6:116)
LEIDEBACH, Godfried - 3 July 1759 (Laws, ch. 1089)
LEINHART, Michael - 24 Mar. 1772 (Laws, ch. 1564)
LEMAN, Cleman, of Ulster Co. - 8/9 Sept. 1715 (Deed Book BB:387)

LEMAN, Wilhelm, of Ulster Co. - 8/9 Sept. 1715 (Deed Book BB:387)

LEMBERT, Daniel, of New Rochell, yeoman - 16 Aug. 1715 (MCRM:92)

LENDE, Ernst Ludewig - 11 Sept. 1761 (Laws, ch. 1154)

LENGEVELDER, Coenraadt - 3 July 1759 (Laws, ch. 1089)

LENING, Christopher - 11 Sept. 1761 (Laws, ch. 1154)

LENTZ, Frederick, Sigismund, Lutheran, of NYC, gentleman - 18 Oct. 1763 (C.O. 5:1071; SCJ)

LEONARD, George - 11 Sept. 1761 (Laws, ch. 1154); Lutheran, of NYC, butcher; cert. min. J. A. Weygand; witnesses: Casper Reisper, Henry Datliff - 21 Oct. 1761 (NYPL; Oo:63; SCJ)

LEONHARD, Wilhelm/William, High German Reformed Congregation, of NYC, baker - 21 Oct. 1765 (C.O. 5:1072; Qq:63; SCJ)

LE ROY, Jacob - 3 May 1755 (Laws, ch. 975)
    A Jacob LeRoy, of NYC, merchant, was bondsman in 1772 for the administrator of the estate of Garret Roos (Scott, Adm. Bonds: 117). A Jacob Le Roy, of Amsterdam, Holland, was residing in Dutchess Co. when on 22 Apr. 1781 he was appointed one of the administrators of the estate of Jacob Henry Chabanel (apparently his father-in-law) (Scott, Adm. Papers:53)

LERVER, Tobias, Lutheran, of Orange Co., husbandman - 20 Apr. 1763 (C.O. 5:1071; SCJ)

LETRER, Johan - 11 Sept. 1761 (Laws, ch. 1154)

LEUNINGBECKER, Johan Phillip - 24 July 1724 (Laws, ch. 461)

LEUZ, John - 8 Mar. 1773 (Laws, ch. 1638)

LEVY, Gershom Moses - see introd.

LEVY, Haeman - 24 Nov. 1750 (Laws, ch. 902)
    A Haman Levy was made freeman of NYC 29 Dec. 1750 as a merchant (CNYHS 1885:171). Hayman Levy, of NYC, merchant, was a bondsman in Sept. 1760 and Feb. 1763 (Scott, Adm. Bonds: 37,65); see introd.

LEVY, Isaac/ Isaac Moses, Jew, of NYC, merchant - nat. between 1 June 1740 and 1 June 1741 (NYPL; Gg:68; Huhner:6; NYHS Oath Roll, 1741)

LEVY, Moses, Jew, of NYC, merchant - 19 Apr. 1743 (NYPL; Gg:97; Huhner:6)

LEVY, Myer - see introd.

LEVY, Samuel, Jew, of NYC, merchant - nat. between 1 June 1740 and 1 June 1741 (NYPL; Huhner:6; NYHS Oath Roll, 1741)

LEWIS, John, Church of England, of NYC, mariner; cert. min. Henry Barclay; witnesses: Coenradt Ten Eyck, Abraham Ten Eyck - 18 Jan. 1748 (NYPL; Hh:70)

LEYDERBACH, Godfrey - 11 Sept. 1761 (Laws, ch. 1154)

LEYNSEN, Joost, baker - 26 July 1715 (MCRM:88)

L'HOMMEDIEU, Benjamin - petition to be naturalized 19 Aug. 1687 (CEM:167)

L'HOMMEDIEU, Jean - petition to be naturalized 19 Aug. 1687 (CEM:167)

LIEBHARDTS, Tobias - 11 Sept. 1761 (Laws, ch. 1154)

LIEPE, Hans Casper, of Albany Co. - 31 Jan. 1715/6 (Alb. CCM 6:116)

LIESLAER, Martin - 3 July 1759 (Laws, ch. 1089)

LIGHTHERT, Johan Barent, of Ulster Co. - 8/9 Sept. 1715 (Deed Book BB: 387)

LINK, Willem, of Albany Co. - 14 Feb. 1715/6 (Alb. CCM 6:117)

LINDER/LINDNER, Benjamin, Lutheran, of NYC, practitioner in Physic; cert. min. J. A. Weygand; witnesses: David Fairley, Jacob Epply - 29 July 1761 (NYPL; Oo:63; SCJ) - 11 Sept. 1761 (Laws, ch. 1154)

Benjamin Lindner was made freeman of NYC 7 Aug. 1761 as a practitioner in Physic (CNYHS 1885:109)

LINDER, George, Lutheran, of Montgomery Ward of NYC,- 20 Apr. 1774v

LINK, Matthias - 3 July 1759 (Laws, ch. 1089)   (SCJ)

LISSENMAN, Hane - 16 Dec. 1737 (Laws, ch. 662)

LOAKES, Nicolas, of Ulster Co. - 8/9 Sept. 1715 (Deed Book BB:387)

LOAKS, Peter, of Ulster Co. - 8/9 Sept. 1715 (Deed Book BB:387)

LODWICH, Johan Pieter, of Albany Co. - 28 Feb. 1715/6 (Alb. CCM
6:118)

LODWICK, Hendrick, of Albany Co. - 17 Jan. 1715/6 (Alb. CCM 6:115)

LODZ/LOW, Reynold, French Protestant, of Oyster Bay, Queens Co,
"gardiner" - 15 Oct. 1765 (C.O. 5:1072; Qq:63; SCJ)

LOECKSTEEN, Jurie, of Ulster Co. - 8/9 Sept. 1715 (Deed Book BB:386)

LOFLAND/LOSLAND, Adrian (son of Henry Lofland by Adriana his wife),
born at Rotterdam, Holland - 12 June 1689 (Shaw II:3; Deeds 9:703)

LOMBARDY, Peter - 23 Dec. 1765 (Laws, ch. 1295)

LOON, David - 16 Dec. 1737 (Laws, ch. 662)

LOPEZ, Moses, Jew - nat. according to Act of 1740 (NYPL; Gg:68;
Huhner:6; NYHS Oath Roll, 1741)

LORENTZ, John Peter, Reformed Dutch Protestant Church, of Dutchess
Co., yeoman -- 22 Oct. 1768 (C.O. 5:1074; Ss:59; SCJ)

LORILLARD/LORILLAND, John George, French Protestant, of NYC, yeoman;
cert. min. Jean Carle; witnesses: Peter Vallade, Jaque Desbrosses
- 27 Oct. 1760 (NYPL; Oo:63); took oath 28 Oct. 1760 (SCJ)

LORIN, Peter - 24 Nov. 1750 (Laws, ch. 902)
A Peter Lorin, jeweller, from London, in Nov. 1746 was at the
house of Thauvet Besly, goldsmith, on Golden Hill; in May 1751
he was working in Crown St., NYC (Gottesman: 30,70)

LOTT, Baltus, of Ulster Co. - 8/9 Sept. 1715 (Deed Book BB:387)

LOUCK, Abraham, of Albany Co. - 31 Jan. 1715/6 (Alb. CCM 6:116)

LOUCKS, Diedrich, of Albany Co. - 31 Jan. 1715/6 (Alb. CCM 6:116)

LOUCKS, Johan Hendrick, of Albany Co. - 3 Jan. 1715/6 (Alb. CCM
6:113)

LOUCKS, Philip, of Albany Co. - 17 Jan. 1715/6 (Alb. CCM 6:115)

LOUILLARD, Peter, French Protestant, of NYC, stocking-weaver; cert.
min. J. Carle; witnesses: Daniel Bonet, Peter Vallade - 21 Apr.
1762 (NYPL; Rec. 94:142)

LOUNDERT, Jurich, of Albany Co. 14 Feb. 1715/6 (Alb. CCM 6:117)

LOUNHERT, Philip, of Ulster Co. - 8/9 Sept. 1715 (Deed Book BB:387)

LOUWER, Konrat - 27 Jan. 1770 (Laws, ch. 1462)

LOWEN, Jacob - 31 Dec. 1761 (Laws, ch. 1170)

LOWEN, Jury - 31 Dec. 1761 (Laws, ch. 1170)

LUCAM, George, German Lutheran, of NYC, butcher - 18 Oct. 1765 (C.O.
5:1072; Qq:63; SCJ)

LUNEMAN, Carl, Antient Lutheran Church, of NYC, carpenter - 18 Oct.
1768 (C.O. 5:1074; Ss:59; SCJ)

LUSHAR, Charles - 16 Dec. 1737 (Laws, ch. 662). Took oath NYC
Mayor's Court 10 Jan. 1737/8 and the same afternoon was made
freeman of NYC as a victualler (CNYHS 1885:135; MCM)

LUYCASSE, Jan. of Albany Co - 6 Dec. 1715 (Alb. CCM 6:111)

LYDYUS, Geertruy Isabella, of Albany Co. - 28 Feb. 1715/6 (Alb.
CCM 6:118)

LYDYUS, Maria Adrianata, of Albany Co. - 28 Feb. 1715/6 (Alb.
CCM 6:118)

LYNSEN, Joost, baker - 26 July 1715 (MCRM:88)
LYON, Benjamin - see introd.

MACK, Jury - 20 Oct. 1764 (Laws, ch. 1272)
MAERSCHALCK, Andries, bolter - 26 July 1715 (MCRM:88)
MAGENS, Jochum Melchior - 11 Oct. 1750, petition of Magens that the
    Council would pass the bill for his naturalization, the same hav-
    ing already passed the General Assembly (CEM:595) - 12 Oct. 1750
    (Laws, ch. 878); took oath 18 Oct. 1750 (SCJ)
MAINSER, John - 3 May 1755 (Laws, ch. 975)
MAINSER, Lowrens - 3 May 1755 (Laws, ch. 975)
MALLEVILLE, Jean/John - 6 July 1723 (Laws, ch. 444; NYHS Oath Roll,
    1723)
MALLEVILLE, Pieter/Piter - 6 July 1723 (Laws, ch. 444; NYHS Oath
    Roll, 1723)
MAN, George, Antient Lutheran Church, of Orange Co., farmer - 24
    Apr. 1767 (C.O. 5:1073; Rr:30; SCJ)
MANCIUS, Georgius Wilhelmus - 16 Dec. 1737 (Laws, ch. 662)
MANCK, Casper - 11 Sept. 1761 (Laws, ch. 1154)
MANNEL, John, Lutheran, of Orange Co., husbandman - 20 Apr. 1763
    (Rec. 94:143; SCJ)
MANNHARD, Philip, Lutheran, of NYC, house-carpenter - 21 Oct. 1765
    (C.O. 5:1072; Qq:63); took oath 23 Oct. 1765 (SCJ)
MANOK, Jacob, of Ulster Co. - 8/9 Sept. 1715 (Deed Book BB:387)
MARCHE, Dina - 6 July 1723 (Laws, ch. 444)
MARCHE, Lieven - 6 July 1723 (Laws, ch. 444; NYHS Oath Roll, 1723)
MARCHEL, John - 27 Feb. 1770 (Laws, ch. 1462)
MARCKELL, Martinus, Dutch Reformed, of Ulster Co., farmer; cert.
    min. Georgus Wilhelmus Mancius; witnesses: Martin Snyder,
    Zacharias Becker - Oct. 1740 (Rec. 94:135)
MARCINHAS, Andrie - 11 Sept. 1761 (Laws, ch. 1154)
MARKEL, Frederick, of Ulster Co. - 8/9 Sept. 1715 (Deed Book BB:387)
MARKS, Anthony - 20 Mar. 1762 (Laws, ch. 1179)
MARQUAT, Hend - 11 Sept. 1761 (Laws, ch. 1154)
MARSEQUIE, Honore, of NYC, merchant - 20 May 1769 (Laws, ch. 1404;
    Ss:79); took oath 28 July 1769 (SCJ)
MARTIN, Jean, of New Rochell, yeoman - 16 Aug. 1715 (MCRM:92)
MARTIN, John - 24 Mar. 1772 (Laws, ch.1564)
    A John Martin was made freeman of NYC 1 Nov. 1786 as a whitesmith
    (CNYHS 1885:277)
MASSON, John - 6 July 1723 (Laws, ch. 444)
MATCHKER, Jacob - 24 Nov. 1750 (Laws, ch. 902); see introd.
MATERSTOCK, Dedrich, of Ulster Co. - 8/9 Sept. 1715 (Deed Book
    BB:387)
MATHYS, Jury, of Albany Co. - 28 Feb. 1715/6 (Alb. CCM 6:118)
MATTYSEN, Jan, of Ulster Co. - 8/9 Sept. 1715 (Deed Book BB:387)
MAY, Peter, of Ulster Co. 8/9 Sept. 1715 (Deed Book BB: 387)
MAYER, Felix - 11 Sept. 1761 (Laws, ch. 1154)
MAYER, Hans, Geerlag, Jr. - 11 Sept. 1761 (Laws, ch. 1154)
    On 23 May 1784 Elizabeth Nistell (wife of George Nistell and late
    widow of Gerlach Mayer, of the Palatine District, Montgomery Co.)
    was appointed administratrix of the estate of Gerlach Mayer
    (Scott, Adm. Papers: 216)
MAYER, Hendrick - 11 Sept. 1761 (Laws, ch. 1154)
MAYER, Jacob - 11 Sept. 1761 (Laws, ch. 1154)

MAYER, Johan Geerlag - 11 Sept. 1761 (Laws, ch. 1154)
MAYER, Joseph - 11 Sept. 1761 (Laws, ch. 1154)
MAYER, Solomon - 11 Sept. 1761 (Laws, ch. 1154)
MEINTZER, John - pet. 16 Nov. 1739; see introd.
MEINTZER, Lawrence - pet. 16 Nov. 1739; see introd.
MELIN, Simon - 19 Oct. 1730 (Laws, ch. 556)
MELLOW/MELLO, David Henry, Lutheran, of NYC, mariner; cert. min.
    J. A. Weygand; witnesses: Jacob Funck, John George Sheffield -
    21 Jan. 1761 (NYPL; Oo:63; SCJ)
MELSBACH, Nicholas, Dutch Reformed, of Ulster Co., farmer; cert.
    min. G. W. Mancius; witnesses: William Smith, Christian Rocke-
    feller - 18 Oct. 1750 (NYPL; Hh:142: SCJ)
MELSBACH, Peter, Dutch Reformed of Wallkill, Ulster Co., farmer;
    cert. min. B. Vrooman; witnesses: Johannes Krans, Johan Philip
    Spies - 17 Oct. 1753 (NYPL; Oo:62; SCJ)
MELSBAGH, Matys - 8 Nov. 1735 (Laws, ch. 634)
MELSBAGH, Phillip - 8 Nov. 1735 (Laws, ch. 634)
MENGES, Hieronimus, of Ulster Co. - 8/9 Sept. 1715 (Deed Book
    BB:387)
MENGES, Johanis, of Ulster Co. - 8/9 Sept. 1715 (Deed Book BB:387)
MENOLD, Martin, Lutheran, of NYC, shoemaker - 18 Oct. 1765 (C.O.
    1072; Qq:63); German Reformed (SCJ)
MENTI, Firdinand, of Albany Co. - 17 Jan. 1715/6 (Alb. CCM 6:115)
MERCIER, Isaac - petition to be naturalized 19 Aug. 1687 (CEM:167)
MERCIER, Isaac, of New Rochell, gentleman - 25 Oct. 1715 (MCRM:114)
MERDELE, Christoph - 20 Mar. 1762 (Laws, ch. 1179)
MERDELE, Michel - 20 Mar. 1762 (Laws, ch. 1179)
MERKLER, Christopher, of Ulster Co. - 8/9 Sept. 1715 (Deed Book
    BB:387)
MERKLEY, Jacob - 8 Mar. 1773 (Laws, ch. 1638)
MERKWAT, Hans Jury - 23 Dec. 1765 (Laws, ch. 1295)
MERLIN, Paul - petition to be naturalized 19 Aug. 1687 (CEM:167)
MERSCHET, Jean Peletrau - petition to be naturalized 19 Aug. 1687
    (CEM:167)
MERTE (or MERLE ?), Johanis, of Ulster Co. - 8/9 Sept. 1715 (Deed
    Book BB:387)
METSIGER, Jacob, Dutch Reformed, of NYC, yeoman; cert. min. G. Du
    Bois; witnesses: Willem Corcilius, Willem Crolius - 17 Apr. 1750
    (NYPL; Hh:142)
METZ, Bartholomew - 3 May 1755 (Laws, ch. 975)
MEYARS, Jacob - 16 Feb. 1771 (Laws, ch. 1508)
MEYER, Christian, of Ulster Co. - 8/9 Sept. 1715 (Deed Book BB:387)
MEYER, Christopher, Lutheran, of NYC, cartman; cert. min. M. C.
    Knoll; witnesses: Fredericus Oesterman, Casparus Hertz - 30 July
    1747 (NYPL; Gg:213)
MEYER, Felix - 3 July 1759 (Laws, ch. 1089)
MEYER, Fredrich, of Ulster Co. - 8/9 Sept. 1715 (Deed Book BB:386)
MEYER, Gerlach - 3 July 1759 (Laws, ch. 1089)
MEYER, Hendrich, of Albany Co. - 28 Feb. 1715/6 (Alb. CCM 6:118)
MEYERS, Salomon - 6 July 1723 (Laws, ch. 444)
    A Solomon Meyers was made freeman of NYC 12 May 1724 as shop-
    keeper (CNYHS 1885:104)
MICHELL, Andries, Dutch Reformed, of NYC, labourer; cert. min. J.
    Ritzema; witnesses: Johannes Myer, Daniel Smith - 21 Apr. 1748
    (NYPL; Hh:22)

MICHIEL, Anthony, of Albany Co. - 17 Jan. 1715/6 (Alb. CCM 6:114)

MICHIEL, Hendrich, of Albany Co. - 17 Jan. 1715/6 (Alb. CCM 6:114)

MICHIEL, Hendrich, Jr., of Albany Co. - 17 Jan. 1715/6 (Alb. CCM 6:114)

MIDDAGH, Joris, of Ulster Co. - 8/9 Sept. 1715 (Deed Book BB:386)

MIELER, Bartell - 6 July 1723 (Laws, ch. 444; NYHS Oath Roll, 1723)
    A Bartell Miller was made freeman of NYC 10 Sept. 1723 as a
    cordwainer (CNYHS 1885:104)

MIESICK, Fiet, of Albany Co. - 17 Jan. 1715/6 (Alb. CCM 6:115)

MIGEL, Nicolas, of Ulster Co. - 8/9 Sept. 1715 (Deed Book BB:387)

MILDENBERGEN, Johan Adam, Lutheran, of NYC, husbandman; cert. min.
    M. C. Knoll; witnesses: Matthys Knecht, Willem Bauman - 2 Aug.
    1750 (NYPL; Hh:142)

MILLER, Christoffel - 31 Dec. 1768 (Laws, ch. 1385)
    A Christopher Miller was made freeman of NYC 11 Sept. 1770 as a
    mariner (CNYHS 1885:235). In 1774 a Christopher Miller had
    carpets for sale (Gottesman:126)

MILLER, Cornelius - 3 May 1755 (Laws, ch. 975)

MILLER, David, of Ulster Co. - 8/9 Sept. 1715 (Deed Book BB:387)

MILLER, Faltin - 8 Mar. 1773 (Laws, ch. 1638)

MILLER, Filb, of Ulster Co. - 8/9 Sept. 1715 (Deed Book BB:387)

MILLER, Godfery - 24 Nov. 1750 (Laws, ch. 902)
    A Godfrey Miller was made freeman of NYC 5 Feb. 1750/1 as a
    labourer (CNYHS 1885:172); see introd.

MILLER, Jacob - 3 May 1755 (Laws, ch. 975)
    On 28 Feb. 1786 Eve Miller was appointed administratrix of the
    estate of her deceased husband, Jacob Miller, late of Beekmans
    Precinct, Dutchess Co., currier (Scott, Adm. Papers: 218)

MILLER, Johan - 16 Dec. 1737 (Laws, ch. 662)
    At the Nov. Sessions 1738 of the Court of Ulster Co. "Johannis
    Miller, on the basis of Act of Assembly published 10 Dec. last
    for his naturalization, subscribed the test and abjuration
    oaths." (National Genealogical Society Quarterly 61 (1973):4)

MILLER, Johan Christ., of Albany Co. - 17 Jan. 1715/6 (Alb. CCM 6:115)

MILLER, Johannes, Protestant - nat. between 1 June 1740 and 1 June
    1741 (NYPL; Gg:68); see also introd.

MILLER, Johannis, of Albany Co. - 3 Jan. 1715/6 (Alb. CCM 6:113)

MILLER, John, German Reformed, of NYC, Doctor of Physic - 15 Oct.
    1765 (SCJ)

MILLER, John Daniel - 3 July 1759 (Laws, ch. 1089)

MILLER, John Godfrey - 3 May 1755 (Laws, ch. 975)
    A Godfrey Miller was made freeman of NYC 27 May 1755 as a
    britches-maker (CNYHS 1885:182)

MILLER, John Thomas - 3 July 1759 (Laws, ch. 1089)

MILLER, Paul, of NYC, mariner - 15 Nov. 1715 (MCRM:119)

MILLER, Philip, Protestant - nat. between 1 June 1740 and 1 June
    1741 (NYPL; Gg:68); see also introd.

MILLER, Philip - 20 Mar. 1762 (Laws, ch. 1179)
    A Philip Miller was a watchmaker in NYC in 1763 (Gottesman:154).
    A Philip Miller, of NYC, watchmaker, was a bondsman in July
    1770 (Scott, Adm. Bonds:69)

MILLUR, Samuel - 8 Mar. 1773 (Laws, ch. 1638)

MINCKLAER, Josias, of Albany Co. - 17 Jan. 1715/6 (Alb. CCM 6:115)

MINCKLAER, Killiaen, of Albany Co.- 17 Jan. 1715/6 (Alb. CCM 6:115)

MINEMA, Benjamin, Dutch Reformed, of Dutchess Co., clerk; cert.
min. Benjamin Minema; witnesses: John Alsop, Bartholomew
Crannel - 24 Oct. 1753 (NYPL; Oo:62; SCJ)

MINNELEY, Albert, of Tappan, yeoman - 23 Aug. 1715 (MCRM:94)

MINVIELLE, David (son of Peter and Paule Minvielle), born at
Montauban, France - 19 Mar. 1705/6 (Shaw II:50; Deeds 10:151-7)

MISPAGH, Nicholas - pet. 16 Nov. 1739; see introd.

MOHR, Frederick - 11 Sept. 1761 (Laws, ch. 1154)

MOLECK, Jonas, Lutheran, of NYC, baker; cert. min. Mich. Christian
Knoll; witnesses: Hans Pfeffer, Henrick Behr - 23 Apr. 1744
(Gg:118,161)

MONIE, Jacob - 20 Mar. 1762 (Laws, ch. 1179)

MONIS, Judah, of NYC, merchant - 28 Feb. 1715/6 (MCRM:146)

MONIS, Peter, Jr., of Ulster Co. - 8/9 Sept. 1715 (Deed Book BB:387)

MOOR, Philip, of Albany Co. - 17 Jan. 1715/6 (Alb. CCM 6:115)

MOORE, Blazey, Lutheran, of NYC, innholder; cert. min. J. A. Weygand; witnesses: David Fairley, Henry Price - 21 Oct. 1761
(NYPL; Oo:63; SCJ)

MOORE, Conradt - 16 Feb. 1771 (Laws, ch. 1508)

MOORE, Henrich, of Ulster Co. - 8/9 Sept. 1715 (Deed Book BB:387)

MOORE, Jacob, Lutheran, of the Outward of NYC, farmer - 20 Apr.
1769 (C.O. 5:1075; Tt:4); German Evangelical Congregation (SCJ)

MOORE, Jacob - 8 Mar. 1773 (Laws, ch. 1638)

MOORE, Johannis, of Albany Co. - 13 Mar. 1715/6 (Alb. CCM 6:119)

MORRELL, Mathew, French Protestant, of NYC, labourer; cert. min.
J. Carle; witnesses: Peter Vallade, James Desbrosses, Daniel
Bonet - 22 Apr. 1761 (NYPL; Oo:63; SCJ)

MORRISON, John - 3 May 1755 (Laws, ch. 975)

MORRISSET, Alexander, French Protestant - petition to be made
burgher and citizen in 1691 (CEM:206)

MORROS, John, of New Rochell, yeoman - 16 Aug. 1715 (MCRM:92)

MOSES, Isa - 3 Feb. 1768 (Laws, ch. 1350)
An Isaac Moses was made freeman of NYC 22 Oct. 1766 as a cordwainer (CNYHS 1885:213). An Isaac Moses, of NYC, merchant, was
a bondsman in Apr. 1775, May 1789 and Nov. 1795 (Scott, Adm.
Bonds: 17, 54, 101)

MOSES, Isaac, Jew, of NYC, merchant - 25 Apr. 1771 (SCJ)

MOSES, Jacob, of NYC, trader - 20 May 1769 (Laws, ch. 1404; Ss:79);
took oath 18 Oct. 1769 (SCJ)

MOSES, Levy - 3 July 1759 (Laws, ch. 1089)

MOSES, Simon, of NYC, merchant - 28 Feb. 1715/6 (MCRM:146)

MOTS, Johannes, of Tappan, yeoman - 23 Aug. 1715 (MCRM:94)

MOULE, Christoffel, of Ulster Co. - 8/9 Sept. 1715 (Deed Book BB:387)

MOULE, Fredrick, of Ulster Co. - 8/9 Sept. 1715 (Deed Book BB:387)

MOULE, Jacob, of Ulster Co. - 8/9 Sept. 1715 (Deed Book BB:387)

MOUSSIER, Hans Jury, of Albany Co. - 3 Jan. 1715/6 (Alb. CCM 6:113)

MOUSSIER, Jacob, of Albany Co. - 3 Jan. 1715/6 (Alb. CCM 6:113)

MOWER, Jurick, of Albany Co. - 17 Jan. 1715/6 (Alb. CCM 6:115)

MULDRUP, Christian - 3 May 1755 (Laws, ch. 975)

MULLEDALLER/MULLIDALLER, John, Reformed German Church, of NYC,
cordwainer; cert. min. F. Rothenbuhler; witnesses: John Remmy,
John Philip Spies - 21 Oct. 1761 (NYPL; Oo:63; SCJ)

MULLER, Adam, Dutch Reformed, of Manor of Cortlandt, farmer -
19 Oct. 1763 (C.O. 5:1071)

MULLER, Andries, Dutch Reformed, of Manor of Cortlandt, farmer -
19 Oct. 1763 (C.O. 5:1071)

MULLER, Jacob, Dutch Reformed, of Manor of Cortlandt,farmer - 29
Oct. 1762 (C.O. 5:1071; SCJ)

MULLER, Johan Jurch, of Albany Co. - 17 Jan. 1715/6 (Alb. CCM 6:114)

MULLER, John, Lutheran, of NYC, labourer; cert. min. J. A. Weygand;
witnesses: John George Auch, Jacob Epply - 29 July 1761 (NYPL;
Oo:63; SCJ)

MULLER, John, Reformed German Church, of NYC, Doctor of Physic -
15 Oct. 1765 (C.O. 5:1072; Qq:63)

MULLER, Peter - 11 Sept. 1761 (Laws, ch. 1154)
One Muller, a leather-breeches-maker, lived before 1770 nearly
opposite Flattenbarrack-Hill in the Broadway (Gottesman:367)

MULLER, Samuel, of Albany Co. - 17 Jan. 1715/6 (Alb. CCM 6:115)

MULTER, Peter - 8 Mar. 1773 (Laws, ch. 1638)

MUNDERBACH, Johannes - 8 Mar. 1773 (Laws, ch. 1638)

MUSCULUS, William - 23 Dec. 1765 (Laws, ch. 1295)

MUTTEE, Peter - 11 Sept. 1761 (Laws, ch. 1154)

MUZELIUS, Frederikus - 16 Dec. 1737 (Laws, ch. 662)

MYAR, Michael - 16 Feb. 1771 (Laws, ch. 1508)

MYER, Frederick - 16 Feb. 1771 (Laws, ch. 1508)

MYER, Hermanus - 20 Oct. 1764 (Laws, ch. 1272)

MYER, Jacob - 3 May 1755 (Laws, ch. 975)

MYER, Jacob - 8 Mar. 1773 (Laws, ch. 1638)

MYER, Solomon - 3 May 1755 (Laws, ch. 975)
In 1741 a chirurgeon named Elias Wollin was living in a house in
Stone St. lately occupied by a Solomon Myers (Gottesman:316)

MYERS, Hyam, Jew, of NYC, butcher - 16 Jan. 1759 (NYPL; Oo:63;
Huhner:4 & 6; NYHS Oath Roll, 1741; SCJ)

MYERS, Manuel, Jew, of NYC, trader - 16 Jan. 1759 (NYPL; Oo:63;
Huhner: 4 & 6; NYHS Oath Roll, 1741; made his mark; SCJ)

MYERS, Napthaly Hart, Jew, of NYC, merchant - 27 Apr. 1764 (C.O. 5:
1072; Qq:63; Huhner:6; SCJ)

MYERS, Samuel - 12 July 1729 (Laws, ch. 538). Took oath NYC Mayor's
Court 9 Sept. 1729 (MCM)
A Samuel Myers was made freeman of NYC 6 Oct. 1730 as a shop-
keeper (CNYHS 1885:114)

MYERS, Solomon - 1723 (NYHS Oath Roll, 1723)

MYERS, Solomon, Jew, of NYC, merchant - nat. by Act of 1749 (NYPL;
Gg:68; Huhner:6)

NARE, Solomon, Jew - nat. by Act of 1740 (NYPL; Huhner:6)

NARKE, Jacob - 20 Mar. 1762 (Laws, ch. 1179)

NAYER, Johan Frans, of Ulster Co. - 8/9 Sept. 1715 (Deed Book
BB:387)

NAYER, Nicolas, of Ulster Co. - 8/9 Sept. 1715 (Deed Book BB:387)

NEDMER, Anthony - 29 Mar. 1762 (Laws, ch. 1179)

NEIHER, Carel, of Ulster Co. - 8/9 Sept. 1715 (Deed Book BB:386)

NEITHE, John Frederick - 24 Nov. 1759 (Laws, ch. 902); see introd.

NEIUKIRCH, Johanis, of Ulster Co. - 8/9 Sept. 1715 (Deed Book BB:387)

NELLES, Christian, of Albany Co. - 31 Jan. 1715/6 (Alb. CCM 6:116)

NELLES, William, of Albany Co. - 31 Jan. 1715/6 (Alb. CCM 6:116)

NESSEL, Martin - 20 Mar. 1762 (Laws, ch. 1179)

NESTEL, Jasper, Antient Lutheran Trinity Church, of NYC - 20 Jan.
1776 (SCJ)

NEUFEILE/NEWFUILE, Rachel, of New Rochell, widow - 15 Nov. 1715
  (MCRM:119)
NEUKERCK, Henrick, of Ulster Co. - 8/9 Sept. 1715 (Deed Book BB:387)
NEUPPENNYE, Adam - pet. 16 Nov. 1739; see introd.
NIES, Hendrick, of Albany Co. - 22 Nov. 1715 (Alb. CCM 6:109)
NIETS, Hans George, Dutch Reformed, of Ulster Co., farmer; cert.
  min. J. H. Goetschius; witnesses: Lawrence Alsdorf, Hans George
  Ranck - 29 July 1752 (NYPL; Ii:52)
NISTELL, Michael - 3 July 1759 (Laws, ch. 1089)
  A Michael Nistel (or Nestel), of NYC, blacksmith, was a bondsman
  in Oct. 1774, June 1780, Nov. 1792, Nov. 1795 and Nov. 1798
  (Scott, Adm. Bonds: 7,68,114,137,150)
NOLD, Bernard, of Ulster Co. - 8/9 Sept. 1715 (Deed Book BB:386)
NUYTUBER, Nicholas (son of Quirinus Nuytuber) - 10 Jan. 1715/6
  (MCRM:135)
NUYTUBER, Querinus, of Phillipsburgh, yeoman - 10 Jan. 1715/6
  (MCRM:135)

OASTERMAN, John Fredrick, of NYC, labourer - 16 Apr. 1750 (SCJ)
OEL, John Jacob, Lutheran, of Albany Co., clerk; cert. min. Henry
  Barclay; witnesses: Jacob Glen, Jacob H. Ten Eyck - 28 July 1743
  (NYPL; Gg:97)
OERTLY, Henrick, High German Reformed Church, of NYC, yeoman - 21
  Oct. 1765 (C.O. 5:1072; Qq:63; SCJ)
OOSTERHOUT, Teunis, of Ulster Co. - 8/9 Sept. 1715 (Deed Book BB:387)
ORTMAN, Francis - 20 May 1769 (Laws, ch. 1404; Ss:79)
OSWALD, Philip - 20 May 1769 (Laws, ch. 1404; Ss:79)
  A Philip Oswald was made freeman of NYC 20 June 1769 as a baker
  (CNYHS 1885:227)
OTT, Jacob, German Lutheran, of NYC, butcher - 18 Oct. 1765 (C.O. 5:
  1072; Qq:63; SCJ)
OTTO, Frank - 20 Mar. 1762 (Laws, ch. 1179)
OTTO, Frans - 20 Mar. 1762 (Laws, ch. 1179)
  A Frans Otto, of Albany Co., in Feb. 1761 was bondsman for the
  administrator of the estate of a deceased carpenter of Albany
  (Scott, Adm. Bonds:79)
OUGH, George - 8 Mar. 1773 (Laws, ch. 1638)
OUTMAN, Johannes, of NYC, merchant - 23 Aug. 1715 (MCRM:94)
OVERACKER, Micheal - 3 May 1755 (Laws, ch. 975)
OVERACKER, Wendel - 3 May 1755 (Laws,ch. 975)
OVERBACH, Jorg, of Ulster Co. - 8/9 Sept. 1715 (Deed Book BB:387)
OVERBACH, Peter, of Ulster Co. - 8/9 Sept. 1715 (Deed Book BB:387)
OVERPACH, Johan Peter, of Ulster Co. - 8/9 Sept. 1715 (Deed Book
  BB:387)
OVERYSER, Casper - 3 July 1759 (Laws, ch. 1089)
  On 25 Apr. 1780 Barnet Overheiser was appointed one of the ad-
  ministrators of the estate of Casper Overheiser, late of Beek-
  mans Precinct, Dutchess Co., yeoman (Scott, Adm. Papers:238)
OWLE, Carel, of Ulster Co. - 8/9 Sept. 1715 (Deed Book BB:387)
OWLE, Henrich, of Ulster Co. - 8/9 Sept. 1715 (Deed Book BB:387)
OXBURY, Alexander, Church of England, of NYC, cordwainer; cert.
  min. H. Barclay; witnesses: William Mucklevain, Henry Ustick
  21 Apr. 1762 (NYPL; C.O. 5:1071)

PAINTER, John, Lutheran, of NYC, shopkeeper; cert. min. J. A.
Weygand; witnesses: Charles Beekman Jr., George Gorgus - 31
July 1760 (NYPL; Oo:63; SCJ)
A John Painter was made freeman of NYC 29 Oct. 1765 as a shop-
keeper (CNYHS 1885:211)

PANET, Johannes, Dutch Reformed, of NYC, gentleman - 29 July 1762
(C.O. 5:1071)

PARIS, Isaac - 20 Mar. 1762 (Laws, ch. 1179)
In Feb. 1787 Johan Daniel Gros and Catharine Paris were executors
of the estate of Isaac Paris, late of Stone Arabia, Montgomery
Co., Esq., deceased (Scott, Adm. Papers:240)

PARIS, Isaac, Jr. - 20 Mar. 1762 (Laws, ch. 1179)

PARISIEN, Otho, French Protestant, of NYC, silversmith - 18 Jan.
1763 (C.O. 5:1071; SCJ)
Otto Parisien was made freeman of NYC 31 Jan. 1769 as a silversmith (CNYHS 1885:222)

PART, Johannes - 11 Sept. 1761 (Laws, ch. 1154)

PAYER, Leonard - 11 Sept. 1761 (Laws, ch. 1154)

PEKER, Ernst - 11 Sept. 1761 (Laws, ch. 1154)

PEMART, Francis - 20 Dec. 1763 (Laws, ch. 1236)

PERE, John Casper - 16 Feb. 1771 (Laws, ch. 1508)

PEREIRA, Abraham, of NYC, tallow chandler - 28 Feb. 1715/6 (MCRM:146)
An Abraham Pereira was made freeman of NYC 28 Feb. 1715/6 as a
tallow chandler (CNYHS 1885:95)

PETERIZ, Jan Dewit - 20 Sept. 1728 (Laws, ch. 520)

PETERSON, George, Lutheran, of NYC, sugar baker (sugar boiler);
cert. min. Mich. Christian Knoll; witnesses: Charles Beekman,
Johan David Wolf - 17 Apr. 1744 (NYPL; Gg:118 & 161)
George Peterson was made freeman of NYC 1 May 1744 as a sugar
baker (CNYHS 1885:149)

PETRIE, Johan Coenraet, of Albany Co. - 22 Nov. 1715 (Alb. CCM
6:109)
A Coenradt Petre, blacksmith, of the Manor of Livingston, Albany
Co., was a bondsman on 1 Apr. 1779 (Scott, Adm. Papers:147)

PETRIE, William - 27 Jan. 1770 (Laws, ch. 1462)

PFEFFER, Michael, of NYC, labourer - 23 Aug. 1715 (MCRM:94)
A Michael Peffer was made freeman of NYC 23 Aug. 1715 as a
labourer (CNYHS 1885:94)

PHENUS, Philip, Lutheran, of New Town, Queens Co., tailor - 31 July
1766 (SCJ)

PHIFSTER, Francis - 24 Mar. 1772 (Laws, ch. 1564)

PHILIPS, Jonas, of NYC, merchant - 25 Apr. 1771 (SCJ)

PHILIPS, Niecolas, of Albany Co. - 17 Jan. 1715/6 (Alb. CCM 6:115)

PHILIPS, Peter, of Albany Co. - 17 Jan. 1715/6 (Alb. CCM 6:115)

PILET, Philip - 27 Jan. 1770 (Laws, ch. 1462)

PINAUD, Paul, labourer - 26 July 1715 (MCRM:88)

PINTO, Abraham, of NYC, merchant - 28 Feb. 1715/6 (MCRM:146)

PINTO, Joseph Jesurum, Jew, of NYC, minister of the Jewish Congregation - 22 Jan. 1766 (C.O. 5:1072; Qq:63; Huhner: 4 & 6);
took oath 21 Jan. 1766 (SCJ)

PIT, Jan - 3 July 1718 (Laws, ch. 356; NYHS Oath Roll, 1718)

PIT, Jacob - 3 July 1718 (Laws, ch. 356); subscribed 5 Aug. 1718
(NYHS Oath Roll, 1718)

PLANK, Adam - 16 Feb. 1771 (Laws, ch. 1508)

PLANSZ, Johannes - 11 Sept. 1761 (Laws, ch. 1154)

PLANTIN, John - 19 Dec. 1766 (Laws, ch. 1319)
   A John Plantin was a tavernkeeper in NYC in 1770 (Scott, Adm.
   Bonds: 42)
PLAS, Johan Hend., of Albany Co. - 17 Jan. 1715/6 (Alb. CCM 6:115)
POLFER, Micheal - 3 May 1755 (Laws, ch. 975)
POLFER, Peter - 3 May 1755 (Laws, ch. 975)
POLT, Michael - 3 July 1766 (Laws, ch. 1299)
POLTZ, Micheal - 3 May 1755 (Laws, ch. 975)
PONTIUS, Adam - 3 July 1759 (Laws, ch. 1089)
PONTIUS, Christian, Lutheran, of NYC, tailor; cert. min. J. A.
   Weygand; witnesses: William Mucklevain, Henry Ustick - 21 Apr.
   1762 (NYPL; C.O. 5:1071)
   A John Christian Pontius was made freeman of NYC 29 Oct. 1765
   as a tailor (CNYHS 1885:210)
POPELSDORF, William - 8 Nov. 1735 (Laws, ch. 634)
   A William Popelsdorf was made freeman of NYC 4 Oct. 1737 (CNYHS
   1885:133). On 20 Jan. 1758 a Wilhelmus Poppelsdorff married
   Elizabeth Walter (N.Y. Marriages: 304). On 2 Aug. 1758 a Wilhelmus
   Poppelsdorff, of NYC, baker, was one of the signers of an ad-
   ministration bond on the estate of George Mospeh, of Sussex Co.,
   N.J., labourer (Scott, Adm. Bonds:99)
POST, Daniel, of Albany Co. - 17 Jan. 1715/6 (Alb. CCM 6:115)
POST, Johan Hend., of Albany Co. - 17 Jan. 1715/6 (Alb. CCM 6:115)
POUCHER, Anthony - 11 Sept. 1761 (Laws, ch. 1154)
POUNTENAY, Henry, of NYC, butcher - 27 Mar. 1716 (MCRM:152). He
   was made freeman of NYC 27 Mar. 1716 as a butcher (CNYHS 1885:95)
POUTCHER, Tunis - 3 May 1755 (Laws, ch. 975)
POWERS, George - 20 May 1769 (Laws, ch. 1404; Ss:79)
POYSHERT, Peter, Lutheran, of NYC, blacksmith - 21 Oct. 1765 (C.O.
   5:1072; Qq:63; SCJ)
   Peter Poyshart was made freeman of NYC 29 Oct. 1765 as a black-
   smith (CNYHS 1885:212)
PRIEGEL, Hans Jorg, of Ulster Co. - 8/9 Sept. 1715 (Deed Book BB:387)
PRIEN, Christopher - 3 July 1759 (Laws, ch. 1089)
PROPER, Johan Frederick, of Albany Co. - 22 Nov. 1715 (Alb. CCM 6:
   109)
PROPER, Johan Joseph, of Albany Co. - 22 Nov. 1715 (Alb. CCM 6:109)
PROPER, Johan Pieter, of Albany Co. - 22 Nov. 1715 (Alb. CCM 6:109)
PROSIUS, Peter - 20 Mar. 1762 (Laws, ch. 1179)
PRYL, Dewaeld, of Albany Co. - 3 Jan. 1715/6 (Alb. CCM 6:113)
PULVER, Johannis, of Albany Co. - 17 Jan. 1715/6 (Alb. CCM 6:115)
PUSCHART, John George - 25 Nov. 1727 (Laws, ch. 508)
PYGEL, Jacob - 20 Mar. 1762 (Laws, ch. 1179)
PYPPER, David, Lutheran, of NYC, tailor; cert. min. M. Christian
   Knoll; witnesses: Johan George Windlinger, Valentine Lambert -
   18 Apr. 1749 (NYPL; Hh:90)

QUACKENBOSS, Wouter, of Albany Co. - 6 Dec. 1715 (Alb. CCM 6:111)
QUANTEIN, Isaac, of Manor of Pelham, yeoman - 16 Aug. 1715 (MCRM:92)
QUERAUD, Joshua, of NYC, blacksmith - 4 Oct. 1715 (MCRM:109)
   A Joshua Quereau was made freeman of NYC 16 May 1721 as a black-
   smith (CNYHS 1885:101)
QUITHLOT, John - 16 Feb. 1771 (Laws, ch. 1508)

RAFF, Fredrick - 20 Dec. 1763 (Laws, ch. 1236)

RAFF, John - 20 Dec. 1763 (Laws, ch. 1236)
   On 3 July 1766 a John Raaf, of Albany, was a bondsman for Isaac
   Paris, of "Steen Rabe," administrator of the estate of Mathew
   Ward (Scott, Adm. Papers:351). A John Raff, of the Manor of
   Rensselaerwyck, Albany Co., trader, on 8 Feb. 1781 was appointed
   administrator of the estate of William Reagal, late of Albany,
   baker, deceased (Scott, Adm. Papers:259)

RAISNER, Casper - 3 July 1759 (Laws, ch. 1089)

RAM, John - 23 Dec. 1765 (Laws, ch. 1295)

RANCK, Hans George, Dutch Reformed, of Ulster Co., shoemaker; cert.
   min. J. H. Goetschius; witnesses: Lawrence Alsdorf, Hans George
   Niets - 29 July 1752 (NYPL; Ii:52)

RANDEKER/RANDECKER, John, Lutheran, of NYC, cartman - 26 July 1769
   (C.O. 5:1075: Tt:4; SCJ)

RANKEL, Cornelius - 11 Sept. 1761 (Laws, ch. 1154)

RANZIER, Frederick, Lutheran, of NYC, cooper - 29 July 1762 (C.O.
   5:1071)
   A Frederick Ranshier was made freeman of NYC 29 Oct. 1765 as a
   cooper (CNYHS 1885:210)

RASPER, Johannis - 20 Dec. 1763 (Laws, ch. 1236)

RATENHOUWER, Godfrey - 20 Mar. 1762 (Laws, ch. 1179)

RAVAUD, Daniel, of NYC, weaver - 6 Mar. 1715/6 (MCRM:148)

RAYMON, Isaac, of New Rochell, yeoman - 16 Aug. 1715 (MCRM:92)

REBER, Andreas, Lutheran, of NYC, shopkeeper; cert. min. M. C.
   Knoll - 5 Nov. 1745 (Rec. 94:137)

RECHTER, Andries, of Ulster Co. - 8/9 Sept. 1715 (Deed Book BB:387)

REDECKER, Henry - 31 Dec. 1768 (Laws, ch. 1385)

REES, William, of Albany Co. - 17 Jan. 1715/6 (Alb. CCM 6:114)

REGLER, Andreas, Lutheran, of NYC, butcher; cert. min. John Nicholas Kurts; witnesses: Peter Grimm, Philip Lydig, John Ekbert -
   21 Apr. 1762 (NYPL; C.O. 5:1071)
   An Andries Regler was made freeman of NYC 31 Jan. 1769 as a
   butcher (CNYHS 1885:222)

REIGLER, Andreas - 11 Sept. 1761 (Laws, ch. 1154)

REITER, Paul - 3 July 1759 (Laws, ch. 1089)

REITER, Paul - 11 Sept. 1761 (Laws, ch. 1154)

RELJE, Johanis, of Ulster Co. - 8/9 Sept. 1715 (Deed Book BB:387)

REMERSE, Johan - 27 July 1721 (Laws, ch. 418); as John Remerse made
   freeman of NYC 26 Sept. 1721 as a "gardiner" (CNYHS 1885:101)

REMMY, John, Reformed German Church, of NYC, potter; cert. min.
   F. Rothenbuhler; witnesses: John Christian Armpriester, Hendrick
   Schwatz - 21 Oct. 1761 (NYPL; Oo:63; SCJ)
   On 16 June 1780 John Remmy, potter, and Elizabeth his wife, both
   of NYC, were appointed administrators of the estate of John
   Armbrister, of NYC, tanner and innkeeper (Scott, Adm. Bonds:7).
   Nov. 1792 John and Henry Remmy were appointed administrators of
   the estate of John Remmy, late of NYC, potbaker, dec'd (Scott,
   ibid.:114)

REMSEN, Adam Leonard - 24 Mar. 1772 (Laws, ch. 1564)

RENEAU, Mary (wife of Andrew Reneau) - 20 Sept. 1728 (Laws, ch. 520)

RENEAU, Stephen, of New Rochell, boatman - 2 Aug. 1715 (MCRM:90)

RENNER, Frederick Christian, Antient Lutheran, of NYC, sugar baker-
   16 Jan. 1771 (SCJ)

RESLER, Jacob, Lutheran, of NYC, tallow chandler; cert. min. J. A.
Weygand; witnesses: David Fairley, Henry Datliff - 21 Oct. 1761
(NYPL; SCJ)
On 7 July 1770 Jacob Rossler, of NYC, tallow chandler, was one
of the bondsmen for Barbara Du Bronner, widow and administratrix
of Ferdinand H. A. Du Bronner, of Dutchess Co., practitioner in
physic, dec'd (Scott, Adm. Bonds:46). On 21 Oct. 1795 Frederick
Resler (son of the deceased) and Baltus Moore (son-in-law of the
deceased) were appointed administrators of the estate of Jacob
Resler, of NYC, tallow chandler (ibid.:114)
RESLER, Teunis, of NYC, baker - 17 Jan. 1753
REVERA, Jacob Rodrigues, Jew, of NYC, merchant - 21 Jan. 1746/7
(NYPL; Gg:213)
REYFENBURGER, Jurich, of Albany Co. - 14 Feb. 1715/6 (Alb. CCM 6:
117)
RHINEHART, Valentine, Lutheran, of NYC, innholder - 29 July 1762
(C.O. 5:1071)
RHINELANDER, William, German, Church of England, of NYC, yeoman; cert.
min. H. Barclay; witnesses: John Ellis, William Ustick - 31 July
1754 (NYPL; Oo:62; SCJ)
A William Rhinelander was made freeman of NYC 6 Aug, 1754 as a
cordwainer (CNYHS 1885:180)
RHUELL, Gustav/Gustaph Martin - 16 Dec. 1737 (Laws, ch. 662). He
took oath in NYC Mayor's Court 10 Jan. 1737/8 (MCM) and that
afternoon was made freeman of NYC as a tallow chandler (CNYHS
1885:135)
RHYMA, John - 8 Mar. 1773 (Laws, ch. 1638)
RHYNE, Honnicol - 8 Mar. 1773 (Laws, ch. 1638)
RYNLANDER, Bernard, Church of England, of Westchester Co., tanner;
cert. min. P.Stouppe; witnesses: Isaac Varian, Willem Rhinlander
- 21 Apr. 1750 (NYPL)
RICE, Hannis - 11 Sept. 1761 (Laws, ch. 1154)
RICHARDS, Samuel - 3 July 1718 (Laws, ch. 356); subscribed 5 Aug.
1718 (NYHS Oath Roll, 1718) and was that day made a freeman of
NYC as a distiller (CNYHS 1885:98)
RICHART, Joseph, of Ulster Co. - 8/9 Sept. 1715 (Deed Book BB:387)
RICHE, Michael - 16 Feb. 1771 (Laws, ch. 1508)
RICHERS, John Michael - 20 May 1769 (Laws, ch. 1404; Ss:79)
RIEGELER, Leonarat - 6 Dec. 1746 (Laws, ch. 844)
RIEMESNYDER, Hendrick - 20 Mar. 1762 (Laws, ch. 1179)
RIES, John, Antient Lutheran Church, of the Outward of NYC, farmer
- 20 Apr. 1769 (C.O. 5:1075; Tt:4; SCJ)
A John Ries was made freeman of NYC 20 June 1769 as a farmer
(CNYHS 1885:227)
RIET, Michiel Goewy, of Albany Co. - 13 Mar. 1715/6 (Alb. CCM 6:119)
RIGHTMEYER, Coenradt, Dutch Reformed, of Ulster Co., farmer; cert.
min. Georgus Wilhelmus Mancius; witnesses: Martin Snyder, Zach-
arias Becker - Oct. 1740 (NYPL; Gg:68)
RIGHTMIER, Coenraet - 22 June 1734 (Laws, ch. 605)
RIHT MEYER, Jorg - 16 Dec. 1737 (Laws, ch. 662)
RIM, George - 11 Sept. 1761 (Laws ch. 1154)
RING, Christopher - 3 May 1775 (Laws, ch. 975)
RINGLAND, John Christian, of Ulster Co., boatman - 3 Feb. 1768
(Laws, ch. 1350); took oath 23 Apr. 1768 (SCJ)
RINGLE, Lawrence - 8 Mar. 1773 (Laws, ch. 1638)

RINGSDORP, Johannes, of Ulster Co. - 8/9 Sept. 1715 (Deed Book
BB:386)

RISLAR, Jacob, Lutheran, of NYC, tallow chandler - 21 Oct. 1761
(Oo:63)

RISLER, Tunis, Dutch Reformed, of NYC, baker; cert. min. L. DeRonde;
witnesses: William Crolius, William Crolius, Jr. - 17 Jan. 1753
(NYPL; Oo:62)

RITMAN, David, Lutheran, of NYC, carpenter; cert. min. J. A. Weygand; witnesses: Henry Keysler, Jacob Reysler - 21 Apr. 1762
(NYPL; C. O. 5:1071)

RITMAN, Michael, Lutheran, of NYC, weaver - 20 Apr. 1763 (C.O. 5:
1072; SCJ)

RITSMAN, Johannis - 11 Sept. 1761 (Laws, ch. 1154)

RITTER, Henry, Lutheran, of NYC, cordwainer; cert. min. J. A. Weygand; witnesses: John Goodpertel, Alexander Augspurger - 19 Apr.
1759 (NYPL; Oo:63; SCJ)
A Henry Ritter was made freeman of NYC 29 Oct. 1765 as a cordwainer (CNYHS 1885:211). A Henry Ritter, of NYC, shoemaker, was
a bondsman on 8 Sept. 1766 (Scott, Adm. Bonds:126). A Henry
Ritter, of Montgomery Co., was a bondsman on 20 July 1786 (Scott,
Adm. Papers: 264). A Henry Ritter witnessed a renunciation on
28 Dec. 1786 (ibid.:15)

RITTER, Michael, Lutheran, of NYC, tailor; cert. min. J. A. Weygand;
witnesses: John Goodpertel, Alexander Augspurger - 19 Apr. 1759
(NYPL; Oo:63; SCJ)

RITZEMA, Rudolphus - 3 July 1766 (Laws, ch. 1299)
A Rudolphus Ritzema, gentleman, was made freeman of NYC 7 June
1768 as an attorney-at-law (CNYHS 1885:215). Rudolphus Ritzema,
of NYC, attorney-at-law, was a bondsman in Mar. 1775 (Scott,
Adm. Bonds:11)

RIVERA, Abraham Rodregos - 17 June 1726 (Laws, ch. 476)
An Abraham Rodregos Rivera was made freeman of NYC 19 July 1726
as a merchant (CNYHS 1885:108)

RIVERA, Jacob Rodrigues, Jew, of NYC, merchant - 21 Jan. 1746 (Huh-
ner:6)

ROBINSON, Barns - 24 Nov. 1750 (Laws, ch. 902)

RODRIGUES/RODRIGNES, Isaac Raphael - 16 Dec. 1737 (Laws, ch. 662)
He took oath NYC Mayor's Court 10 Jan. 1737/8 (MCM) and the same
afternoon was made freeman of NYC as a shopkeeper (CNYHS 1885:135)

RODRIGUES, Isaack - 6 July 1723 (Laws, ch. 444; NYHS Oath Roll, 1723)

ROETERS, Abraham - 6 July 1723 (Laws, ch. 444; NYHS Oath Roll, 1723)

ROETTIG, Christoph - 20 Mar. 1762 (Laws, ch. 1179)

ROGE/ROG, John, Church of England, of NYC, merchant; cert. min.
William Vesey; witnesses: Thomas Duncan, James Lyno - 24 Jan.
1740/1 (NYPL; Gg:68)

ROGGEN, Frans Petrus - 20 Oct. 1764 (Laws, ch. 1272)
A Frantz P. Roggen, of Kingston, Ulster Co., yeoman, was a bondsman on 6 July 1785 (Scott, Adm. Papers:90)

ROGGEN, John Jacob - 20 Oct. 1764 (Laws, ch. 1272)

ROHEFELLER, Diel - 16 Dec. 1737, ch. 662)

ROKHEFFELLER/ROKKEFELLER, Johannes Petrus, Reformed Dutch Church
at the Camp, Albany Co., farmer; cert. min. G. W. Mancius, witnesses: Tiels Rokhefeller, Simon Rokhefeller - 21 Oct. 1761
(NYPL; Oo:63; SCJ)

ROKHEFFELLER/ROKKEFELLER, Simon, Dutch Reformed Church at the Camp,
Albany Co., farmer; cert. min. G. W. Mancius; witnesses: Tiels
Rokhefeller, Michael Blass - 21 Oct. 1761 (NYPL; Oo:63; SCJ)
ROKKENFELDER, Christian, Dutch Reformed, of Ulster Co., blacksmith;
cert. min. G. W. Mancius; witnesses: Nicholas Milsbach, Phillipus
Zinsebach - 18 Oct. 1750 (NYPL; Hh:142: SCJ)
RONIS (?), Thomas, of Ulster Co. - 8/9 Sept. 1715 (Deed Book BB:386)
RONKILL, John - 3 May 1755 (Laws, ch. 975)
RONLAFF, John - 8 Mar. 1773 (Laws, ch. 1638)
ROORBAGH, Johannes - 17 June 1726 (Laws, ch. 476)
A Johannes Roorback was made freeman of NYC 25 Mar. 1728/9 as
a baker (CNYHS 1885:112). Barent Visscher, of Albany, Indian-
trader, in his will dated Apr. 1769 mentioned his stepfather,
Johannes Roorbach (Scott, Adm. Papers:346)
ROOS, Arien, of Ulster Co., farmer, age 42 - 2 Dec. 1689 (Deed
Book BB:87)
ROOS, Gerret, baker - 19 July 1715 (MCRM:87)
Anthony Rutgers (nephew of Garret Roos, of NYC, merchant, dec'd)
on 10 Dec. 1772 was appointed administrator of his late uncle's
estate (Scott, Adm. Bonds:117)
ROOS, Guert, cordwainer - 19 July 1715 (MCRM:87)
ROOS, Heyman, of Hurly, Ulster Co., shoemaker, age 45 - nat. before
1715 (Deed Book BB:215)
ROOS, Lodowick, German - 31 July 1754 (NYPL; Oo:62; SCJ); a Lode-
wick Roos was made freeman of NYC 6 Aug. 1754 as a labourer
(CNYHS 1885:180)
ROOS, Pieter, of Ulster Co. - 8/9 Sept. 1715 (Deed Book BB:386)
ROOSEVELT, Johannis, of NYC, chirurgeon - 20 Oct. 1764 (Laws, ch.
1272); took oath 23 Oct. 1764 (SCJ)
RORIG, Hendrick - 11 Sept. 1761 (Laws, ch. 1154)
ROS, Wilhelm - 20 Mar. 1762 (Laws, ch. 1179)
ROSE, Johan Peter/Johanis Peter, Dutch Reformed, of Albany Co.,
shoemaker - 15 Oct. 1765 (C.O. 5:1072; Qq:63; SCJ)
ROSEKRANS, Abraham - 29 Mar. 1762 (Laws, ch. 1179)
ROSENKRANS, Dirck, of Ulster Co. - 8/9 Sept. 1715 (Deed Book BB:387)
ROSSEL, Henry, German Reformed Congregation, of Outward of NYC,
tanner - 20 Apr. 1769 (C.O. 5:1075; Tt:4; SCJ)
ROSSENER, Jorg - 11 Sept. 1761 (Laws, ch. 1154)
ROTHER, Jacob - 11 Sept. 1761 (Laws, ch. 1154)
ROU, Nikals, of Ulster Co. - 8/9 Sept. 1715 (Deed Book BB:386)
ROUCH, Johan Casper, of Albany Co. - 17 Jan. 1715/6 (Alb. CCM 6:115)
ROUGEON, Peter, French Protestant, of NYC, ship-carpenter - 21 Apr.
1762 (C.O. 5:1071)
ROUGON, Peter - 3 July 1759 (Laws, ch. 1089)
ROUSET, David, of NYC, leather-dresser - 1 Nov. 1715 (MCRM:115)
ROUSMAN, Johannis, of Albany Co. - 22 Nov. 1715 (Alb. CCM 6:109)
ROW, Hans Jurch, of Albany Co. - 17 Jan. 1715/6 (Alb. CCM 6:115)
ROW, Michael Christopher - 8 Nov. 1735 (Laws, ch. 634)
RUBELL, Johannis Casparus - 23 Dec. 1765 (Laws, ch. 1295)
RUCH, Fredrich, of Ulster Co. - 8/9 Sept. 1715 (Deed Book BB:387)
RUCH, Frederich, Jr., of Ulster Co., - 8/9 Sept. 1715 (Deed Book
BB:387)
RUFF, Johan Christian - 20 Mar. 1762 (Laws, ch. 1179)
RUGER, Frederick, Lutheran, of NYC, carman/cartman - 20 Apr. 1763
(C.O. 5:1071; SCJ)

RULLEAU, John (son of John and Mary Rulleau), born at Saumien in
    Saintonge, France - 20 Mar. 1707/8 (Shaw II:62; Deeds 10:326-8)
RUPERT, George - 27 Jan. 1770 (Laws, ch. 1462)
RUPPERT, Adam - 3 July 1759 (Laws, ch. 1089)
RUPPERT, Francis - 3 July 1759 (Laws, ch. 1089)
RURS, Hendrick - 20 Mar. 1762 (Laws, ch. 1179)
RUSH, John, of Bergen Co., N.J., farmer - 16 Feb. 1771 (Laws, ch.
    1508); took oath 22 Jan. 1772 (SCJ)
RUSS, David - 11 Sept. 1761 (Laws, ch. 1154)
RUSSEL, William - 19 Dec. 1766 (Laws, ch. 1319)
    On 7 Dec. 1780 Robert Moore, of NYC, baker, was appointed ad-
    ministrator of the estate of William Russell, late of NYC, baker,
    dec'd (Scott, Adm. Bonds:119)
RUSSELL, Michael - 3 July 1759 (Laws, ch. 1089)
RUTSEN, Jacob, of Ulster Co. - 8/9 Sept. 1715 (Deed Book BB:386)
RUTSEN, Johon, of Ulster Co. - 8/9 Sept. 1715 (Deed Book BB:386)
RUYTER, Henrich, of Ulster Co. - 8/9 Sept. 1715 (Deed Book BB:387)
RYPELL, John, of NYC, baker - 28 Feb. 1715/6 (MCRM:146)
    On 28 Oct. 1761 Catharine Rypele (widow of John Rypele, late of
    NYC, baker) was cited (Scott, Adm. Papers:172)
RYSDYCK, Isaac - 3 July 1766 (Laws, ch. 1299)
RYST, John - 20 Mar. 1762 (Laws, ch. 1179)

SAAND, Christian, Protestant Evangelical Church, of Skohary Town-
    ship - 20 Apr. 1773 (SCJ)
SACOMBEL, Louis - 17 June 1726 (Laws, ch. 476)
ST. GAUDENS, Peter, of New Rochell, yeoman - 6 Mar. 1715/6 (MCRM:
    148)
ST. JOHN, John Hector - 23 Dec. 1765 (Laws, ch. 1295)
SAIT, David - 20 Mar. 1762 (Laws, ch. 1179)
SAIZ, Johannes Michael, Lutheran, of NYC, baker - 17 Oct. 1753 (SCJ)
SALBACK, Jermi, of Ulster Co. - 8/9 Sept. 1715 (Deed Book BB:387)
SALSBERGH, Michael - 31 Dec. 1768 (Laws, ch. 1385)
SAMLER, John, of NYC, sugar refiner - 20 May 1769 (Laws, ch. 1404;
    Ss:79); took oath 27 July 1769 (SCJ)
    A John Samler was made freeman of NYC 6 Mar. 1770 as a sugar
    refiner (CNYHS 1885:228)
SAMSON, Daniell, of Manor of Pelham, yeoman - 16 Aug. 1715 (MCRM:92)
SAMUEL, Levy, Jew - between 1 June 1740 and 1 June 1741 (Gg:68;
    NYHS Oath Roll, 1741); see also introd.
    A Levy Samuel was made freeman of NYC 4 Oct. 1743 as a merchant
    (CNYHS 1885:148)
SANDER, Hendrick - 11 Sept. 1761 (Laws, ch. 1154)
SANDOTS, Leonard - 3 July 1759 (Laws, ch. 1089)
SAUTHIER, Claude Joseph - 24 Mar. 1772 (Laws, ch. 1564)
SAX, Johan Peter, Dutch Reformed, of Albany Co., farmer; cert.
    min. G. W. Mancius; witnesses: Corneles Kneckerbaker, John West
    - 2 Aug. 1750 (NYPL; Hh:142)
SAX, Johannes Michael, Lutheran, of NYC, baker; cert. min. P. Sten-
    rious; witnesses: John Debele, John George Cook - 17 Oct. 1753
    (NYPL; Oo:62)
SAXE, Michael - 20 Oct. 1764 (Laws, ch. 1272)
SBRECKER, Coenraad - 11 Sept. 1761 (Laws, ch. 1154)
SBRECKER, George - 11 Sept. 1761 (Laws, ch. 1154)

SBRECKER, Martin - 11 Sept. 1761 (Laws, ch. 1154)

SCHAAK, Jurian Hansen - 29 Nov. 1745 (Laws, ch. 811)

SCHAD, Theodorus - 11 Sept. 1761 (Laws, ch. 1154)

SCHAD, Ulrick - 11 Sept. 1761 (Laws, ch. 1154)

SCHAFER, Hendrick - 8 Mar. 1773 (Laws, ch. 1638)

SCHAFER, Maria Catharina (widow of Jost Schafer), member German
    Church in Lebanon, West N.J. - 20 Jan. 1776 (SCJ)

SCHAFF, Philip, Lutheran, of NYC, brass-founder; cert. min. Jean
    Frideric Ries; witnesses: Peter Grim, John Ebert - 1 Aug. 1750
    (NYPL: Hh:142)

SCHAFFER, Mattheus - 3 July 1759 (Laws,ch. 1089)

SCHAFFER, Nicholas - 3 July 1759 (Laws, ch. 1089)

SCHAL, Johannes - 11 Sept. 1761 (Laws, ch. 1154)

SCHALL, Fredrick - 20 Mar. 1762 (Laws, ch. 1179)

SCHALL, Johannes - 11 Sept. 1761 (Laws, ch. 1154)

SCHALTZ (= SCHULTZ), Jachen Christian - 20 May 1769 (Laws, ch. 1404;
    Ss:79)
    A Jochem Christian Schultz was made freeman of NYC 20 June 1769
    as a baker (CNYHS 1885:227)

SCHEFFER, Frederick, of Albany Co. - 11 Oct. 1715 (Alb. CCM 6:105)

SCHEFFER, Philip, of Albany Co. - 3 Jan. 1715/6 (Alb. CCM 6:113)

SCHEFFER, Reynhaert, of Albany Co. - 11 Oct. 1715 (Alb. CCM 6:105)

SCHEL, Christian - 11 Sept. 1761 (Laws, ch. 1154)

SCHEL, Christoph, Lutheran, of NYC, cartman - 21 Oct. 1765 (C. O. 5:
    1072: Qq:63); as Christopher Schel, "gardiner" took oath (SCJ)

SCHELD, Carle - 20 Mar. 1762 (Laws, ch. 1179)

SCHELL, Christian - 20 Dec. 1763 (Laws, ch. 1236)

SCHELL, Christian - 20 Oct. 1764 (Laws, ch. 1272)

SCHELL, Johannes - 20 Dec. 1763 (Laws, ch. 1236)

SCHELL, Johannes - 20 Oct. 1764 (Laws, ch. 1272)

SCHENERHINGER, Mathew, Lutheran, of NYC, hatter - 23 Oct. 1765
    (C.O. 5:1072; Qq:63; SCJ)

SCHEPMOES, Dirck, of Ulster Co - 8/9 Sept. 1715 (Deed Book BB:386)
    A Derick Schepmoes on 14 Oct. 1764 was appointed administrator
    of the estate of his only brother, Johannes Schepmoes, Esq., of
    Kingston, Ulster Co. (Scott, Adm. Papers:277)

SCHERP, Jurich Emrig, of Albany Co. - 17 Jan. 1715/6 (Alb. CCM 6:115)

SCHERPE, Andries Hanse, of Albany Co. - 27 Apr. 1716 (Alb. CCM 6:123)

SCHERTS, Jurch, of Albany Co. - 31 Jan. 1715/6 (Alb. CCM 6:116)

SCHEVER, Harme - 20 Mar. 1762 (Laws, ch. 1179)

SCHEVER, Hendrick, of Ulster Co. - 8/9 Sept. 1715 (Deed Book BB:386)

SCHICK, Christian - 16 Feb. 1771 (Laws, ch. 1508)

SCHIEF, William, of Albany Co. - 11 Oct. 1715 (Alb. CCM 6:105)

SCHIEFFER, Jacob, of Albany Co. - 22 Nov. 1715 (Alb. CCM 6:109)

SCHIEFFER, Nicolas, of Albany Co. - 11 Oct. 1715 (Alb, CCM 6:105)

SCHIERTS, Andries, of Albany Co. - 6 Dec. 1715 (Alb. CCM 6:111)

SCHIETS, Hans Adam, of Albany Co. - 22 Nov. 1715 (Alb. CCM 6:109)

SCHIETS, Johannis, of Albany Co. - 22 Nov. 1715 (Alb. CCM 6:109)

SCHINCK, George - 16 Feb. 1771 (Laws, ch. 1508)

SCHITH, Jacob - 16 Feb. 1771 (Laws, ch. 1508)

SCHLIEDORN, Henrick - 27 July 1721 (Laws, ch. 418)
    A Henry Schleydorn was made freeman of NYC 26 June 1722 as a
    tailor (CNYHS 1885:102)

SCHNEIDER, Daniel, Dutch Reformed, of Ulster Co., yeoman; cert.
min. Geor. Wilhelmus Mancius; witnesses: Johan Teunis Sinseback,
Johannes Schneider - 20 Oct. 1747 (NYPL; Hh:22)
On 17 Jan. 1784 a Daniel Snyder, father of Johannis Snyder, of
Shawangunk, Ulster Co., was appointed administrator of his dec'd
son (Scott, Adm. Papers:298)
SCHNEIDER, Henrich - 20 Mar. 1762 (Laws, ch. 1179)
SCHNEIDER, William, German Reformed, of NYC, baker - 19 Jan. 1774
(SCJ)
SCHNEYDER, Jacob - 11 Sept. 1761 (Laws, ch. 1154)
A Jacob Snyder (Schnyder), of Tryon Co., carpenter, was appoint-
ed administrator of the estate of Nicholas Sitz on 27 Feb. 1784
(Scott, Adm. Papers:287). On 27 Jan. 1786 Jacob Snyder, of Mont-
gomery Co., was a bondsman (ibid.:69)
SCHNOG, Johanes - 8 Nov. 1735 (Laws, ch. 634)
SHOEMAKER, Jacob, of Albany Co. - 22 Nov. 1715 (Alb. CCM 6:109)
SHOEMAKER, Thomas, of Albany Co. - 22 Nov. 1715 (Alb. CCM 6:109)
SCHOLDIES, Johannis, of Albany Co. - 31 Jan. 1715/6 (Alb. CCM 6:116)
SCHONMAKER, Egbert, of Ulster Co. - 8/9 Sept. 1715 (Deed Book BB:386)
SCHONMAKER, Jochem, of Ulster Co. - 8/9 Sept. 1715 (Deed Book BB:386)
SCHONNERET/SHONNERET, Frederick, German Lutheran, of NYC, shopkeeper
- 18 Oct. 1765 (C.O. 5:1072; Qq:63; SCJ)
SCHORER, Christian - 8 Mar. 1773 (Laws, ch. 1638)
SCHOTLER, Garret - 20 May 1769 (Laws, ch. 1404)
A Garret Schotler was made freeman of NYC 19 Dec. 1769 as "Paynter
and Glazier" (CNYHS 1885:228)
SCHOUGH, Andreas - 16 Feb. 1771 (Laws, ch. 1508)
SCHRAM, Fredrich, of Ulster Co. - 8/9 Sept. 1715 (Deed Book BB:387)
SCHRAM, Henrich, of Ulster Co. - 8/9 Sept. 1715 (Deed Book BB:387)
SCHRAM, Johanis, of Ulster Co. - 8/9 Sept. 1715 (Deed Book BB:387)
SCHREIBER, Albertus, of Ulster Co. - 8/9 Sept. 1715 (Deed Book BB:
387)
SCHREIBER, Stephen, Lutheran, of Montgomery Ward of NYC - 20 Apr.
1774 (SCJ)
SCHREIT, Jorg Adam, of Ulster Co. - 7/8 Sept. 1715 (Deed Book BB:
387)
SCHUERMAN, Coenraet, of Albany Co. - 17 Jan. 1715/6 (Alb. CCM 6:115)
SCHULER, Lawrence - 19 Dec. 1766 (Laws, ch. 1319)
SCHULTZ, Casparus, Lutheran, farmer; cert. min. G. M. Weiss; wit-
nesses: Johannis Snue, Teunis Snyder - 17 Oct. 1744 (NYPL:
Gg:61) He is also given as of Dutchess Co. (Gg:118)
SCHURRI, Johannes, Dutch Reformed, of Dutchess Co., blacksmith;
cert. min. B. Meynard; witnesses: John Brinckerhoff, William
Cyffer - 18 Oct. 1750 (NYPL; Hh:142; SCJ)
SCHUTTES, Phillip - 16 Dec. 1737 (Laws, ch. 662)
SCHUTZE/SCHUTZ, Johann Michael, tailor - 12 July 1715 (MCRM:85)
SCHYET, Anthony, of Albany Co. - 11 Oct. 1715 (Alb. CCM 6:105)
SEABALT, John - 27 Jan. 1770 (Laws, ch. 1462)
SEBAS, John - 3 July 1759 (Laws, ch. 1089)
SEBER, Jacob - 27 Jan. 1770 (Laws, ch. 1462)
SEEBER, Jacob - 11 Sept. 1761 (Laws, ch. 1154)
A Jacob Sebor, of NYC, merchant, on 3 Feb. 1796 was appointed
administrator of the estate of John Coddington, late of NYC,
mariner, dec'd (Scott, Adm. Bonds:34)

SEEBER, Jacob, Jr. - 11 Sept. 1761 (Laws, ch. 1154)
SEEBER, William - 11 Sept. 1761 (Laws, ch. 1154)
    Henry W. Seeber (son of a dec'd William Seeber) on 29 Sept. 1781
    was appointed administrator of the estate of his father, William
    Seeber, late of Canijohary, Tryon Co. (Scott Adm. Papers:280)
SEGEDORP, Harme, of Albany Co. - 3 Jan. 1715/6 (Alb. CCM 6: 113)
SEIDEL, John - 3 July 1759 (Laws, ch. 1089)
SEIX, Hendrick, of Albany Co. - 11 Oct. 1715 (Alb. CCM 6:105)
SEIXAS, Isaac, Jew, of NYC, merchant - 4 Nov. 1745 (NYPL; Gg:213;
    Huhner:6)
    On 25 June 1756 an Isaac Mendes Seixas, of NYC, merchant, was
    appointed administrator of the estate of Abraham Mendes Seixas
    (otherwise Miguel Pacheco da Silva) (Scott, Adm. Bonds:122)
SELBACH, Arnoldus - 3 July 1759 (Laws, ch. 1089)
SELBACH, Johan Peter - 3 July 1759 (Laws, ch. 1089)
SENSEBACH, Phillipus, Dutch Reformed, of Ulster Co., farmer; cert.
    min. G. W. Mancius; witnesses: Nicholas Milsbach, Hans Ulrich
    Binder - 18 Oct. 1750 (NYPL; SCJ)
SENSENBACH, Jacob - 8 Nov. 1735 (Laws, ch. 634)
SENSIBACH, Frederick, Protestant - nat. by Act of 1740 (NYPL;
    Gg:68)
SENSIBACH, John Christ - nat. by Act of 1740 (Rec. 94:135); see
    also introd.
SERVER, Johan Jacob, of Albany Co. - 17 Jan. 1715/6 (Alb. CCM 6:115)
SERVER, Marte, of Albany Co. - 17 Jan. 1715/6 (Alb. CCM 6:115)
SERVIS, Christopher - 11 Sept. 1761 (Laws, ch. 1154)
SERVIS, Peter - 11 Sept. 1761 (Laws, ch. 1154)
SETEFAN, Johannes - 3 July 1759 (Laws, ch. 1089)
SEVENBERGH, Christian - 3 May 1755 (Laws, ch. 975)
    A Christian Sevenbergh was made freeman of NYC 7 May 1755 as a
    watchmaker (CNYHS 1885:181)
SEVER, Jacob - 11 Sept. 1761 (Laws, ch. 1154)
SEYBERT, Johan Jacob, of Albany Co. - 13 Mar. 1715/6 (Alb. CCM 6:119)
SEYBERT, Johan Martin, of Albany Co. - 13 Mar. 1715/6 (Alb. CCM 6:
    119)
SEYN, Petter, of Tappan, yeoman - 23 Aug. 1715 (MCRM:94)
SHAAD, Theodorus - 3 July 1759 (Laws, ch. 1089)
SHAAD, Ulrick - 3 July 1759 (Laws, ch. 1089)
SHADWELL, David - 16 Feb. 1771 (Laws, ch. 1508)
SHADWELL, Michael - 16 Feb. 1771 (Laws, ch. 1508)
SHAPHER, Philip - 20 Mar. 1762 (Laws, ch. 1179)
SHARPE, George 27 Jan. 1770 (Laws, ch. 1462)
SHARPE, Jacob, of Kingsbury, Dutchess Co., yeoman - 4 Oct. 1715
    (MCRM: 107)
SHAUMAN, John - 3 July 1759 (Laws, ch. 1089)
SHEERHAM, Christoffel - 31 Dec. 1768 (Laws, ch. 1385)
SHEETS, Jacob - 8 Mar. 1773 (Laws, ch. 1638)
SHELTS, Charles - 24 Nov. 1750 (Laws, ch. 902); see introd.
SHENIGH, Fredrick - 23 Dec. 1765 (Laws, ch. 1295)
SHERP, Jacob - 3 May 1755 (Laws, ch. 975)
SHERP, John - 3 May 1755 (Laws, ch. 975)
SHERP, Micheal - 3 May 1755 (Laws, ch. 975)
SHERPENSTONE, Jacob - 20 Dec. 1763 (Laws, ch. 1236)
    On 8 Feb. 1786 a Jacob Sherpenstone, of Charlotte Precinct,

Dutchess Co., farmer, was appointed one of the administrators
of the estate of Daniel Bush (Scott, <u>Adm</u>. Papers:47)

SHEYER, Teunis, of Albany Co. - 13 Mar. 1715/6 (Alb. CCM 6:119)

SHIFF, George - 8 Mar. 1773 (Laws, ch. 1638)

SHINKEL, Johan Hendrich, of Albany Co. - 17 Jan. 1715/6 (Alb. CCM
6:114)

SHINKEL, Jonas, of Albany Co. 17 Jan. 1715/6 (Alb. CCM 6:114)

SCHMIDT, Johan Jurch, of Albany Co. - 17 Jan. 1715/6 (Alb. CCM 6:115)

SCHOALS, John, Church of England, of NYC, mariner; cert. min.
H. Barclay; witnesses: Thomas Grigg, Jr., Jos. Hildreth - 31
July 1750 (NYPL; Hh:142)

SHOE, Godfried - 27 Jan. 1770 (Laws, ch. 1462)

SHOE, Johan Wm., of Albany Co. - 17 Jan. 1715/6 (Alb. CCM 6:115)

SHOE, Johannis, of Albany Co. - 17 Jan. 1715/6 (Alb. CCM 6:115)

SHOE, Martinus, of Albany Co. - 17 Jan. 1715/6 (Alb. CCM 6:115)

SHOEMAKER, Godfried - 11 Sept. 1761 (Laws, ch. 1154)

SHOL, Coenrad - 31 Dec. 1768 (Laws, ch. 1385)

SHOL, Johannes - 31 Dec. 1768 (Laws, ch. 1385)

SHOPF, Henry - 11 Sept. 1761 (Laws, ch. 1154)

SHOUMAN, William - 16 Feb. 1771 (Laws, ch. 1508)

SHOURE, Adam, of Ulster Co. - 8/9 Sept. 1715 (Deed Book BB:387)

SHOURE, Michael, of Ulster Co. - 8/9 Sept. 1715 (Deed Book BB:387)

SHREIB, Hieronimus, of Ulster Co. - 8/9 Sept. 1715 (Deed Book BB:387)

SHREIDER, Simon - 27 Jan. 1770 (Laws, ch. 1462)

SHRIFER, Joseph, of Ulster Co. - 8/9 Sept. 1715 (Deed Book BB:387)

SHURGER, Simon - 19 Dec. 1766 (Laws, ch. 1319)

SHURTER, Frederick - 23 Dec. 1765 (Laws, ch. 1295)

SHUTZ, Christiaen - 16 Feb. 1771 (Laws, ch. 1508)

SHUYMER, Mattys, of Ulster Co. - 8/9 Sept. 1715 (Deed Book BB:387)

SHWEIKERT, Peter - 3 July 1759 (Laws, ch. 1089)
A Peter Shweikert was made freeman of NYC 24 July 1759 as a
chocolate-maker (CNYHS 1885:193). In 1758 Peter Swigard, chocolate-maker, was established in Bayard St., opposite John Livingston's storehouse (Gottesman:295). Swigard was deceased by 26
October 1772 (Gottesman:351)

SICKNEER, Jacob (age 11½ years, son of Apollonia Sickneer) - 21
Feb. 1715/6 (MCRM:143)

SIEFFERT, Johannes - 11 Sept. 1761 (Laws, ch. 1154)

SIEGELER, Pieter - 3 July 1759 (Laws, ch. 1089)

SIELIE, Jacob - 20 Oct. 1764 (Laws, ch. 1272)

SIEMON, Anthony - 11 Sept. 1761 (Laws, ch. 1154)

SIEMON, Johan Wm., of Albany Co. - 17 Jan. 1715/6 (Alb. CCM 6:115)

SIEMON, John, of NYC - 8 Mar. 1773 (Laws, ch. 1638); took oath
28 July 1773 (SCJ)
On 17 Nov. 1798 Jonathan G. Tompkins was appointed administrator
of the estate of a John Siemon, of NYC, furrier, dec'd (Scott,
<u>Adm</u>. Bonds:124)

SILVESTER, Constant (born in Amsterdam, son of Giles Silvester and
Mary his wife, English parents) - 29 Dec. 1660 (Shaw I:79;
Patents 1)

SILVESTER, Giles (born in Amsterdam, son of Giles Silvester and
Mary his wife, English parents) - 29 Dec. 1660 (Shaw I:79;
Patents 1)

SILVESTER, Joshua (born in Amsterdam, son of Giles Silvester and

Mary his wife, English parents) - 29 Dec. 1660 (Shaw I:79; Patents I)

SILVESTER, Nathaniell (born in Amsterdam, son of Giles Silvester and Mary his wife, English parents) - 29 Dec. 1660 (Shaw I:79; Patents 1)

SIMMONS, Anthony - 11 Sept. 1761 (Laws, ch. 1154)
On 30 Nov. 1786 a renunciation was signed by Esther Nicholson, wife of Peter Nicholson but late of an Anthony Simmons, formerly of New York but last of Philadelphia, Pa., cartman (Scott, Adm. Papers:286)

SIMONIS, Harmanus - 24 July 1724 (Laws, ch. 461)

SIMONS, Joseph - 16 Feb. 1771 (Laws, ch. 1508)
A Joseph Simons, seal-cutter and engraver from Berlin, in May 1763 was living in the Fly, next door to Edward Leight, leather-dresser (Gottesman:13)

SIMSON, Joseph - 6 July 1723 (Laws, ch. 444)

SIMSON, Joseph, Jew, of NYC, merchant - nat. by Act of 1740 (NYPL; Gg:68; NYHS Oath Roll, 1741; Huhner:6)
A Joseph Simson was made freeman of NYC 1 Feb. 1742/3 as a shop-keeper (CNYHS 1885:146). A Joseph Simson, of NYC, merchant, was a bondsman in Oct. 1762 and Sept. 1770 (Scott, Adm. Bonds:79,80)

SIMSON, Martin - 16 Feb. 1771 (Laws, ch. 1508)

SINSEBACK, Johan Teunis, Dutch Reformed, of Ulster Co., yeoman; cert. min. Geo. Wilhelmus Mancius; witnesses: Daniel Schneider, Johannes Schneider - 20 Oct. 1747 (NYPL; Hh:22); see also introd.

SKANS, Johannis, of Albany Co. - 3 Jan. 1715/6 (Alb. CCM 6:113)

SKINK, George - 27 Jan. 1770 (Laws, ch. 1462)

SLEGHT, Daniel - 20 May 1769 (Laws, ch. 1404; Ss:79)

SLEGHT, Hendrick - 20 Oct. 1764 (Laws, ch. 1272)

SMALL, Jacob, Evangelical German Lutheran, of NYC, blacksmith - 28 July 1773 (SCJ)

SMEDES, Benjamin, of Ulster Co. - 8/9 Sept. 1715 (Deed Book BB:387)

SMIT, Johan Christ, of Albany Co. - 3 Jan. 1715/6 (Alb. CCM 6:113)

SMITH, Adam Meichel, of Albany Co. - 27 Apr. 1716 (Alb. CCM 6:123)

SMITH, Barent, Reformed Protestant Dutch Church, of NYC, tailor - 27 July 1768 (C.O. 5:1074; Ss:59; SCJ)

SMITH, Christopher, of NYC - 3 May 1755 (Laws, ch. 975); took oath 24 Oct. 1755 (NYPL; Oo:62; SCJ)

SMITH, Coenraad - 11 Sept. 1761 (Laws, ch. 1154)

SMITH, Coenraed, of Albany Co. - 17 Jan. 1715/6 (Alb. CCM 6:114)

SMITH, Conradt - 27 Jan. 1770 (Laws, ch. 1462)

SMITH, Daniel, Dutch Reformed, of NYC, labourer; cert. min. J. Ritzema; witnesses, Johannes Douebach, Andries Michell - 21 Apr. 1748 (NYPL; Hh:22)
A Daniel Smith, of NYC, was a bondsman on 8 Nov. 1798 (Scott, Adm. Bonds:65)

SMITH, Henry - 31 Dec. 1768 (Laws, ch. 1385)

SMITH, Henry - 8 Mar. 1773 (Laws, ch. 1638)

SMITH, Johan - 8 Mar. 1773 (Laws, ch. 1638)

SMITH, Johan Adam, of Albany Co. - 17 Jan. 1715/6 (Alb. CCM 6:114)

SMITH, Johan Georg, of Ulster Co. - 8/9 Sept. 1715 (Deed Book BB:387)

SMITH, Johan Hendrick - 11 Sept. 1761 (Laws, ch. 1154)

SMITH, Johan Nicholas - 11 Sept. 1761 (Laws, ch. 1154)

SMITH, Johan Willem - 16 Nov. 1739. Amendment proposed to act for naturalizing him (CEM:539); see introd.

SMITH, Johannes - 11 Sept. 1761 (Laws, ch. 1154)
SMITH, John - 24 Nov. 1750 (Laws, ch. 902)
   A John Smith was made freeman of NYC 8 Jan. 1750/1 as a baker
   (CNYHS 1885:171); a John Smith, of NYC, baker, was bondsman on
   13 Jan. 1755 and 18 Sept. 1765 (Scott, Adm. Bonds: 96,135);
   see introd.
SMITH, John - 31 Dec. 1768 (Laws, ch. 1385)
SMITH, John - 16 Feb. 1771 (Laws, ch. 1508)
SMITH, John - 16 Feb. 1771 (Laws, ch. 1508)
SMITH, John Conradt - 8 Mar. 1773 (Laws, ch. 1638)
SMITH, Lambert, of Tappan, yeoman - 22 Aug. 1715 (MCRM:94)
SMITH, Martin - 3 July 1759 (Laws, ch. 1089)
SMITH, Matthias, of NYC - 3 May 1755 (Laws, ch. 975); took oath 24
   Oct. 1755 (NYPL; Oo:62; SCJ)
   A Matthias Smith, of Bedford, Westchester Co., hatter, was a
   bondsman on 18 May 1775 (Scott, Adm. Papers:218)
SMITH, Michael - 24 Nov. 1750 (Laws, ch. 902)
   A Michael Smith was made freeman of NYC 7 May 1751 as a labourer
   (CNYHS 1885:173)
SMITH, Niccolas, of Albany Co. - 17 Jan. 1715/6 (Alb. CCM 6:114)
SMITH, Nicolas, of Ulster Co. - 8/9 Sept. 1715 (Deed Book BB:387)
SMITH, Peter, of Albany Co. - 22 Nov. 1715 (Alb. CCM 6:109)
SMITH, Peter, of Albany Co. - 17 Jan. 1715/6 (Alb. CCM 6:115)
SMITH, Philip - 31 Dec. 1768 (Laws, ch. 1385)
SMITH, Philip - 8 Mar. 1773 (Laws, ch. 1638)
SMITH, Poulus, of Ulster Co. - 8/9 Sept. 1715 (Deed Book BB:387)
SMITH, Wilhelmus - 11 Sept. 1761 (Laws, ch. 1154)
   A William Smith was made freeman of NYC 22 Sept. 1761 as a block-
   maker (CNYHS 1885:199)
SMITH, William, of Ulster Co. - 8/9 Sept. 1715 (Deed Book BB:387)
SMITH, William, Dutch Reformed, of Ulster Co., blacksmith; cert.
   min. G. W. Mancius; witnesses: Hans Ulrich Binder, Christian
   Rockefeller - 18 Oct. 1750 (NYPL; Hh:142; SCJ)
   A William Smith, of NYC, blacksmith, on 21 Apr. 1774 was ap-
   pointed administrator of the estate of his brother-in-law, John
   Crawford, Jr., of Westchester Co. (Scott, Adm. Bonds:37)
SMITH, Zacharis - 29 Oct. 1730 (Laws, ch. 556)
   A Zechariah Smith, of Dutchess Co., yeoman, was cited 26 May 1773
   as one of the executors of an estate (Scott, Adm. Papers:301)
SMITT, Jonas, of Albany Co. - 22 Nov. 1715 (Alb. CCM 6:109)
SNECK, George, Jr. - 8 Mar. 1773 (Laws, ch. 1638)
SNEIDER, Andreas - 3 July 1759 (Laws, ch. 1089)
SNEIDER, Christopher, Lutheran, cert. min. G. W. Mancius, witnesses:
   Johannes Weber, Henrick Berringer - 23 Oct. 1741 (NYPL; Gg:81)
SNEIDER, William - 3 July 1759 (Laws, ch. 1089)
SNELL, Jacob, of Albany Co. - 11 Oct. 1715 (Alb. CCM 6:105)
SNEYDER, Henderick, Dutch Reformed of NYC, cartman; cert. min. G.
   DuBois; witnesses: Willem Corcilius, Willem Crolius - 17 Apr.
   1750 (NYPL; Hh:142)
SNEYDER, Hendrick, of Albany Co. - 17 Jan. 1715/6 (Alb. CCM 6:114)
SNEYDER, Johan, of Albany Co. - 14 Feb. 1715/6 (Alb. CCM 6:117)
SNEYDER, Johan Joest, of Albany Co. - 14 Feb. 1715/6 (Alb. CCM 6:117)
SNEYDER, Johan Wm., of Albany Co. - 17 Jan. 1715/6 (Alb. CCM 6:115)
SNEYDER, Michael - 11 Sept. 1761 (Laws, ch. 1154)
SNEYDER, Willem, of Albany Co. - 17 Jan. 1715/6 (Alb. CCM 6:115)

SNIDER, John Wilhelm, of Ulster Co. - 8/9 Sept. 1715 (Deed Book
BB:387)

SNIDER, Martinus, Dutch Reformed, of Ulster Co., farmer; cert. min.
Georgus Wilhelmus Mancius; witnesses: Matis Marckel, Conrad
Myer- Oct. 1740 (NYPL; Gg:68)

SNITER, Jacobus Peter - 8 Nov. 1735 (Laws, ch. 634) listed in
title and on first listing as SUCITER, Jacobus Peter.
A Jacobus Peter Snider was made freeman of NYS 4 Oct. 1737 as a
cordwainer (CNYHS 1885:133)

SNOUS, Johannes - 3 July 1759 (Laws, ch. 1089)

SNYDER, Georg, of Ulster Co. - 8/9 Sept. 1715 (Deed Book BB:387)

SNYDER, George - 31 Dec. 1761 (Laws, ch. 1170)

SNYDER, Hendrick - 24 Nov. 1750 (Laws, ch. 902)
A Hendrick Snyder was made freeman of NYC 31 Aug. 1750 as a
cordwainer (CNYHS 1885:170); see introd.

SNYDER, Hendrick, Reformed Protestant Dutch Church, of Orange Co.,
farmer - 21 Apr. 1769 (C.O. 5:1075; Tt:4)

SNYDER, Johanis, of Ulster Co. - 8/9 Sept. 1715 (Deed Book BB:387)

SOBELL, William - 31 Dec. 1768 (Laws, ch. 1385)

SOLL, Johan - 8 Mar. 1773 (Laws, ch. 1638)

SOLOMON/SOLOMONS, Jonas, Jew, Colony of N.Y., (NYC) merchant - 27
Oct. 1763 (C.O. 5:1071; Huhner: 4 & 6; SCJ); see introd.

SOLOMONS, Levy - 3 May 1755 (Laws, ch. 975)

SOMNER, Peter Nicholaus - 20 Mar. 1762 (Laws, ch. 1179)

SONTS, Dedrick, of Ulster Co. - 8/9 Sept. 1715 (Deed Book BB:387)

SOOY, Yoos (Joost) - 6 July 1723 (Laws, ch. 444; NYHS Oath Roll,
1723)
A Joost Sooy was made freeman of NYC 30 July 1723 as a mariner
(CNYHS 1885:103)

SORNBERGER, Georg Jacob, Lutheran; cert. min. G. W. Mancius; wit-
nesses: Johannes Weber, Henrick Berringer - 23 Oct. 1741 (NYPL)
A George Sornberger on 13 June 1768 was appointed administrator
of the estate of his father, a George Jacob Sornberger, of
Amenia Precinct, Dutchess Co., shopkeeper, dec'd (Scott, Adm.
Papers: 299)

SOULLICE, John, of NYC, baker - 27 Sept. 1715 (MCRM:104)

SOWRESHLER, Hegmerick, of Ulster Co. - 8/9 Sept. 1715 (Deed Book
BB:387)

SPACH, Jonas, French Reformed; cert. min. L. Rou; witnesses: James
Buvelot, Alexander Alaire - 21 Oct. 1741 (NYPL; Gg:81)

SPALER, Johannes - 22 June 1734 (Laws, ch. 605)

SPAN, of Ulster Co. - 8/9 Sept. 1715 (Deed Book BB:387)

SPEDER, Daniel, Dutch Reformed, of NYC, cartman; cert. min. Joan.
Ritzema; witnesses: George Petterson, Dirck Amerman - 18 Oct.
1749 (NYPL; Hh:142)

SPERBECK, Martin - 11 Sept. 1761 (Laws, ch. 1154)

SPEYKERMAN, Bastiaen, of Albany Co. - 13 Mar. 1715/6 (Alb. CCM
6:119)

SPICKERMAN, Johan Harme, of Albany Co. - 31 Jan. 1715/6 (Alb. CCM
6:116)

SPIES, John Philip, Reformed German Church, of NYC, cordwainer; cert.
min. F. Rothenbuhler; witnesses: Abraham Young, Johannes Myers -
21 Oct. 1761 (NYPL; Oo:63; SCJ)
A John Spies, of NYC, was a bondsman on 12 Nov. 1798 (Scott, Adm.
Bonds:145)

SPINGLER, Jacob - 3 July 1759 (Laws, ch. 1089)

SPINGLER, John Balthas - 3 July 1759 (Laws, ch. 1089)

SPORNHEIR, William - 11 Sept. 1761 (Laws, ch. 1154)
    A William Spornheyr, of Knistione, Albany Co., on 20 Feb. 1781
    was appointed administrator of the estate of his brother-in-law,
    William Harris, of Kobeskill, Albany Co. (Scott, Adm. Papers:138)

SPORY, Jacob, German Reformed Congregation, of NYC, gardiner -
    31 July 1770

SPRANGENBERGH, Johannes - 3 July 1759 (Laws, ch. 1089)

SPRECHER, Georg - 11 Sept. 1761 (Laws, ch. 1154)

SPRINGER, Silvester, of NYC, tobacconist - 3 Feb. 1768 (Laws, ch.
    1350); took oath 27 Apr. 1768 (SCJ)

SPYES, Peter, of Albany Co. - 13 Mar. 1715/6 (Alb. CCM 6:119)

SRAMT, Henrich, of Ulster Co. - 8/9 Sept. 1715 (Deed Book BB:387)

SRAMT, Michel, of Ulster Co. - 8/9 Sept. 1715 (Deed Book BB:387)

SRUM, Michael - 20 May 1769 (Laws, ch. 1404; Ss:79)

STAATS, Isabella, of Albany Co. - 28 Feb. 1715/6 (Alb. CCM 6:118)

STAATS, Johannes, Lutheran, of Dutchess Co., farmer; cert. min.
    G. M. Weiss; witnesses: Johannis Snue, Frederick Beringer (NYPL;
    Gg:118, 161)
    On 26 May 1773 the acting executors of the estate of a Johannes
    Staats, of Dutchess Co., yeoman, were cited (Scott, Adm. Papers:
    301)

STALLER, Michael - 24 Mar. 1772 (Laws, ch. 1564)

STAM, George - 11 Sept. 1761 (Laws, ch. 1154)

STAM, George, Jr. - 11 Sept. 1761 (Laws, ch. 1154)

STAM, Lourens - 11 Sept. 1761 (Laws, ch. 1154)

STAMM, George - 3 July 1759 (Laws, ch. 1089)

STAPELL, Johan Jacob - 20 May 1769 (Laws, ch. 1404; Ss:79)
    A John Jacob Staple was made freeman of NYC as a sugar baker on
    20 June 1769 (CNYHS 1885:227)

STARN, Adam, of Albany Co. - 31 Jan. 1715/6 (Alb. CCM 6:116)

STAVER, Jacob Booch - 8 Nov. 1735 (Laws, ch.634)

STECK, Nicholas - 3 May 1755 (Laws, ch. 975)

STEEL, Roelof, of Albany Co. - 11 Oct. 1715 (Alb. CCM 6:105)

STEENBAGH, Anthony, Dutch Reformed, of NYC, baker; cert. min.
    G. D. Bois; witnesses: Henry Heder, William Laurens - 19 Oct.
    1748 (NYPL; Hh:22)
    An Anthony Steenbuck, of NYC, on 7 Nov. 1795, was a bondsman
    (Scott, Adm. Bonds:125)

STEENRNIER, Bastiaan - 11 Sept. 1761 (Laws, ch. 1154)

STEINBRINNER/STEINBRENNER, Jacob, of NYC, blacksmith; cert. min.
    J. F. Ries; witnesses: Peter Grim, Mark Phaffar - 18 Oct. 1750
    (NYPL; Hh:142; SCJ) see introd.

STEINWAS, Arnols - 8 Mar. 1773 (Laws, ch. 1638)

STEIRER, Joseph - 20 May 1769 (Laws, ch. 1404; Ss:79)

STELLINGWERF, Pieter - 6 July 1723 (Laws, ch. 444; NYHS Oath Roll,
    1723)

STEPHANY, John Sebastian - 3 July 1759 (Laws, ch. 1089)

STERENBERGEN, Johan B., of Albany Co. - 31 Jan. 1715/6 (Alb. CCM
    6:116)

STEYGER, Niecolas, of Albany Co. - 14 Feb. 1715/6 (Alb. CCM 6:117)

STEYGER, Stephanis, of Ulster Co. - 8/9 Sept. 1715 (Deed Book
    BB:387)

STICKEL, Lenhart, of Ulster Co. - 8/9 Sept 1715 (Deed Book BB:387)
STICKLEN, John - 20 May 1769 (Laws, ch. 1404; Ss:79)
    A John Sticklin was made freeman of NYC 17 May 1765 as a cord-
    wainer (CNYHS 1885:207). A John Sticklen, of NYC, cordwainer,
    was a bondsman on 17 May 1785 (Scott, Adm. Papers: 211)
STICKLING, Niecolas, of Albany Co. - 14 Feb. 1715/6 (Alb. CCM 6:117)
STIEVER, Baltus, of Albany Co. - 17 Jan. 1715/6 (Alb. CCM 6:115)
STIOP (?), Marten, of Albany Co. - 31 Jan. 1715/6 (Alb. CCM 6:116)
STOLLER, Michael - 20 Dec. 1763 (Laws, ch. 1236)
STOLLER, Michael - 8 Mar. 1773 (Laws, ch. 1638)
STOMF, Hans Jury, of Albany Co. - 31 Jan. 1715/6 (Alb. CCM 6:116)
STONE, John - 27 Jan. 1770 (Laws, ch. 1462)
STOPPELBERT, Peter, of Albany Co. - 17 Jan. 1715/6 (Alb. CCM 6:115)
STOUBER, Christian - 8 Nov. 1735 (Laws, ch. 634)
STOVER, Jacob, Jr. - 3 May 1755 (Laws, ch. 975)
STREBELL/STREBLE, John, Lutheran, of Manor of Livingston, Albany
    Co., farmer - 26 Oct. 1764 (C.O. 5:1072; Qq:63; SCJ)
STREIT, Godfried, Lutheran, of NYC, cordwainer, who has resided in
    N. J. 5 years, in Pa. about 18 mos, in N.Y. 1 yr. and 8 mos;
    cert. min. J. A. Weygand; witnesses: Johan Casper Linche, Joh.
    Matth. Rudolph - 20 Oct. 1758 (NYPL; Oo:62); took oath 28 Oct.
    1758 (SCJ)
STREIT, Johan Friederick, of Ulster Co. - 8/9 Sept. 1715 (Deed Book
    BB:387)
STROOK, Michel - 10 Mar. 1762 (Laws, ch. 1179)
STROOP, Johanis, of Ulster Co. - 8/9 Sept. 1715 (Deed Book BB:387)
STUART, Philip William - 8 Mar. 1773 (Laws, ch. 1638)
STUBARARE/STUBERARE, Peter, Lutheran, of NYC, stocking-weaver - 23
    Oct. 1765 (C.O. 5:1072; Qq:63; SCJ)
STUBER, George, Antient Lutheran Church, of NYC, tailor - 24 Apr.
    1767 (C.O. 5:1073; Rr:30; SCJ)
STUBLE, Christopher - 8 Mar. 1773 (Laws, ch. 1638)
STYERS, John - 20 Oct. 1764 (Laws, ch. 1272)
STYERS, John - 19 Dec. 1766 (Laws, ch. 1319)
SUBER, William, Jr. - 3 July 1759 (Laws, ch. 1089)
SUEVERDIZ, Carl - 3 July 1759 (Laws, ch. 1089)
    A Carl Sweverdiz was made freeman of NYC 24 July 1759 as a tailor
    (CNYHS 1885:193)
SURGET, Peter - 27 Jan. 1770 (Laws, ch. 1462)
SUTS, Baltus, of Ulster Co. - 8/9 Sept. 1715 (Deed Book BB:387)
SUYLANDT, Huybert, of Ulster Co. - 8/9 Sept. 1715 (Deed Book BB:387)
SWARTZ, Peter, Lutheran, Manor of Cortlandt, farmer - 19 Oct. 1763
    (C.O. 5:1071)
SWERE, John, of NYC, joiner - 6 Dec. 1715 (MCRM:127)
SWITTS, Cornelus, of Ulster Co. - 8/9 Sept. 1715 (Deed Book BB:386)
SYBRANDT, John - 25 Nov. 1727 (Laws, ch. 508)
    A John Sybrandt was made freeman of NYC 6 May 1729 as a mariner
    (CNYHS 1885:112)
SYFFERT, Johannes - 3 July 1759 (Laws, ch. 1089)

TADRICK, Christian - 11 Sept. 1761 (Laws, ch. 1154)
TAFT, Nicholas - 3 May 1755 (Laws, ch. 975)
TAUSEHEK, Casper - 20 Mar. 1762 (Laws, ch. 1179)
TAXSTIEDER, Jury, of Albany Co. - 3 Jan. 1715/6 (Alb. CCM 6:113)

TEN BROECK, Dirk Wessels, of Albany Co. - 14 Feb. 1715/6 (Alb. CCM 6:117)

TENNI, Jacob, Dutch Reformed, of NYC, cartman; cert. min. Joan Ritzema; witnesses: Willem Crolius, Willem Lorrens - 17 Oct. 1749 (NYPL; Hh:142)

TERRO, Jacob, Jr., Jew - nat. by Act of 1740 (Gg:68)

TER WILLEGEN, Jan, of Ulster Co. - 8/9 Sept. 1715 (Deed Book BB:386)

TESSON, Marie - 6 Dec. 1746 (Laws, ch. 844)

TESSON, Nicolas - 6 Dec. 1746 (Laws, ch. 844)

TETARD, John Peter, French Protestant, of NYC, clerk - 21 Apr. 1762 (C.O. 5:1071)

THAUVET, Marie Susanne, of New Rochell, widow - 6 Mar. 1715/6 (MCRM: 148)

THEIL, John - 11 Sept. 1761 (Laws, ch. 1154)

THEROUSDE, Jacob - petition to be naturalized 19 Aug. 1687 (CEM:167)

THERUNET, Andre - petition to be naturalized 19 Aug. 1687 (CEM:167)

THEVOU, Abraham, of Ulster Co. - 8/9 Sept. 1715 (Deed Book BB:387)

THEVOU, Daniel, of Ulster Co. - 8/9 Sept. 1715 (Deed Book BB:387)

THOMAS, Andries, of Ulster Co. - 8/9 Sept. 1715 (Deed Book BB:387)

THOMAS, Hans Jury, of Albany Co - 22 Nov. 1715 (Alb. CCM 6:109)

THOMAS, Johan Stoffel, of Ulster Co. - 8/9 Sept. 1715 (Deed Book BB:387)

THOMAS, Mathien - 6 Dec. 1746 (Laws, ch. 844)

TIEDEMAN, Jacobus - 24 Nov. 1750 (Laws, ch. 902)

TIEFENDORPH, Jacob - 3 May 1755 (Laws, ch. 975)

TIEGEL, William - 31 Dec. 1768 (Laws, ch. 1385)

TIEL, Ananias, of Albany Co. - 22 Nov. 1715 (Alb. CCM 6:109)

TIEL, Martin, of Albany Co. - 17 Jan. 1715/6 (Alb. CCM 6:115)

TIER, Daniel, French Protestant/ German Reformed Congregation, of NYC, cartman - 20 Apr. 1769 (C.O. 5:1075; Tt:4; SCJ)

TIERS, Daniel, French Protestant, of NYC, labourer; cert. min. J. Carle; witnesses: Jacques Desbrosses, Pierre Vallade - 21 Jan. 1762 (NYPL; C.O. 5:1071)

TIERS, John Henry, French Protestant, of NYC, labourer; cert. min. J. Carle; witnesses: James Desbrosses, Daniel Bonet - 22 Apr. 1761 (NYPL; Oo:63; SCJ)
A John Hendrick Tier was made freeman of NYC 11 Sept. 1770 as a labourer (CNYHS 1885:235). On 7 Feb. 1784 Daniel Tier, inn-keeper, was appointed administrator of the estate of his father, John Henry Tier, late of NYC, carman, dec'd (Scott, Adm. Papers: 316)

TIERS, Magdalen, French Protestant, of NYC, spinster; cert. min. J. Carle; witnesses: Jacques Desbrosses; Pierre Vallade- 21 Jan. 1762 (NYPL; C.O. 5:1071)

TIERS, Mathew, French Protestant, of NYC, blacksmith; cert. min. J. Carle; witnesses: Jacques Desbrosses, Pierre Vallade - 21 Jan. 1762 (NYPL; C.O. 5:1071)
A Mathew Tiers was made freeman of NYC 1 Oct. 1765 as a black-smith (CNYHS 1885:207)

TILLOU, Peter, French Protestant - petition to be made burgher and citizen, 1691 (CEM:206)

TIMMER, Thomas (a minor) - 20 Sept. 1728 (Laws, ch. 525)

TIMMER, Weit - 8 Nov. 1735 (Laws, ch. 634)
On 19 May 1690 an order was given to Benjamin Blagge, Nicholas Gerritse and Whyte Timber to appraise some guns and patares

belonging to Nicholas Du Maresq for use on board the sloop
Resolution (CEM:196)

TIMMERMAN, Henry, Church of England, of Albany Co., mason - 31
July 1771 (SCJ)

TIMMERMAN, Jacob, of Albany Co. - 3 Jan. 1715/6 (Alb. CCM 6:113)

TIMMERMAN, Nicholas - 19 Dec. 1766 (Laws, ch. 1319)

TITEMA, Johanna Sophia (widow of Jacobus Dekey, late of NYC, dec'd)
- 6 July 1723 (Laws, ch. 444; NYHS Oath Roll, 1723)
On 17 July 1706 Wm. Jackson took Thunis Quick as apprentice in
the presence of a Jacob Dekey (CNYHS 1885:615)

TIVANNI, Antoni, perriwig-maker - 12 July 1715 (MCRM:85)
An Anthony Tivanni was made freeman of NYC 24 Apr. 1716 as a
perriwig-maker (CNYHS 1885:95)

TOBIAS, Christian - 20 Dec. 1763 (Laws, ch. 1236)

TOBIAS, Christopher - 31 Dec. 1761 (Laws, ch. 1170)

TOBIAS, Christopher, Quaker, of Queens Co., yeoman - 23 Jan. 1762
(NYPL; C.O. 5:1071)
On 9 Oct. 1772 Richard Willits and John Whitson, of Queens Co.,
farmers (Executors of the estate of Christopher Tobias, of Queens
Co., farmer, dec'd) were cited upon complaint of Thomas Tobias,
of Queens Co., farmer (Scott, Adm. Papers:317)

TOLLE, John Frederick - 27 Jan. 1770 (Laws, ch. 1462)
On 5 Apr. 1800 Henry Wells, Jr., renounced as one of the executors
of the estate of a John Frederick Tolly, of Coxackie, Albany Co.,
physician, dec'd (Scott, Adm. Papers:318)

TONNEAU, Abraham, French Protestant - petition to be made burgher
and citizen, 1691 (CEM:206)

TOULON, Nicholas, French Protestant, of New Rochelle, Westchester
Co., mariner - 18 Jan. 1764 (C.O. 5:1072; Qq:63; SCJ)

TREVOR, Johan Peter, of Ulster Co. - 8/9 Sept. 1715 (Deed Book
BB:387)

TRIMPER, George - 3 May 1755 (Laws, ch. 975)

TROMPOOR, Johanis Jacob, of Ulster Co. - 8/9 Sept. 1715 (Deed Book
BB:387)

TROMPOOR, Nicolas, of Ulster Co. - 8/9 Sept. 1715 (Deed Book BB:387)

TRUBE, George - 3 May 1755 (Laws, ch. 444; NYHS Oath Roll, 1723)

TRUMPER, Harmanus, Reformed Protestant Dutch Church, of Orange Co.,
farmer - 21 Apr. 1769 (C.O. 5:1075; Tt:4)

TUNDELL, George - 16 Feb. 1771 (Laws, ch. 1508)

TUSSE, Jan/John, of New Rochell, yeoman - 16 Aug. 1715 (MCRM:92)

TYMOT, Juryan, of Ulster Co. - 8/9 Sept. 1715 (Deed Book BB:387)

TYNGES, Jacob - 8 Mar. 1773 (Laws, ch. 1638)

UIN, Helias (Elias EEN), of Ulster Co. - 8/9 Sept. 1715 (Deed Book
BB:386)

UTE, John, Lutheran, of NYC, butcher; cert. min. J. F. Ries; wit-
nesses: Peter Grim, Mark Phaffar - 18 Oct. 1750 (NYPL; Hh:142;
SCJ); see introd.
A John Utt was made freeman of NYC 20 Mar. 1770 as a butcher.
A John Utt, of NYC, butcher, was a bondsman on 20 Mar. 1770, 9
Aug. 1771 and 22 Oct. 1773 (Scott, Adm. Bonds: 83, 19, 111)

VALCKENBURGH, Vallentyn, of Ulster Co. - 8/9 Sept. 1715 (Deed Book
   BB:387)
VALLADE, Peter, French Protestant, of NYC, merchant; cert. min.
   J. Carle; witnesses: James Desbrosses, Daniel Bonet - 21 Apr.
   1762 (NYPL; C. O. 5:1071)
VALLARDE, Mary Elizabeth - 25 Nov. 1751 (Laws, ch. 921)
VALLARDE, Piere - 25 Nov. 1751 (Laws, ch. 921)
VALLEAU, Jesaias - 6 July 1723 (Laws, ch. 444: NYHS Oath Roll, 1723)
   On 2 May 1761 Isaiah Valleau, feltmaker, was appointed adminis-
   trator of the estate of his father, Isaiah Valleau, late of NYC,
   baker, dec'd. Fauconier Valleau, of NYC, sadler, was one of the
   bondsmen (Scott, Adm.Bonds: 138). Petition (9 Sept. 1723) of
   Jesaias Valleau, of NYC, merchant (only son of Jesaias Valleau,
   late of the Island of St. Thomas, son of another Jesaias Valleau,
   of New York), for relief against Peter Valleau, executor (CEM:480)
VALLOS, Estienne - petition to be naturalized 19 Aug. 1687 (CEM:167)
VAN AKEN, Marinus, of Ulster Co. - 8/9 Sept. 1715 (Deed Book BB:387)
VAN BEVERHOUDT, Berand Langemack - 24 Nov. 1750 (Laws, ch. 902)
VAN BEVERHOUDT, Bertrand - 24 Nov. 1750 (Laws, ch. 902)
VAN BEVERHOUDT, Claudius - 24 Nov. 1750 (Laws, ch. 902)
VAN BEVERHOUDT, Johanes - 24 Nov. 1750 (Laws, ch. 902)
VAN BEVERHOUDT, Margarette - 24 Nov. 1750 (Laws, ch. 902)
VAN DALFSEN, Jan, of Tappan, weaver - 23 Aug. 1715 (MCRM:94)
VAN DALSEN (or VAN DALSEMO), Willem, Lutheran, of NYC, schoolmaster;
   cert. min. Johannes Ritzema; witnesses: Elbert Haring, Ahasuerus
   Turck - 1 Aug. 1745 (NYPL; Gg:161, 213)
VAN DEN HAM, Henry, Church of England, of NYC, vintner; cert. min.
   H. Barclay; witnesses: Joseph Hildreth, Joseph Greswold - 15
   Jan. 1750/1 (NYPL; I1:52)
   A Henry Van Denham was made freeman of NYC 5 Feb. 1750/1 as an
   innholder (CNYHS 1885:172). A Henry Van Den Ham, of NYC, inn-
   holder, was a bondsman on 22 June 1757 and 10 May 1764 (Scott,
   Adm. Bonds: 143, 137); see introd.
VANDERBERG, Frans - 24 July 1724 (Laws, ch. 461)
   A Francis Vanderberg was made freeman of NYC 11 Aug. 1724 as a
   brazier (CNYHS 1885:105)
VANDER LYN, Pieter - 24 June 1719 (Laws, ch. 381)
VAN DER VOLGEN, Claes, of Albany Co. - 11 Oct. 1715 (Alb. CCM 6:105)
VAN DRIESEN, Petrus, of Albany Co. - 11 Oct. 1715 (Alb. CCM 6:105)
VAN DYCK, Johanes - 6 Dec. 1746 (Laws, ch. 844)
VAN ETTEN, Jan, of Ulster Co. - 8/9 Sept. 1715 (Deed Book BB:386)
VAN FLYEREN, Jeron, of Albany Co. - 28 Feb. 1715/6 (Alb. CCM 6:118)
VAN GELDER, Ary - 3 July 1759 (Laws, ch. 1089)
   Could this be the Abraham Van Gelder who was made freeman of
   NYC 3 July 1759 as a gunsmith (CNYHS 1885:193)?
VAN HAEREN, Isaac - 24 Nov. 1750 (Laws, ch. 902); see introd.
VAN HARLINGEN, Johannes Martinus - 6 July 1723 (Laws, ch. 444; NYHS
   Oath Roll, 1723)
VAN HERTSBERGEN, Johannes, merchant - 19 July 1715 (MCRM:87)
VANHEYTHUSEN, Gerard (son of Bernhard Vanheythusen), born at Waert
   in Brabant, now dwelling in the Parish of St. Martin's Orgars,
   London - 29 Dec. 1660 (Shaw I:77; Patents 1)
VAN INGEN, Dirck - 31 Dec. 1768 (Laws, ch. 1385)
   On 7 Nov. 1770 a Dirk Van Ingen, of Schenectady, Doctor of Physic

was appointed one of the administrators of the estate of Philip
Truax, late of Schenectady, dec'd (Scott, Adm. Papers:322)

VAN KAMPEN, Jan, of Ulster Co. - 8/9 Sept. 1715 (Deed Book BB:386)

VAN KINSWILDER, Geertruyda, wife of Herman Winkler - 29 Oct. 1730
(Laws, ch. 556)

VAN LOO, John - 6 July 1723 (Laws, ch. 445)

VAN NIMWEGEN, Harmanis, of Ulster Co. - 8/9 Sept. 1715 (Deed Book
BB:387)

VAN OBLINIS, Peter, of NYC, yeoman - 13 Dec. 1715 (MCRM:129)

VAN OLINDA, Peter, of Albany Co. - 27 Apr. 1716 (Alb. CCM 6:123)

VAN PETTEN, Claes, of Albany Co. - 17 Jan. 1715/6 (Alb. CCM 6:114)
A Claes Van Petten and Eva his wife were among the heirs of Claes
Janse Van Bockhoven, of Schenectady, Albany Co., whose estate
was settled in 1713 (Scott, Adm. Papers: 331)

VAN RANST, Gerrit, painter - 19 July 1715 (MCRM:87)
A Gerrit Van Ranst was made freeman of NYC 19 July 1715 as a
painter (CNYHS 1885:94)

VAN RANST, Pieter, of NYC, sailmaker - 13 Dec. 1715 (MCRM:129)
A Pieter Van Ranst was made freeman of NYC 12 Mar. 1727/8 as a
sail-maker (CNYHS 1885:110)

VAN SANTVOORD, Cornelius - 6 July 1723 (Laws, ch. 444; NYHS Oath
Roll, 1723)
A Cornelius Van Santford was made freeman of NYC 16 Feb. 1724/5
as a merchant (CNYHS 1885:105; see CEM:478)

VAN SOOLINGEN, Johannes - 27 July 1721 (Laws, ch. 418)
A Johannes Van Soolingen was made freeman of NYC 21 May 1728 as
a chirurgeon (CNYHS 1885:111)

VAN TAERLING, Floris - 6 July 1723 (Laws, ch. 444; NYHS Oath Roll,
1723)

VAN TAERLINGH, Jan - 24 June 1719 (Laws, ch. 381)

VAN TAERLINGH, Nicholaus - 17 June 1726 (Laws, ch. 476)

VAN VARICK, Jacobus, of NYC, bolter - 2 Aug. 1715 (MCRM:90)

VAN WYCK, Johannes - 22 June 1734 (Laws, ch. 605)
A Johannes Van Wyck was made freeman of NYC 11 Mar. 1734/5 as a
cooper (CNYHS 1885:126)

VAS, Diederick, of Ulster Co. - 8/9 Sept. 1715 (Deed Book BB:387)

VAS, Petrus, of Ulster Co. - 8/9 Sept. 1715 (Deed Book BB:387)

VEDDERLIN, Johannes - 22 June 1734 (Laws, ch. 605)

VELDEN, HIERONIMUS, Protestant - nat. by Act of 1740 (Gg:68)

VELDTMAN, Geertruyda - 14 Oct. 1732 (Laws, ch. 586)

VELDTMAN, Hans - 14 Oct. 1732 (Laws, ch. 586)

VELDTMAN, Hendrick - 14 Oct. 1732 (Laws, ch. 586)

VELDTMAN, John, Church of England, of Richmond Co., farmer; cert.
min. R. Charlton; witnesses: Richard Lawrence; Andrew Puckitt,
Thomas Price - 31 July 1754 (NYPL; Oo:62)

VELDTMAN, Maria - 14 Oct. 1732 (Laws, ch. 586)

VELLER, Flip, of Ulster Co. - 8/9 Sept. 1715 (Deed Book BB:387)

VENUS, Philip - 3 July 1766 (Laws, ch. 1299)

VERGEREAU, Bertram Gideon, of NYC - 27 Sept. 1715 (MCRM:104)

VERNEZOBRE, Christopher Abraham - 20 Oct. 1764 (Laws, ch. 1272)

VERNOOY, Cornelis, of Ulster Co. - 8/9 Sept. 1715 (Deed Book BB:387)

VETTER, Lucas - 3 July 1759 (Laws, ch. 1089)

VEZIEN, John, gardener - 19 July 1715 (MCRM:87)

VINERA, Daniel Rodrigues, Jew - nat. by Act of 1740 (NYPL; Gg:68;
Huhner:6)

VINGER, Johannis, of Albany Co. - 17 Jan. 1715/6 (Alb. CCM 6:114)
VINGLER, Philips, of Albany Co. - 17 Jan. 1715/6 (Alb. CCM 6:115)
VINK, Andries, of Albany Co. - 22 Nov. 1715 (Alb. CCM 6:109)
VINK, Christian, of Albany Co. - 3 Jan. 1715/6 (Alb. CCM 6:113)
VISCHER, Johannis, of Ulster Co. - 8/9 Sept. 1715 (Deed Book BB:386)
VISSER, Theunis - see introd.
VOEDIREN, Johan Bernard - 27 July 1721 (Laws, ch. 418)
VOERMAN, Jacob, of Ulster Co. - 8/9 Sept. 1715 (Deed Book BB:387)
VOGEL, John, Lutheran, of NYC, vintner - 19 Oct. 1763 (C.O.5:1071)
VOLCK, Andrew, of Ulster Co. - 8/9 Sept. 1715 (Deed Book BB:386)
VOLK, Johannis Bartel - 3 Feb. 1768 (Laws, ch. 1350)
VOLLENWYSER, Jacob - 11 Sept. 1761 (Laws, ch. 1154)
VOLMAR, John - 3 May 1755 (Laws, ch. 975)
VOLTS, Melgert, of Albany Co. - 3 Jan. 1715/6 (Alb. CCM 6:113)
VOLZ, Johan Jost - 8 Mar. 1773 (Laws, ch. 1638)
VONK, Peter, of Orange Co., yeoman - 3 Apr. 1716 (MCRM:153f)
VONK, Pieter, of Albany Co. - 22 Nov. 1715 (Alb. CCM 6:109)
VOOGT, William - 24 Nov. 1750 (Laws, ch. 902)
VOSHEE, Daniel, Lutheran, of NYC, tobacco-cutter; cert. min. J. A.
    Weygand; witness: Nicholas Killman (Rec. 94:145); took oath 23
    Oct. 1765 (SCJ)
    A Daniel Forshea was made freeman of NYC 29 Oct. 1765 as a
    tobacconist (CNYHS 1885:210)
VOSS, Jurian, Dutch Reformed, of Manor of Cortlandt, farmer - 19
    Oct. 1763 (C.O. 5:1071)
VROMAN, Adam, of Albany Co. - 22 Nov. 1715 (Alb. CCM 6:109)

WACHTEL, George - 31 Dec. 1761 (Laws, ch. 1170)
WAGENAER, Fallerus - 3 July 1759 (Laws, ch. 1089)
WAGGENAER, Peter, of Albany Co. - 31 Jan. 1715/6 (Alb. CCM 6:116)
WAGGONER, Frederick - 27 Jan. 1770 (Laws, ch. 1462)
WAGGONER, Jacob - 16 Feb. 1771 (Laws, ch. 1508)
WAGGONERZ, Jacob - 9 Mar. 1773 (Laws, ch. 1638)
WALDORPH, Jacob - 3 May 1755 (Laws, ch. 975)
WALDORPH, William - 3 May 1755 (Laws, ch. 975)
WALLACE, Willem Peter - 20 Mar. 1762 (Laws, ch. 1179)
WALLISER, Michal - 16 Feb. 1771 (Laws, ch. 1508)
WALTER, Jacob - 3 May 1755 (Laws, ch. 975)
WALTER, Jacob - 16 Feb. 1771 (Laws, ch. 1508)
WALTER, Jacob - 8 Mar. 1773 (Laws, ch. 1638)
WALTER, Johannes - 16 Feb. 1771 (Laws, ch. 1508)
WALTER, Johannes Franciscus - 14 Oct. 1732 (Laws, ch. 586)
    A John Francis Walter was made freeman of NYC 4 Oct. 1737 as a
    carpenter (CNYHS 1885:133)
WALTER, John - 11 Sept. 1761 (Laws, ch. 1154)
    John Schuyler on 18 Jan. 1786 was appointed administrator of the
    estate of a John Walter, of NYC, Esq., dec'd (Scott, Adm. Bonds:
    143)
WALTMAYER, George - 3 May 1755 (Laws, ch. 975)
WALZ, Coenraed-20 Mar. 1762 (Laws, ch. 1179)
WANNER, Lodwich, of Albany Co. - 31 Jan. 1715/6 (Alb. CCM 6:116)
WARNAER, Christophel, of Albany Co. - 13 Mar. 1715/6 (Alb. CCM 6:119)
WARNER, Michael - 8 Mar. 1773 (Laws, ch. 1638)
WARRAVEN, Johan Adolph, of Albany Co. - 28 Feb. 1715/6 (Alb. CCM 6:
    118)

WATSELL, John - 24 Nov. 1750 (Laws, ch. 902)
WAYGER, Barent - 3 May 1755 (Laws, ch. 975)
WAYGER, Everard - 3 May 1755 (Laws, ch. 975)
WAYGER, Hans Jury - 3 May 1755 (Laws, ch. 975)
WAYGER, Leonard - 3 May 1755 (Laws, ch. 975)
WEAVER, Hendrick - pet. 16 Nov. 1739; see introd.
WEAVER, Johannis, of Orange Co., tailor - 20 Dec. 1763 (Laws, ch.
    1236); took oath 18 Apr. 1764 (SCJ)
WEBER, Johannes, Lutheran; cert. min. G. W. Mancius; witnesses:
    Jacob Sornberger; Henrich Berringer - 23 Oct. 1741 (NYPL; Gg:81)
WEBER, Michael, Lutheran, of NYC, shoemaker - 21 Oct. 1765 (C.O.5:
    1072; Qq:63; SCJ)
WEEDER, Johannis Joost - 20 Mar. 1762 (Laws, ch. 1179)
WEESENER, Henry, of Orange Co., yeoman - 28 Feb. 1715/6 (MCRM:146)
WEESENER, Johannes, of Orange Co., yeoman - 28 Feb. 1715/6 (MCRM:146)
WEEVER, Jacob, of Albany Co. - 11 Oct. 1715 (Alb. CCM 6:105)
WEGELE, Johan Michel, of Ulster Co. - 8/9 Sept. 1715 (Deed Book
    BB:387)
WEGER, Jacob - 11 Sept. 1761 (Laws, ch. 1154)
WEIGIESER, Andreas - 3 July 1759 (Laws, ch. 1089)
WEISS, Friedrick - 3 July 1759 (Laws, ch. 1089)
    A Frederick Weiss was made freeman of NYC 24 July 1759 as a
    cutler (CNYHS 1885:193)
WELLER, Hieronimus, of Ulster Co. - 8/9 Sept. 1715 (Deed Book BB:387)
WELP, Gerrit, of NYC, painter - 20 Oct. 1764 (Laws, ch. 1272); took
    oath 23 Oct. 1764 (SCJ)
WEMER, Philip - 3 July 1759 (Laws, ch. 1089)
WENDELL, John - 31 Dec. 1768 (Laws, ch. 1385)
WENSS, Jorg - 16 Dec. 1737 (Laws, ch. 662)
WERT, Johannes - 3 July 1759 (Laws, ch. 1089)
WERTH, Johann Jacob, Dutch Reformed, of Schohary, Albany Co.,
    Doctor of Physic; cert. min. J. Schuyler; witnesses: Johan
    Willem Dietz, Willim Brown - 29 July 1752 (NYPL; Ii:52)
WESNER, Adam, son of Johannes Wesner or Weesener, of Orange Co.,
    yeoman - 3 Apr. 1716 (MCRM:153f)
WESSELS, Hendrick - 29 Nov. 1745 (Laws, ch. 811)
    A Hendrick Wessells was made freeman of NYC 1 July 1746 as a
    sail-maker (CNYHS 1885:156)
WESSELSE, Jacobus - 6 July 1723 (Laws, ch. 444; NYHS Oath Roll,
    1723)
WESTBROECK, Johannes, of Kingston, Ulster Co., "shewmaker"- before
    1715 (Deed Book BB:215)
WESTERLO, Eildardus - 11 Sept. 1761 (Laws, ch. 1154)
    On 13 Feb. 1788 a petition was signed by, among others, Eilardus
    Westerlo, of Albany, clerk, and Catharine his wife (Scott, Adm.
    Papers:195)
WESTERMEYER, John, Lutheran, of NYC, baker - 26 July 1769 (C.O. 5:
    1075; Tt:4; SCJ)
WESTPHAL, Fredrick, deacon of Antient Lutheran Trinity Church, of
    NYC - 18 Oct. 1774 (SCJ)
WETTERHAN, John, Reformed German Congregation, of NYC - 27 July
    1774 (SCJ)
WEVER, Jacob, of Ulster Co. - 8/9 Sept. 1715 (Deed Book BB:386)
WEVER, Niccolas, of Albany Co. - 11 Oct. 1715 (Alb. CCM 6:105)

WEYANT, Magiel, of Ulster Co. - 8/9 Sept. 1715 (Deed Book BB:386)

WEYGAND, John Albert, Lutheran, of NYC, Minister of the Gospel, in
New York about 16 years - 21 Apr. 1767 (C.O. 5:1073; SCJ)

WEYNIGER, Hans Gerhard, of Albany Co. - 14 Feb. 1715/6 (Alb. CCM 6:
117)

WEYNIGER, Uldrich, of Albany Co. - 14 Feb. 1715/6 (Alb. CCM 6:117)

WEYS, Andrew, Lutheran, of Dutchess Co., carpenter ; cert. min.
M. C. Knoll; witnesses: Johannes Snyder, Christian Haver - 18
Oct. 1744 (NYPL; Gg:118, 161)

WEYTMAN, Hans Marte, of Albany Co. - 31 Jan. 1715/6 Alb. CCM 6:116)

WHADELL, Johannes - 3 July 1759 (Laws, ch. 1089)

WHITEMAN, Henry - 3 May 1755 (Laws, ch. 975)
A Henry Whiteman was made freeman of NYC 14 Oct. 1765 as a button-
maker (CNYHS 1885:208). In 1760 he lived near the lower end of
the Oswego Market (Gottesman:204)

WHITEMAN, Jacob - 31 Dec. 1761 (Laws, ch. 1170)

WHITMORE, Peter - 8 Mar. 1773 (Laws, ch. 1638)

WICK, Johan - 11 Sept. 1761 (Laws, ch. 1154)

WICKHUYSEN, Pieter, of Ulster Co. - 8/9 Sept. 1715 (Deed Book BB:387)

WIDERSTEIN, Henry - 20 Dec. 1763 (Laws, ch. 1236)

WIDERSTEIN, Henry - 20 Oct. 1764 (Laws, ch. 1272)

WIEDERSHEIN/WIEDERSHINE, (John) Daniel, Lutheran, of NYC, butcher -
23 Oct. 1765 (C.O. 5:1072; Qq:63; SCJ)

WIEDERWAX, Hendk. Christopel, of Albany Co. - 22 Nov. 1715 (Alb.
CCM 6:109)

WIEDERWAX, Johan And., of Albany Co. - 22 Nov. 1715 (Alb CCM 6:109)

WIEMER, Andries - 31 Dec. 1761 (Laws, ch. 1170)

WIEST, Conraet, of Ulster Co. - 8/9 Sept. 1715 (Deed Book BB:387)

WILEMAN, Rachel, wife of Henry Wileman, of NYC, gent. - 3 Apr.
1716 (MCRM:153f)

WILGUS/WILIGS/WILIGAS, Jan, turner - 26 July 1715 (MCRM:88)

WILL, Christian, German Reformed Congregation, of NYC, pewterer -
18 Oct. 1769 (C.O. 5:1075; Tt:4; SCJ)
A Christian Will, of NYC, pewterer, was a bondsman on 25 Nov.
1784 (Scott, Adm. Papers:94)

WILL, Hendrick William - 16 Dec. 1737 (Laws, ch. 662)

WILL, Henry, Reformed German Church, of NYC, pewterer; cert. min.
F. Rothenbuhler; witnesses: Frederick Schwatz, Johannes Myers -
21 Oct. 1761 (NYPL; Oo:63; SCJ)
A Henry Will was made freeman of NYC 14 Oct. 1765 as a pewterer
(CNYHS 1885:208). Henry Will, of NYC, pewterer, was a bondsman
in 1773, 1789, 1790 and 1795 (Scott, Adm. Bonds: 68, 103, 100,84)

WILL, John - 3 July 1759 (Laws, ch. 1089)
A John Will was made freeman of NYC 24 July 1759 as a pewterer
(CNYHS 1885:193). John Will, from Germany, pewterer, was work-
ing in NYC in 1756 and 1760 and living in Smith's Fly, opposite
Robert Livingston's (Gottesman:105). See introd.

WILL, John Michel, Lutheran, of NYC, cordwainer; cert. min. M. C.
Knoll; witnesses: Jacob Boss, Jacob Foerster, Jeronimus Riegler -
31 Oct. 1745 (NYPL; Gg:213)
A John Michael Will was made freeman of NYC 6 May 1760 as a
cordwainer (CNYHS 1885:194)

WILL, Philip, Reformed German Church, of NYC, pewterer; cert. min.
E.Rothenbuhler; witnesses:Hendrick Schwatz, Abraham Young - 21
Oct. 1761 (NYPL; Oo:63; SCJ)

WINCKLE, John - 11 Sept. 1761 (Laws, ch. 1154)
WINDRICH, Baltus, of Ulster Co. - 8/9 Sept. 1715 (Deed Book BB:387)
WINKLER, Hans Willem Van Kinswilder - 29 Oct. 1730 (Laws, ch. 556)
WINKLER, Herman - 29 Oct. 1730 (Laws, ch. 556)
   See also Geertruyda Van Kinswilder his wife.
WINKLER, Jacomina Geertruyda Isabella - 29 Oct. 1730 (Laws, ch. 556)
WINKLER, Lewis Adolph - 29 Oct. 1730 (Laws, ch. 556)
WINKLER, Maria Magtelda - 29 Oct. 1730 (Laws ch. 556)
WINKLER, Nicolaas Verkuyle - 29 Oct. 1730 (Laws, ch. 556)
WINTER, Hendrick, of Albany Co. - 17 Jan. 1715/6 (Alb. CCM 6:115)
WINTHROP, Balthazar, Lutheran, of NYC, mariner; cert. min. John
   Albert Weygand; witnesses: Samuel Beeckman, George Petterson -
   23 Oct. 1755 (NYPL; Oo:62; SCJ)
   On 12 Jan. 1764 Elizabeth Thompson (wife of Patrick Hynes, form-
   erly widow of Belthazar Winthrop) was appointed administratrix
   of the estate of Belthazar Winthrop, late of NYC, mariner, dec'd
   (Scott, Adm. Bonds:150). On 31 Jan. 1765 Catharine Van Wyck (sis-
   ter of Balthazar Winthrop, late of NYC, mariner) signed an ad-
   ministration bond in relation to his estate (Scott, Adm. Papers:
   368)
WHITEMAN/WITEMAN, Hendrick, Dutch Reformed, of NYC, brass-button-
   maker; cert. min. G. DuBois; witnesses: Jacob Boshart, Hannes
   Huber 18 Oct. 1750 (NYPL; Hh:142; SCJ)
   A Henry Whiteman was made freeman of NYC 14 Oct. 1765 as a
   button-maker (CNYHS 1885:208)
WITHERICK, George - 8 Mar. 1773 (Laws, ch. 1638)
WITHERICK, Michael - 8 Mar. 1773 (Laws, ch. 1638)
WITMUR, Peter - 16 Feb. 1771 (Laws, ch. 1508)
WOESTER, Simon - 3 May 1755 (Laws, ch. 975)
WOHLGEMUTH, Hannes - 11 Sept. 1761 (Laws, ch. 1154)
WOLF, Coenraed - 20 May 1769 (Laws, ch. 1404 = WOLFE, Coenrad,
   Ss:79)
   On 4 Jan. 1772 administrators were appointed for the estate of
   Conraet Wolfe, late of NYC, butcher, dec'd (Scott, Adm. Bonds:
   150). On 21 Feb. 1774 Hinrich Ditloff (administrator of the
   estate of Conrodt Wolfe) was cited upon complaint of Jane Weath-
   ershine, formerly widow of Conrodt Wolfe (Scott, Adm. Papers:368)
WOLF, Johannes - 8 Mar. 1773 (Laws, ch. 1638)
WOLFE, Frederick - 16 Feb. 1771 (Laws, ch. 1508)
WOLFF, Johan David - 29 Oct. 1730 (Laws, ch. 556)
   A Johann David Wolff was made freeman of NYC 2 Mar. 1730/1 as a
   tailor (CNYHS 1885:116). David Wolfe, of NYC, gentleman, on
   10 Apr. 1770, was appointed administrator of the estate of his
   father, Johan David Wolfe, late of NYC, tailor, dec'd (Scott,
   Adm. Bonds:150)
WOLGEMOOTH, Johannes - 3 July 1759 (Laws, ch. 1089)
WOLHAUPTER, David, Lutheran, of NYC, turner - 23 Apr. 1765 (C.O. 5:
   1072; Qq:63; SCJ)
   A David Woolhofter was made freeman of NYC 29 Oct. 1765 as a
   turner (CNYHS 1885:211)
WOLHAUPTER, Gottliep - 3 July 1759 (Laws, ch. 1089)
   A Gottfried Woolhauper was made freeman of NYC 24 July 1759 as
   a turner (CNYHS 1885:193). A Gottlieb Wolhaupter, maker of
   musical instruments, in 1761 was living opposite Adam Vander-

berg's (Gottesman: 367-368); see introd.

WOLLASEN, Johon Petter, of Ulster Co. - 8/9 Sept. 1715 (Deed Book BB:386)

WOLLEBEN, Fillib, of Ulster Co. - 8/9 Sept. 1715 (Deed Book BB:386)

WOLLEBEN, Johan Jacob, of Ulster Co. - 8/9 Sept. 1715 (Deed Book BB:387)

WOLLEBEN, Peter, of Ulster Co. - 8/9 Sept. 1715 (Deed Book BB:387)

WOLLEVEN, Vallentyn, of Ulster Co. - 8/9 Sept 1715 (Deed Book BB:386)

WONDERLY, Egydius, Lutheran, of NYC, joiner - 20 Apr. 1763 (C.O. 5:1071; SCJ)

WOOLRICE, George - 20 May 1769 (Laws, ch. 1404)
    A George Woolrick was made freeman of NYC 20 June 1769 as a labourer (CNYHS 1885:226)

WORKHARD, George, Lutheran, of NYC, baker - 21 Oct. 1762 (C.O. 5:1071; SCJ)

WOYNAT, Cornelis, of NYC, boatman - 22 Nov. 1715 (MCRM:121)

WURTMAN, Hans Harmon, of Ulster Co. - 8/9 Sept. 1715 (Deed Book BB:387)

WYNKOOP, Johanis, of Ulster Co. - 8/9 Sept. 1715 (Deed Book BB:387)

WYSE, Andries - pet. 16 Nov. 1739; see introd.

YONCKER, Rudolph - 3 July 1759 (Laws, ch. 1089)

YORDAN, John George - 3 July 1759 (Laws, ch. 1089)

YOUNG, Adolph - 11 Sept. 1761 (Laws, ch. 1154)

YOUNG, Christian - 20 Mar. 1762 (Laws, ch. 1179)

YOUNG, Peter - 27 Jan. 1770 (Laws, ch. 1462)
    A Peter Young, pewterer, in Dec. 1775 was living at the house of Mr. Fisher, barber, in Spring Garden, commonly called Chatham St., in NYC (Gottesman:106). On 20 June 1781 Ann Flegley (wife of John Flegley but late widow of Peter Young, soldier in Col. Lamb's Regt. of Artillery) was appointed administratrix of Young's estate (Scott, Adm. Papers:375)

YOUNG, Tebald, of Albany Co. - 3 Jan. 1715/6 (Alb. CCM 6:113)
    On 9 Oct. 1771 Margaret Young was appointed administratrix of the estate of her dec'd husband, Teobalt Young, late of Canajorie, Albany Co. (Scott, Adm. Papers:375)

YORDAN, John George - 3 July 1759 (Laws, ch. 1089)

YSAACKS, Abraham - 6 July 1723 (Laws, ch. 444; NYHS Oath Roll, 1723)
    An Abraham Isaacs was made freeman of NYC 6 Aug. 1723 as a merchant (CNYHS 1885:101). An Abraham Isaacs, of NYC, merchant, was a bondsman in Dec. 1783 (Scott, Adm. Papers:191)

YUNG, Pilus - 16 Dec. 1737 (Laws, ch. 662)

ZEEGAARD, Andries - 20 Dec. 1763 (Laws, ch. 1236)

ZEEGAERD, Andries - 31 Dec. 1761 (Laws, ch. 1170)

ZEEGER, Michael - 3 May 1755 (Laws, ch. 975)

ZENGER, John - 17 June 1726 (Laws, ch. 476)

ZENGER, John Pieter/Peter - 6 July 1723 (Laws, ch. 444; NYHS Oath Roll, 1723)
    John Pieter Zenger was made freeman of NYC 10 Sept. 1723 as a printer (CNYHS 1885:104). His printing press was offered for sale in July 1751, as he was lately deceased (Gottesman:242)

ZIBBERLING, Bernthtt, of Ulster Co. - 8/9 Sept. 1715 (Deed Book BB:386)

ZIEGLER, Gotthart - 3 July 1759 (Laws, ch. 1089)
   A Gotthart Ziegler was made freeman of NYC 24 July 1759 as a
   butcher (CNYHS 1885:193)
ZIMMERMAN, Henry, Lutheran of NYC, carpenter - 21 Oct. 1765
   (C.O. 5:1072; Qq:63; SCJ)
ZINCKE, Johan Casper, see introd.
ZIPPERLING, Bernhert, Jr., of Ulster Co. - 8/9 Sept. 1715 (Deed
   Book BB:387)
ZIPPERLING, Fredrik, of Ulster Co. - 8/9 Sept. 1715 (Deed Book
   BB:387)
ZIPPERLING, Michael, of Ulster Co. - 8/9 Sept. 1715 (Deed Book
   BB:387)
ZOLLINGER, Andreas - 11 Sept. 1761 (Laws, ch. 1154)
ZOLLINGER, Casper - 11 Sept. 1761 (Laws, ch. 1154)
ZUERIGHER, Johannes, Dutch Reformed, of NYC, yeoman; cert. min.
   G. DuBois; witnesses: Evert Pels, Willem Corcilius - 17 Apr.
   1750 (NYPL; Hh:142)
   A Johannes Zuricker was made freeman of NYC 14 Oct. 1765 as a
   stone-cutter (CNYHS 1885:208). A John Zuricher witnessed a
   will on 29 Nov. 1756 (Scott, Adm. Papers:95)
ZU VELT, Gorg, of Ulster Co. - 8/9 Sept. 1715 (Deed Book BB:386)
ZUVELT, George Adam, of Ulster Co. - 8/9 Sept. 1715 (Deed Book
   BB:387)

OATHS OF ALLEGIANCE

I Dutch Period

Since New Netherland was situated between English possessions, it was not remarkable that the Dutch authorities were apprehensive about such British subjects as might live among them. In the Seventeenth Century people were inclined to take oaths seriously. Thus, in August 1639 the following oath was formulated to be taken by all Englishmen dwelling in or about the Island of Manhattan: "You swear that you will be loyal and faithful to their High Mightinesses the Lords States General, his Highness of Orange and the honorable director and council of New Netherland; that you will follow wherever the director or anyone of the council shall lead; that you will immediately faithfully report all treason and injury to the country of which you receive any knowledge; and that you will to the best of your ability help to protect with your life and property the inhabitants thereof against all enemies of the country. So help me God." Eight Englishmen promptly took the above oath and signed the same, four of them by mark. They were George Homs (by mark), Richard Brudnill, Abraham Newman, Jan Habbeson (John Hobson, by mark), John Hathaway, Ffrancis Lastley, Eduart Wilson (by mark) and Willem Willemsz (by mark) (NYHMD 4:58). In like manner, when "Governor Onderhil," (John Underhill), residing in the North, requested permission to settle here with some families under Dutch protection, his petition was granted on September 8, 1639, on condition that he and his associates take the oath of allegiance to their High Mightinesses the Lords States General and His Highness of Orange (ibid. 4:59).

Similarly, on June 6, 1641, the Council of New Netherland granted to a considerable number of respectable Englishmen, with their clergyman, leave to settle in New Netherland on condition that they be "bound to take the oath of allegiance to the honorable States General and the West India Company under whose protection they will reside" (ibid. 4:110). Such was the general pattern in the case of Englishmen - and probably other foreigners - desirous of living in the Dutch colony. In November 1647 it was decreed that persons from the colony of New Haven should be free to come and go and enjoy liberty and freedom "on condition...of taking the proper oath of allegiance"(ibid. 4:472). Two years later it was provided that "No person shall be allowed to keep a public or private store on shore ... or to carry on trade by the small weight and measure within our jurisdiction in this province of New Netherland, except our good and dear inhabitants who first have taken the oath of allegiance..." (ibid. 4:491). Again, in March 1656, the petition of Thomas Wheeler and fifteen other settlers, requesting permission to reside at Vreedland (Westchester) was granted "on (their) taking the oath of allegiance" (CDM 163). Likewise town officials, as was the case in Flushing, had to take the oath of allegiance (NYHMD 4:516), while English officers and soldiers in the Dutch service in 1643 took the following oath: "We promise and swear allegiance to the High and

Mighty Lords the States General, the Prince of Orange, the Chartered
West India Company and the honorable director general and council of
New Netherland, to risk life and limb for them and in the country's
service and furthermore to obey the honorable director as faithful
officers and soldiers are bound to obey their commander. So truly
help us God Almighty" (ibid. 4:205). Citizenship was of the utmost
importance, whether of the colony or a town, as is shown by the
order of the council on July 3, 1664, that the merchants from the
South River desiring to carry on trade at New Amsterdam "must take
out citizenship" (CDM 266). Indeed as early as September, 1662,
persons who came to New Netherland without leave were required to
take the oath of allegiance within six weeks after their arrival
and to register their names at the office of the provincial secretary
in New Amsterdam (Laws and Ordinances of New Netherland: 428-30).

II English Period

The capture of New Netherland by the English in 1664 led to
the requirement that the non-English inhabitants of New York take
an oath of allegiance to the new regime. The third article of surrender, of August 27, 1664, was as follows: "All people shall still
continue free Denizens and enjoy their Lands, Houses, Goods, Shipps,
wheresoever they are within this Country and dispose of them as they
please" (ECM I:65, note 2).

On October 18, 1664, Governor Richard Nicolls felt constrained
to make to the burgomasters and other magistrates of New York a declaration concerning the oath to be taken to his Majesty. His mes-
sage was couched in these terms: "Whereas there is a false & In-
jurious aspersion cast upon the oath of obedience to his Ma^{ty}, his
Royall Highnesse the Duke of Yorke, & the Governo^{rs} or offic^{rs} appointed by his Ma^{tyes} Authority, and that some persons have mali-
ciously sought to distract the mindes of the Inhabitants of New
Yorke by suggesting that the Articles of peace so late, and so sol-
emnly made, signed & sealed, were intended by that oath to bee made
null, & of none effect. To the end that such wicked practises may
not take the effect, for which they are designed, and that all now
under his Ma^{tyes} obedience as Denizens of this Towne, may bee un-
deceived and not give any longer Creditt to the Disturbers of the
peace of this Government. I do thinke fitt to declare, that the
Articles of Surrender are not in the least broken or intended to
bee broken by any words, or expressions in the said Oath: And if
any person or persons hereafter shall presume to give any other
Construction of the said Oath, then is herein declared, I shall
account him or them disturbers of the peace of his Ma^{tyes} Subjects,
and proceed accordingly; I do further appoint, and order, That
this Declaration bee forthwith read to all the Inhabitants & reg-
istred. As also that every Denizen under my Government do take the
said oath, who intend to remaine here under his Ma^{tyes} Obedience;
Given under my hand this 18th day of October in the yeare of our
Lord God. 1664" (General Entries V.I, State Library Bulletin,
History No. 2 [May 1899]: 118f).

The required oath read: "I sweare by the name of Almighty God, that I will bee a true subject, to the King of Great Brittaine, and will obey all such commands, as I shall receive from His Majestie, His Royall Highnesse James Duke of Yorke, and such Governors and Officers, as from time to time are appointed over me, by His authority, and none other, whilst I live in any of his Maj[ties] territoryes; SO HELPE ME GOD." The following signed the above oath October 21, 22, 24, 26, 1664 (CDNY 3:74-77):

Abrahamzen, Izaac
Abrahamzen, Willem van der
    Borden
Adamzen, Abraham
Adamzen, Jan
Albertzen, Egbert (from
    Amsterdam)
Aldricks, Peter
Andrizen, Andries
Andriezen, Ariaan
Andriezen, Lucas
Andriezen, Paulus
Anthony, Allard
Appell, Arien
Arenzen, Frederic
Arianzen, Jan
Ascen, Jan
Assuerus, Hendrick

Backer, Claes Janssen
Backer, Jacob
Backer, Reinier Willemzen
Barentzen, Cornelius van der
    Kuyl
Barrenzen, Meindert
Barentzen, Simon
Bartelzen, Jonas
Bayard, Nicholas
Beeckman, Joghim
Beakman, William (of
    "Esopies")
Bedlow, Isaac
Benaat, Garrit
Blanck, Jurien
Bogardus, Willem
Boon, Francis
Bos (=Bush), Hendrick
Briell, Toussein

Carelzen, Joost
Chambers, Thomas
Claerhoudt, Walraven
Claesen, Andries
Claesen, Sibout
Clock, Abraham

Clopper, Cornelis Yanzen
Coninck, Aldert
Coninck, Thomas
Cossar, Jacob
Coster, Jan
Costurier, Jacques
Course, Barren
Cousseau, Jacques
Cray, Teunis
Cregier, Martin

Danielzen, Jacob
David, James
De Forrest, Isaac
De Haart, Balthazar
De Hayen, Isaac
De Honde, Coutrie Daniel
De Honneur, Guillaume
Dela Montagne, Johann[s] (of Albany)
Dela Montagne, William (of Albany)
De La Plaine, Nicolas
De Meyer, Nicolaus
De Milt, Anthony
De Peister, Johannes
Desille, Lourens
De Weerhem, Ambrosius
De Wiit, Johannes
Dirckzen, Lucas
Dirckzen, Meyer Jan
Doeckles (Douglass?), William
Dopzen (Dobson?), Joris
Douzen, Herman
Drisius, Samuel
Dupuis, Nicholaus
Duyckings, Evert
Dydelofzen, Claes

Ebbinck, Jeronimus
Ebell, Peter
Etsal, Samuel
Evertzen, Dirck

Fedder, Harman
Fell, Simon
Filipzen, Frederick

Fries, Jan
Fulwevez, Gerrit

Gabry, Timotheus
Gerritson, _____
Goderus, Joost
Goukes, Reinier
Grevenraat, Isaac
Guindan, Estienne

Hagener, Jeremias Janssen
Hall, Thomas
Hardenbroeck, Abell
Harderbroeck, Johannes
Heinse, Jacob
Hendrickzen, Fredric
Hendrickzen, Gerrit (from
  Amsterdam)
Hendrickzen, Hendrick (from
  Ireland)
Hendrickzen, Hubert (from
  Ceulen (Cologne))
Hermel, Abraham
Hermzen, Pieter
Holst, Barent
Hoogheland, Christoffle
Huges, Jacob

Isaackzen, Arent
Isaackzen, Denys
Israel, Jacob

Jacobs, Crains
Janzen, Abraham
Janzen, Claes
Janzen, Claes (from Langendick)
Janzen, Cornelis (from Hoorn)
Janzen, Cors
Janzen, Frans (from Hooghten)
Janzen, Galma Sibrant
Janzen, Hendrick (the baker)
Janzen, Jan (from Brestec)
Janzen, Jan (from Langedick)
Janzen, Jurien
Janzen, Pieter
Janzen, Pieter ("of the Long
  Street")
Janzen, Roeloff (from
  Meppelen)
Janzen, Sick
Jogkimzen, Andries
Joosten, Jacob
Joosten, Jan
Jurianzen, Lantsman Arent

Keeren, Jacob
Keuninck, Albert
Kierstede, Hans
Kipp, Hendrick, d'oude (Sr.)
Kipp, Isaac
Kipp, Jacob
Knoesvelt, Bay
Kock, Jan Jelezen
Kool, Barrent Jacobzen

Laurens, Jan
Laurens, Thomas
Lawrenzen, Arien
Leisler, Jacob
Leunizen, Jacob
Levi, Asser
Loockermans, Govert
Luyck, Egidius

Maan, Bartholdus
Meet, Pieter
Megapolensis, Johannes
Megapolensis, Samuel
Meindertzen, Jan
Meindertzen, Jan
Mens, Jacob
Mens, Johannes
Merrit, William
Migkielzen (Michelson), Stoffell
Mindertse, Egbert
Moesmans, Arent Janssen
Moesman, Jacob Jansen
Mol, Lambert Huybertzen
Molengraaff, Thomas
Moyer, Thomas

Nevius, Johannes
Nys, Pieter

Obe, Hendrick
Onckbauck, Adam

Pauluzen, Claes
Pieter, Abraham
Pieterzen, Albert (Trompetter
  (trumpeter))
Peterson, Jacob
Pieterzen, Nathanael
Pieters, Reintse (from Bolsart)
Pluvier, Cornelius
Pos, Lodowick
Provost, Johannes (of Albany)

Quick, Teunis Thomazen

Reddel, (name not given)
Rees, Andries
Reinier, Pieter
Reinoutzen, Reinout
Renzlaer, Jeremias
Renzlaer, Richard
Reycken, Reinier
Richard, Paulus
Roelofzen, Boele
Roelofzen, Jan
Romein, Simon Janzen
Roos, Gerrit Janzen

Sanderzen, Thomas
Schaafbanck, Pieter
Schivelbergh, Johannes
Scruyver, Jan
Simkam, Pieter
Slictenhorst, Gerrit
Spygelaar, Jan
Staets, Abraham
Steenwick, Cornelius B.
Sticken, Dirck
Still, Cornelys Jacobzen
Stoll, Pieter Janzell
Stoutenbergh, Pieter
Stuyvesant, Pieter G.

Tades, Mighiel
Ten Eyck, Coenraut
Teunizen, Jan
Tonneman, Pieter
Tyler, Andries
Tyler, William

Van Bommel, Hendrick
Van Bommel, Jan Hendrickzen
Van Brugh, Carel
Van Brugh, Johannes
Van Brussum, Egbert
Van Buytenhuysen, Jan Gerritzen
Van Campen, Lambert Hendrickzen
Van Cortland, Oloffe Stevenzen
Van Couwenhoven, Johannes
Van Den Bergh, Frederick Gys-
bertzen

Van Der Borden, see William
Abrahamzen
Van Der Cleffe, Dirck
Van Der Grist, Paulus Leendert-
zen
Van Der Kuyl, see Cornelius
Barentzen
Van Der Schuyren, Willem
Van Der Vin, Hendrick Janzen
Van De Water, Hendrick
Van Dyck, Hendrick
Van Elsland, Claes de Jonge (Jr.)
Van Elsland, Claes d'oude (Sr.)
Van Gelder, Jan
Van Haerlem, Jan
Van Laar, Arien
Van Laar, Stoffel
Van Ruyven, Cornelius
Van Schuiller, Philip Peterson
Van Tricht, Gerrit
Varetanger, Jacob Hendrickzen
Vermoon, Jacob
Verplank, Abraham
Verveel, Daniel
Videt, Jan
Vincent, Adrian
Ving, Jan
Vis, Jacob

Waldron, Resolveert
Wanshaer, Jan (from St. Aubin)
Wesselzen, David
Wessels, Herman
Wessell, Warnar
Willemzen, Ratger
Winster, Pieter
Witthart, Johannes
Wouterzen, Egbert
Wouterzen, Jan
Wouterzen, Willem

Yanzen (Jansen), Gerrit Stavast
Yanzen (Jansen), Martin

In January, 1664/5, was recorded an oath, called "The Oath of Allegiance," which was presumably to be taken by officials of New York. It reads: "I A. B. Do truly and Sincerely acknowledge, professe Testifie, and declare in my Conscience, before God and the World; That Our Soveraigne Lord King Charles, is Lawfull and Rightfull King of this Realme, and of all other his Maties Dominions and Countryes, and that the Pope neither of himselfe, nor by any Authority, by the Church or See of Rome, or by any other meanes with any other, hath any Power or Authority to depose the King, or to dispose of any of his Maties Kingdomes, or Dominions, or to Authorize any fforaigne Prince, to invade or annoy him, or his Countryes, or to discharge any of his Subjects of their allegiance and obedito his Matie or to give licence or leave to any of them to beare Armes, raise Tumults, or to offer any violence or hurt, to his Maties Royall Person, State, or Governm^t, or to any of his Ma^{tyes} Subjects within his Maties Dominions.

Also, I do Sweare from my heart, That notwithstanding any declaracon, or Sentence of Excommunicacon, or deprivation, made or granted, or to be made or granted by the Pope, or his Successors or by any Authority derived, or pretended to be derived from him, or his See, against the said King, his heires or Successo^{rs}, or any absolucon of the said Subjects from their obedience: I will beare faith and true allegiance to his Matie his heires and Successors, and him, and them will defend to the uttermost of my Power, against all conspiracyes & attempts whatsoever, wch shall be made against his, or their psons, their Crowne and Dignity, by reason, or Colour of any such Sentence, or Declaracon, or otherwise, and will do my best endeavo^{rs}, to disclose and make knowne unto his Ma^{ty}, his, heires and Successo^{rs}, all Treasons, or Traiterous conspiracyes, which I shall know, or hear of, to be against him, or any of them.

And I do further Sweare, That I do from my heart, abhorr, detest, and abjure, as impious and hereticall, this dammable Doctrine and Posicon, That Princes wch be excomunicated, or deprived by the Pope, may be deposed, or murthered by their Subjects, or any other whatsoever.

And I do believe, and in Conscience am resolved, that neither the Pope, nor any Person whatsoever, hath Power to absolve me of this Oath, or any part thereof, which I acknowledge; by good and full Authority, to be Lawfully ministered unto mee, and do renounce all pardons, and dispensacons to the contrary,

And all these things, I do plainly and Sincerely acknowledge and Sweare, according to these words by me Spoken, & according to the plaine and Common Sence & understanding of the same words, wthout any equivocation or mentall evacon, or Secret reservacon whatsoever. And I do make this Recognicon & acknowledgm^t heartily, willingly, and truely, upon ye true faith of a Christian; So helpe mee God" (General Entries, State Library Bulletin, History No. 2: 145f).

III Dutch Period

On Monday, July 28, 1673, a Dutch fleet under Evertsen and Benckes arrived at New York and on July 30 obtained the surrender of the English. They then appointed Captain Anthony Colve as governor-general. New officials were chosen for the city of New Orange, formerly New York, and they, after taking an oath of allegiance themselves, were required to take a census of the residents and tender to each the oath of allegiance (RNA 6:400f). Two oaths of fidelity were formulated, one for the English and the other for non-

English. The English residing in the city were obliged to take this oath: "Wee do Sweare in the Presence of the Almighty God that wee schall bee tru an faittfull to the heigh en Migty Lords the Staetes Genner[1] of the United Provinces and his Serene heighnesse the prince of Orangien and to thier Govern[r] heere for the time beingh and tho behaive o[r]selves upon all occasieons as true en faitfull subjet provided onely that wy schall not be forced in armss aginst our onwe Natieon if they be sent by authoriety of his majestie of Engelandt Except they bee accopaned by a Commission en of other Natieons then Wee doo obligde o[r]selves to take up armes aginst them.. Soo help us God." The oath taken by non-English residents read: "We promise and swear in the presence of Almighty God to be faithful to their High Mightinesses the Lords States General of the United Netherlands and his Illustrious Highness, the Prince of Orange, and their Governour already appointed or hereafter to be appointed here; and on all occasion to demean ourselves as loyal and dutiful subjects are bound to do. So truly help me God Almighty." (The form of both oaths is given in RNA 7:2.)

By September some persons had not complied, for it was ordered that all strangers in New Orange who had not taken the oath of allegiance or obtained a license were to depart within one day (CDNY 2:603f). In December it was provided that all persons not yet bound by the oath of allegiance to the Dutch were to depart from New Netherland within twenty-four hours (CDNY 2:666-7).

The fidelity of the inhabitants of New Netherland to the new government was, of course, of concern to Colve and his associates. At a council of war held on August 29 Capt. Willem Knyff and Lt. Jeronimus de Hubert, together with Ephraim Herman (a clerk in the office of Secretary Bayard), were directed to administer oaths of allegiance to the inhabitants of the towns at the western end of Long Island. The oath to be taken by the Dutch was "We do promise and swear, in the presence of Almighty God, to be loyal and faithful to their High Mightinesses the Lords States-General of the United Netherlands, and his Serence Highness the Prince of Orange and their Governor already, or hereafter to be appointed here, and to comport ourselves on all occasions as loyal and faithful subjects are bound to do. So Truly help me God." The English, however, swore the oath but with this proviso: "that wee shall not be forced in armes against our owne nation if they be sent bij authority of his Majesty of England, except they be accompanied by a commission of force of other nations when wee do oblidge o[r]selves to take up armes against them. So help us God." (Both oaths are given in CDNY 2:589).

Little or no difficulty was encountered in the towns at the western end of Long Island, for Colve's commissioners on Sept. 1 made the following report concerning the number of men in each settlement and the number who took the oath:

 Midwout (Flatbush) - 73, all of whom took the oath
 Amesfoort (Flatlands) - 48, all of whom took the oath
 Breukelen and dependencies - 81, of whom 52 took the oath
 New Utrecht - 41, all of whom took the oath
 Bushwyck - 35, all of whom took the oath except Humphrey Clay,
                 a Quaker.

Gravesend - 31, all of whom took the oath
Hemstede - 107, of whom 51 took the oath
Flushing - 67, of whom 51 took the oath
Rustdorp (Jamaica) - 63, of whom 53 took the oath
Middelborgh (Newtown) - 99, of whom 53 took the oath (CDNY 2:596)

Delinquents, of course, were ordered to comply, those at Hemstede, for example, within four days (CDNY 2:616).

Towns to the east, however, presented a more serious problem. As a result of their protests the Dutch government prescribed a modified oath (CDNY 2:602) and commissioned Capt. Knyff and Lt. Anthony Malypart, together with Abram Varlett, clerk, to call town meetings in the eastern towns and administer the oath to the inhabitants (CDNY 2:620, 626). On Oct. 19 the commissioners returned and reported that the townspeople refused to take the oath, except those of Oysterbay, where it was taken, and of Huntington, "where the inhabitants requested to be excused from the oath on promising fidelity in writing to the government" (CDNY 2:638).

The following day the Dutch authorities debated the proposal to send an armed force against the eastern towns but decided such a move was not practical (CDNY 2:642). Instead, on October 25, a commission was issued to Capt. Knyff and Ensign Nicolaes Vos to visit Huntington and Setalcot. This was a success, for three days later the commissioners reported that the inhabitants of both towns promised fidelity and that their names were deposited in the office of the secretary (CDNY 2:645-7).

Governor Colve, doubtless encouraged by the news, on Oct. 30 dispatched Cornelis Steenwyck, Capt. Carel Epesteyn and Lt. Charles Quirynsen to Easthampton, Southold and Southampton, there to administer the oath. It was all in vain, for on Nov. 8 they reported that the townspeople in all three places "exhibited an utter aversion to the oath and made use of gross insolence, threats, etc." (CDNY 2:648,654).

Presumably, however, Capt. Epesteyn and Ensign Sol, who were sent on December 21 to Staten Island to administer the oath, were successful in their attempt (CDNY 2:671).

Fortunately some lists of persons who subscribed to the oath have been preserved. They are the following:

Town of Oyster Bay (NY Col Mss 23:227e. Other names have been
    burned away.):
Aron Furman, Senr. (by mark)
Joseph Ludlam
Adem Wright
Jan Cock (by mark)
[N] icholas Simkins
[Richard (T. R.]] Kerby (by mark)
[Abra] ham Kraft (by mark)
Edman Hid....

Town of Eastchester (NY Col Mss 23:277 a-b):

William Hiden
(Thom)as Cur... (perhaps for
   Thomas Keurkin?)
Moses Hide
Philip Pinckne
John Hoitt
Joseph Purdy
(....)311 Purdy
Richard Shout
William Esq(...)e (probably
   for William Squire)

Samuel Hoit, "quacker"
John Jacson
Samuell Godwin
John God....(?)
Samuell Drake
John Drake
Nathanaell Tompkins
John Tompkins
John Hilljard

Town of Westchester (NY Col Mss 23:277 a/b, in very bad condition):

(Ric)hard Panton
(Tho)mas Hunt, Senr
Joseph Palmer
John Hunt
Joseph Hunt
Josias Hunt
Edward Waters
Samuell Barret
.....phell Oockley
John Hidgekock
(Dir)ck Gerritson
       icki
    s Ge....
(possibly Consider) Wood
      ealle
      Stebens
      (Hi) dgecock
        att
       hield
        ers, "quacker"

(possibly Samuell?) (Pa)lmer
       is
Robbert Huestis, "quacker"
Niclaes Balye
(Natha?)n Bayly
4 illegible names
(John?) (Qui)mby, Sen[r]
(John?) (Qu)imby, Jun[r]
2 illegible names
(Joseph?) Taylor
      man
(Thomas?) Bacxter
illegible name, "quacker"
3 illegible names
Thomas Hunt, Junr.
Thomas Veale, Junr.
Thomas Bedienct
(Joh)n Forgison
      Platt
      Gard

A number of Quakers in Westchester on September 28, 1673,
signed a document in which they promised to be faithful to the
States General and the Prince of Orange and not to take up arms
against them. They stated that they would endeavor to keep their
promise to the best of their ability and that they would be liable
to the same punishment as those persons would be who broke their
oaths. The manuscript is so badly burned away that only the first
four names have been preserved. These are Francis French, Th[o]
Mollennex, John Feeris and (Robe)rt Huestis (NY Col Mss 23:277c).

Town of New Harlem

1 Resolvert Waldron
2 David Des Marest
3 Joost Van Oblinus
4 Arent Hermensz
5 Lubbert Gerritsz
6 Cornelis Jansz
7 Meyndert Journee

8   Adolph Meyer
9   Simeon Courier
10 Jan Laurens v. Schoonrewt[t]
11 Jean Des Marest
12 Jan Dyckman
13 Daniel Tourneur
14 Jan Nagel

15	Samuel Pell	24	Coenraet Hendrichsz
16	Robbert Halles	25	Cornelis Theunisz
17	John Smith	26	Gabriel Carbosie, miller
18	Jan Le Maistre	27	Glaude Le Maistre
19	David Des Marest, de Jonger	28	Pieter Cresson
20	Samuel Des Marest	29	Jean Le Roy
21	Isaco El Roey	30	Claes Carstensz
22	Evert Alrichs	31	Isaacq Vermlje
23	Jochem Engelbert	32	Henrich Jansz

Of the above, nos. 1-26 were aged between 16 and 60, 27-32 aged
over 60, nos. 15-17 were Englishmen, nos. 18-25 were unmarried
and 1-4 were magistrates, all as classified by the town secretary,
Hendrick J. Vander Vin (New Harlem Records, III: 94-95, ms. in the
New York Public Library). The transcription of the list as pub-
lished by James Riker, History of Harlem, pp. 337-338, is in places
incorrect; a similar list (NY Col Mss 23:276, ms. in the N Y State
Library in Albany) partly burned, gives only four men as over 60,
namely (Glaude) Le Maistre, (Pieter) Cresson, (Jean L)e Roy and
(Claes C)arstens "nourman," while Isaacq Vermlje and Henrich Jansz
do not appear at all.

Persons who took the oath of allegiance at Fordham or Yonkers
at a meeting held Oct. 10, 1673, by Cornelis Steenwyck:

Mester Jan Artter [i.e., John Archer]
Johannes [Verveelen?]
[Mi]chiel Bastianss
[G?]e ...er Harmens
Hendrick Kiersen
Reyer Michielss
Valetyn Classen
Jan Gerritsen ...
Art Piterss
Cornelis Adrianss Viervan
Hendrick Janss (van Beest "from Beest")
[R?] ...ger Agoris
Davit [illegible], mullenaer op de Jonkers mullen "miller at the
                                            Yonkers mill"
Joris Jans(woont op de Yonkers "lives at Yonkers")
Marcus Janchon (woont op Daniel Tourneurs Land "lives on Daniel
                                            Tourneur's land")
Thomas Higges
Jan Lambert
Koster Essing
Jans Meyers

A manuscript in the State Library in Albany (NY Col Mss 23:275)
is a list of persons apparently in or between the Bowery and the
Fresh Water. It had been incorrectly calendared as "Names of persons residing between the Fresh water and Harlem, and of negroes"
(CEM: 20). It seems likely that the list is one of persons who
took the oath of allegiance or were supposed to take it. The names
are as follows:

[...] [...] bertsen
Jacob Fredricksen De Groot
[Nicho]laes Stuyvesant
Gerrit Hendricksen
Hans Jacob
[...]erry Pers
[Jan?] Tiebout
[Car]stren Cornelissen
Cosyn Gertsen
Jan Tonussen
Basteiaen De Hamaecker
Andries Juriaense
Tuenis Jedense
Jan Hendricksen
Hendrick Jansen
Jacob Cornelissen Pillen
Claes Jansen Van Heninge
Davit De Voor
Jan Davitsen
Jan Tuenissen
Hendrick Basteiansen
[H]endrick Cornelissen
[...] Pers
[...] [...]olynsen
[Hendr]ick Jochense
[De?]rick Evertsen
[Ger]rit Basteiaensen
[Juria]en Anderiesen
[Tu]enis Barentsen
[L]eendert Jacobsen
Jan Cornelissen Du Ryck

List of Negroes

Klaes Manewel
Manewel Pietersen
Manewel Sandersen
Jan
Willem Antonisse
Machiel Manewelse
Minkes Poulissen
Evert Andriesse
Antony Antonisse
Loures Jansen
Fransisko Ankolen
Pieters Inboer
Agustinen Fordonck
Salemon Pietersen
Louies Gene
Jan ... ginie
... Van Ankole
... ent Kaspersen
Domickes Van Ankole
Manewel De ...
Manewel Spanien
... Flipsen

Free Negroes

Louies Ankole
Luykes Pietersen

IV English Period

By the Peace of Westminster in 1674 New Netherland was re-
stored to the English. The non-English inhabitants were now required to swear allegiance to the King of England. Forty-four took
the oath on March 17, 1675, and 193 more on March 18 and 19 (Stokes,
Icon. IV: 306. This is based, according to Stokes, upon a manuscript of minutes of the Common Council of New York City). A number
of other persons swore allegiance in the city on November 24, 1675,
taking the following oath: "You doe sweare by the name of the Almighty God that you and every one of you will bee true Subjects to
the King of Great Brittaine; and will obey all such commandements
as you Shall receive from his Majestie his Royall Highnesse James
Duke of Yorke and such Governours and Officers as from time to time
are appointed over you by his authority and none other, whilst you
Live in any of His Majesties Territoryes. So helpe you God." The
list of individuals, sworn November 24 before Gabriel Minvielle,
is as follows: Peter Windsor, John Laurens, Junior, William Sidnam,
Thomas Taylor, William Pinhorne, Andries Meyer, Patrick Arnott,
Hendrick Van Burssen, John Janssen, Peter Janssen, Francis Wessells,
Domine Jacobus Fabricius, Johannes Meyer, Asserus Hendricks, Nicho-

las Du Puy, Hans Scoderus, Hendrick Ten Eyck, John Van Loney, Justice Whitefield, Nicholas Blanke, Hendrick Dusbrough, Junior, Andries Res, John Charles Russel, Robert Witty, Matthew Hilliard, Samuel Whiteway, John Chesam, Clement Sebrach, George Delloe, Englebart Lot, Matthys Blanchon and John Tuder. On December 7 three others took the oath, namely John Cooley, John Henry and David Jochemse (MCC 1:12; CNYHS 1885:39-40). Further, on November 4, 1678 Cornelius Jacobsen and Matthias Van Der Heathen took the oath of fidelity and were made free burghers of the City and Colony of New York (ibid.: 42).

The coveted freedom of a city, which enabled its possessor to carry on his trade or profession, was regularly preceded by taking an oath of allegiance as above. When Governor Dongan on April 20, 1686, granted a charter to the City of New York, it was specified that except at the time of fairs, only freemen might practise a trade or occupation. Further it was provided "that no person or persons Shall be made free . . . but Such as are his Majestys natural born Subjects or Such as Shall first be naturalized by Act of general Assembly or Shall have Obtained Letters of Denization under the hand of the Lieutenant Governour or Commander in Chief for the time being and Seal of the province." A person made free might be required to pay a fee but not in excess of five pounds (CNYHS 1885: 48).

On June 13, 1687, a proclamation in regard to naturalization was ordered and the next day commissioners were appointed to administer the oath of allegiance in various places (CEM:166). The lists of persons who took the oath of allegiance in three counties are preserved. That for Ulster County, taken September 1, 1687 (the date of 1689 in DHNY 1:279 is incorrect; the names are on pages 279-282), is as follows:

Beekman, Capt. Hennery	Sluitt[r], Claes Claes
Matthison, Capt. Matthis	Powlas, Powlas
Haesbrock, Lt. Abraham	Quick, Thomas
Bouier, Lowies	Anthony, Nicolas
Hendricks, John	Wincop, Johanas
V. Steenwicke, Albert Johnson	Jansin, Jost
Hoffeman, Marten	Arsin, Jacob
Van Fredingborch, William	Slecht, Matthies
Van der Bush, Lowranc.	Middag, John
Tenbrock, Wessell	Bogard, Hendrick Cornelis
Boorehanc, John	Albortsa, Gisbort
Hogetilen, John Willianson	Van Fleitt, Gerrit
Arsin, Gerritt	Slecht, Cornelis
Elison, Tunis	Haesbrock, John
Focken, John	Sweitts, Cornelius
DeMy[r]s, William	Mind[r]son, Burgar
Schencke, Johanas	Albertsa, Hendrick
De Lamontanij, William	Franckford, Abraham
Van Osternhoudt, John Johnson	Danswick, William
Hendricks, Jochijam	Depuis, Moses
Hendricks, Harrama	Hoogtilin, William
Johnson, Pett[r]	Wincoop, Gerritt

Cool, Symon
Dibois, Isack
Provorist, Benj^a
Valleij, Jesely
Laffever, Andries
Dovo, Pett^r
Deboijs, Abraham
Laconta, Moses
Hellibrandts, Petter
Laffever, Symon
Roesinkranc, Sander
Cool, Cornelis
France, Arrie
Osternhoudt, John, Jr.
Traphager, Hendrick
Decker, Jacob
Hendricks, Roloff
VerNoij, Cornelis
Van Wien, Hendrick
Freri, Hiuge, Sr.
Freri, Hiuge, Jr.
Cornelis, Pett^r
Johnson, Gerritt
Criupill, Anthony
Carrmar, Abraham
Winniy, Pett^e
Cool, Jacob
Rutton, Abraham
Westfalin, Abl
Lamiater, Abraham
Jacobs, Pett^r
Van Fredinborch, Isack
Cornelis, Gerrit
Lamiater, Jacob
Tunis, Arrian
Westfalin, Claes
Cottin, John
Westfalin, Johannas
Johnson, Thomas
Van Bush, Hendrick Johnson
Petters, Andries
Decker, Gerritt Jansa
Cool, Lendart
Finehoudt, Cornelis
Jacobs, Tunis
Schutt, Jacob
Jacobs, Leury
Elting, John
Swartwout, Rollof
Westbrock, Dirrick
Hendricks, Agbert
Berrey, Saml
Heybertsin, Lambert

Claes, Hendrick
Hendricks, Brown
Pier, Harrama
David, John
Blanchard, John
Gerritts, Cornelis
Smedis, John
Cuinst, Barrant
Lazer, Hellebrandt
Bush, Johanas
Lhommedieu, Pietter
Jay, August
Rulland, John
Traphager, William, Jr.
Van Ama, Jochyam
Canchi, Aimi
Besteyansa, Jacob
Larew, Abraham
Blanzan, Matthis, Jr.
Lazier, John
Pett^rson, John
Josten, John
DeMont, Wallraven, Jr.
Traphager, Johanas
[No Surname], Hendrick (in the
                              Feelt)
Criupill, Petter
Gisborts, Gerrit
Hendricks, Hendrick
Gerrittsa, John (of New Church)
Arreyn, Hendrick
Van Fleitt, John
Tunis, Claes
Dewitt, Andries
Van Etta, Jacob
Schutt, John
Dewitt, John
Johnson, Hendrick
Swardtwout, Thomas
Van Etta, John
Swartwoudt, Anthony
Stoll, John Jacosa
Lambertsa, Heybert
Jacobs, William
Deboyes, David
Deboyes, Sallomon
Wincoope, Evert
Westbrock, Johanas
Peteet, John
Jores, Rutt
Sealand, Heibort
Tunies, Jury
Decker, John Broerson

Johnson, Roulof
Matthies, John
Roos, Heymon
Roos, John
Roos, Arrie
Pettersin, Petter
Agbortsin, Gerritt
Roosinffelt, Claes
Evedin, Jno
Lambertsin, Cornelis
Harramansa, Thomas
Dehogos, Johanas
Cantine, Moses
Deboyes, Isack
Mastin, Cornelis
Bonamiz, James
Hendricks, Dirrick
Gerrittsa, John
Cordaback, James
Powlason, Powlas, Jr.

Williamson, John (yᵉ Duitcher,
            "the German")
Schutt, William
Tacke, Cornelis
Poast, John Johnson
Demarr, Petter
Doon, Privie go
Deboyes, Lowies, Sr.
Deboyes, Jacob
Evertsa, John
Elvendorop, Coinradt
Petterson, Cornelis
Jacobs, Barrant
Van Acar, Marinos
Lazier, Claes
Coll, Barrant
Westfallin, Symon
Jacobs, Arrent
Doorn, Artt Martenson
Bogardos, Cornelis
Van Dick, Arrent

The following were present when the oath was given but refused to take it:

Tilba, Antony
Van der Marrick, Thomas
Focker, Joseph
Horne, Jacob

The following did not appear:

Archer, John
Larrow, Livie
De Mott, Maghell
Pelce, Evert
Pelce, Symon
Dewitt, Terrick Claes
Demont, Wallraven, Sr.
Schepmous, Dirrick
Tennick, Matthis
Tunis, Claes
Crum, Gisbert
Van Fleitt, Arre Gerritt
Van Fleitt, Dirrick
Lodtman, Jno:
Lodtman, Jury
Lodtman, Hellebrandt
Brown, Jacob (Alis yᵉ Noorman,
    "alias the Norman"?)

Hornebeak, Warnar
Lowrance, John
Larow, Symon
Hogoboom, Cornelis
(no surnam), Cornelis (yᵉ
    Duitcher, "the German")
Powlasin, Gombart
Meueson, Jno: (Alis Jn. De pape,
    i.e. "John the Papist")
Wallaffish, William
Pollin, Jnᵒ
Bussalin, Antony
Aylberts, Gerritt
Keizer, Dirrick

List made by Thomas Chambers

The names of those who took the oath of allegiance in Kings County, 26-30 September, 1687, with indication whether native born or the number of years in the country, are the following (DHNY 1: 659-661):

Of Flackbush

Van Boerem, Willem Jacobs, 38
Probasco, Christoffel, 33
Rijcken, Hendrick, 24
Strycker, Pieter, native
Pieterse, Cornelis, native
Luijster, Cornelis Peters, native
Van Vliet, Dirck Jansn, 23
Lubberse, Gerrit, native
Albertse, Ruth, 25
Beakman, Gerrardus, native
Hafften, Jacob Henk., 23
Dorlant, Gerrit, native
Lott, Engelbert, native
Hanssen, Simon, 48
Van Bueren, Jacob Willem, 38
Aertsen, Reynier, 34
Lott, Pieter, 35
Van Wyck, Cornelis Barense, 27
Remsen, Jacob, native
Harmenssen, Jan (from Amesfoort), 29
Hendrickse, Willem, native
Hegeman, Joseph, 37
Willkens, Claes, 25
Janse, Willem Guil, 47
Reijnierse, Auke, native
Remssen, Jooris, native
Van Bosch, Jan Wouterse
Jansen, Lambert, native
Remsen, Jan, native
Van Vliet, Jan Dircks, 23
Hegeman, Hendrickus, 36
Spigelaer, Jan, 25
Aaten, Adriaen Hend., 36
Pieterse, Lefferd, 27
Hegeman, Isaack, native

Janse, Pieter Guil., 45
Willemsen, Pieter, native
Seeu, Cornelis Jansse, 27
Lott, Hendrick, native
Polhemius, Daniel, native
Van Ditmaertz, Jan, native
Theunissen, Denijs, native
Strycker, Jan, 35
Van Cassant, Isaac, 35
Blom, Jan Barense, native
Reyerse, Adriaen, 41
Vanderbilt, Aris, native
Van Nuys, Auke Janse, 36
Adriaense, Elbert, native
Remsen, Daniel, native
Vanderbilt, Jacob, native
Adriaense, Marten, native
Snediker, Christiaen, native
Hegeman, Abram, native
Vander Veer, Jan Cornelissen native
Van Wijck, Theodorus, native
Aaten, Thomas, native
Snediker, Gerrit, native
Janse, Hendrick, native
Verkerck, Roeloff, 24
Janssen, Barent, native
Hegeman, Jacobus, 36
Willemse, Hendrick, 38
Hooglant, Dirck Jan, 30
Hooglant, Jan Dircks, native
Hooglant, Willem Dircks, native
Oake, Jan, 36
Strijker, Gerrit Janse, 35
Remssen, Rem, native

Of Breucklijn

Lamberse, Thomas, 36
Hanssen, Jooris, native
Vechten, Hendrick, 27
Vechten, Claes Arense, 27
Aertsen, Jan, 26
Claaesen, Hendrick, 33
Bergen, Jacob Hanssen, native
Martens, Jooris, native
Thyssen, Hendrick, 21

Couverts, Mauritius, native
Huijcken, Willem, 24
Bogaert, Theunis Gysbertse, 35
Bennitt, Willem, native
Lamberse, Hendrick, native
Fredricks, Jan, 35
Couverts, Jan, native
Couverts, Luijcas, 24
Abramse, Frans, native

Middag, Gerrit Aerts, native
Aertsen, Simon, 23
Cornelisen, Matthys, 24
Hendricks, Ephraim, 33
Van Dyck, Claes Thomas, native
D'Rapale, Jeronimus, native
Remsen, Jeronimus, native
Janssen, Casper, native
Vandijck, Achias Janse, 36
Joorisen, Jacob, native
D'Beauvois, Jacobus, 28
Joorissen, Harmen, native
Bennit, Jacob Willemse, native
Brouwer, Jacob, native
Broulaet, Bourgon, 12
Damen, Jan, 37
Subrink, Cornelis, native
Sleght, Hendrick, 35
Vanderbreets, Juriaen, native
Staats, Pieter, native
Remsen, Abram, native
Hanssen, Machiel, native
Tobiassen, Theunis, native
Corsen, Pieter, native
Couverts, Theunis Janse, 36
Simonssen, Aert, native
Brouwer, Adam, Jr., native
Schaers, Alexander, native
Pos, Willem, native
Dorland, Jan Gerrise, 35

Casperse, Johannis, 35
Blom, Claes Barentse, native
Brouwer, Pieter, native
Brouwer, Abram, native
Bennit, Jan, native
Sleght, Barent, native
Vande Water, Jacobus, 29
Vande Water, Benjamin, native
Weijnants, Pieter, native
Franssen, Joost, 33
Aaten, Hendrick, native
Staats, Jan Janse, native
Simons, Claes, native
Souso, Anthonij, 5
Casperse, Joost, 35
Lubberse, Thijs, 50
Dirckse, Paulus, 36
Brouwer, Adam, 45
Dreths, Josias, 26
Van Nesten, Pieter, 40
Theunisen, Jan, native
Woertman, Dirck Janse, 40
D'Rapale, Daniel, native
Boomgaert, Gijsbert, native
Vanderbrats, Volkert, native
Buijs, Jan, 39
Dorlant, Gerrit, native
Bennit, Abriaen, native
Verdon, Thomas, native
Staats, Pieter Janse, native

Of New Uijtreeht

Vandermij, Tielman, 13
Vandijck, Karel Janse, 35
Vandijck, Jan Janse, 35
Tierckse, Thomas, 35
Van Pelt, Wouter, 24
Christiaense, Jacob, native
Janse, Lambert, 22
Van Deventer, Jan, 25
Vandeventer, Cornelis Janse,
    native
Laenen, Gijsbert Thysen, 24
Laenen, Theunis Janse Van
    Pelt, 24
Van Pelt, Anthony, 24
Clement, Jan, 22
Wijnhart, Cornelis, 30
Van Meteeren, Kreijn Janse, 24
Van Brent, Joost Rutsen, native
Van Pelt, Aert Theunissen,
    native
Du Chaine, Anthonij, 24

Laenen, Jan Thijssen, native
Laenen, Jacob Thijssen, native
Janse, Laurens, native
Van Cleeff, Jan, 34
Klinckenberg, Wellem, native
Vandergrifft, Nicolase, native
Van Kerck, Jan, Jr., native
Van Kerck, Jan, Sr., 24
Ridder, Barent Joosten, 35
Smack, Hendrick Matthysse, 33
Van Kleeff, Cornelis, native
Van Sutphen, Dirck Janse, 36
Kierson, Jan, 38
Van Voorhuys, Gerrit Courten,
    native
Van Brunt, Rooth Joosten, 34
Francisco, Pieter, native
Cortejou, Jacques, 35
Corteljou, Jacques, Jr., native
Corteljou, Cornelis, native
Corteljou, Pieter, native

Corteljouw, Willem, native
Van Duyn, Gerrit Cornelis, 38
Vanduyn, Cornelis Gerris, native
Vanduyn, Denijs Gerrisse, native
De Camp, Laurens Janse, 23
Thyssen, Pieter, native
Janssen, Swaen, 33
Stoffelse, Gerrit, 36

Bruynenburgh, Jan Hanssen, 48
Gerritse, Stoffel, native
Debaene, Joost, 4
Kamminga, Hendrick Janse, 9
Van Brunt, Cornelis Rutsen,
    native
Verkerck, Barent, native

Of Boswijck

Dirckse, Volkert, native
De Witt, Pieter Janse, 35
Daniel, Pieter, 10
La Forge, Adriaen, 15
Kockuyt, Joost, 27
La Febre, Issack, 4
Schamp, Pieter, 15
Verschier, Wouter Gysbert, 38
Loyse, Pieter, native
Fontaine, Jacques, native
Klock, Pelegrom, 31
Witt, Volkert, native
Waldron, Daniel, 35
Haecks, Simon, 16
Loyse, Cornelis, 36
Le Quie, Jean, 30
Cockevaer, Alexander, 30

Hendrickse, Albert, 25
Miseroll, Jean, Jr., 20
Kat, Claes Cornelissen, 25
Palmentier, Michiel, 23
Bale, Vincent, 4
Para, Pieter, 28
Fontaine, Johannis, native
De Consilie, Jean, 25
Durie, Joost, 12
Janse, Jan, 36
Janse, Jacob, native
Simonse, Peter, native
Rosekrans, Jacob Dirckse, native
VerSchuer, Jochem, native
Verschuer, Hendrick, native
Koeck, Laurens, 26

Of Flackland

Elbertse, Elbert, 50
Shenck, Roeloff Martense, 37
Schenck, Jan Roeloffs, native
Schenck, Jan Martense, 37
Van Dyckhuys, Jan Theunis, 34
Van Voorhuys, Court Stevense, 27
Nevius, Pieter, native
Willemson, Abram, 25
Schenck, Marten Roeloffe,
    native
Janssen, Hans, 47
Van Voorhuijs, Albert Courten,
    native
Wijckoff, Pieter Claasen, 51
Van Aerts Daalen, Simon
    Janse, 34
Van Aerts Daalen, Cornelis
    Simonsen, native
Wijckoff, Gerrit Pieterse,
    native
Brower, Jan, 30
Hanssen, Gerrit, native
Van Wickelen, Evert Jans-
    sen, 23

Wijckoff, Claes Pieterse, native
Brouwer, Dirck, native
Bresse, Gerrit Hendrickse, native
Brouwer, Pieter, native
Ammerman, Dirck Janssen, 37
Kume, Adriaen, 27
Stoothoff, Gerret Elberts, native
Strijcker, Jacob, 36
Stoffelse, Dirck, 30
Dirckse, Stoffel, native
Van Sichgelen, Ferdinandus, 35
Wijckoff, Hendrick Pieterse,
    native
Van Couwenhooven, Willem
    Gerritse, native
Van Couwenhooven, Gerrit Willem-
    sen, native
Wijckoff, Jan Pieterse, native
Wanshaer, Anthony, native
Stevense, Luycas, 27
Luyster, Pieter Cornelis, 31
Stevense, Jan, 27
Bruynsen, Ruth, 34
Borcklo, Willem Willemse, native

Tull, Pieter Pieterse, 30
Brouwer, Hendrick, native
Monfoort, Pieter, native
Van Amach, Theunis Janse, 14

Luyster, Thys Pieterse, 31
Terhuen, Jan Albertse, native
Davies, Willem, 34
Willemse, Johannis, 25

Of Gravens End

Van Siegelen, Renier, native
Romeyn, Stoffel Janse, 34
Machielse, Johannis, native
Boisbilland, John 2 ("had
  letters of denisatie")
Juriaense, Barent, 29
Barense, Jan (Van Zutphen "from
  Zutphen"), 30
Pieterse, Marten, native

Gulick, Jochem, 34
Buys, Cornelis, native
Van Borcklo, Jan Willemsen,
  native
Gerritse, Rem, native
Messcher, Adam Machielse, 40
Willemse, Willem, 30
Carstense, Jan, native
Brouwer, Johannis, native

The third list, heretofore unpublished, is that of persons who took
the oath of allegiance in Orange County on September 26, 1687.
Their names are as follows (NY Col Mss 35:144):

Minne, Johannes
Rynard, Johnis
Lammerts, Adriaen
Crom, Florus
Van Texel, John
Brower, Matthis
Gillisz, John
Caspars, Melchior
Storm, Dirck
Du Pue, Francois
Abramsz, Hendrick
Joosten, Caspar
Gerritsz, Huybart
Roeloffs, Teunis
Gerrits, Johannes
Du Voor, Daniel

Dowsen, Harmen
Dowsen, Teunis
Minne, Albertt
Harinck, Peter
Clarcke, Daniel
De Vries, Jean
De Groot, Staes
Barier, John
Serwaes, Thys
Gerrits, Abram
Claesz, Cornelis
Manuel, Claes
Adriaens, Lammert
Fransz, Thys
Gerritsz, Hendrick

Sometime in March 1688, on board the ship Beaver a number of
persons were said to have taken, before Father Smith, an oath of
allegiance to King James. The names of three of the men are known,
namely James Emott, Thomas Stevens and Daniel Whitehead (CDNY 3:747)

On November 23, 1698, a proclamation was made requiring the
inhabitants to take the oaths prescribed by act of Parliament and
to sign the test and association. Accordingly, in October 1699 the
association and test oath were taken in Queens County, with some
persons from New York City, and the rolls, with original signatures
were in existence up to the time of the disastrous fire in the State
Library in Albany in 1911 (CEM:265, 272). On January 11, 1699, the
Mayor of New York City presented to the Common Council a letter
from the governor, the Earl of Bellomont, in which it was directed
that the oath of allegiance be administered to the inhabitants and
that the test and association be signed by them. It was ordered
that the names and addresses of all who refused be reported, in

order that a discrimination might be made "between Good and Lowall Subjects and those that by ill principles Are prevailed Upon to be Enemies to his Majesties person and Government." (MCC 2:68-69)

Oaths taken later have been discussed in connection with denizations and naturalizations, with, however, one exception. On February 11, 1777, Governor Tryon of New York wrote to Lord George Germain that the oath of allegiance and fidelity to his Majesty and his government had met with his, Tryon's, warmest wishes. In New York City some 3,000 took the oath "without a shadow of compulsion" and on Staten Island, three counties on Long Island and Westchester County 2,600 more. (CDNY 8:697)

Fortunately the rolls of signers on Staten Island have been preserved, with signatures. The date is July 9, 1776, and the form of the oath is the following: "I do sincerely promise and Swear, that I will be faithful and bear Allegiance to His Majesty King George the Third; and Him will defend to the utmost of my Power against all traiterous Conspiracies and Attempts whatsoever which shall be made against his Person, Crown, or Dignity; And I will do my utmost Endeavor to disclose and make known to His Majesty, & His Successors, all Treasons, and traiterous Conspiracies, which I shall know to be against Him, or any of Them. So help me God." (E P)

The following took the oath before Roger Barnes:

Keteltas, Jno.
Jacobson, Christian
Egberts, Tuness (by mark)
Schrit, Rich^d (by mark)
Corbey, Rich^d (by mark)
Cubberley, Isaac
Gifford, John
Lakerman, Isaac
Egberts, Anthony
Egberts, Tunis
Sweane, Mattus
Wood, Stephen
Latourrette, Henry
Colon, Jonas
Limmer, Owen (by mark)
Burbank, Abraham (by mark)
Saunders, Richard
Barton, Joseph
Scharit, James
Doughtey, Tho. (by mark)
Rezeau, Jacob
Baker, John
Silvester, John
Vandeventer, Cornelius
Simonson, Jeremiah
Josephson Maur. (?)
Fountain, Anthony
Howell, James
Howell, Richard

Burke, Tobias
Forrest, James
Perine, Joseph
Lewiss, Isack "was sowrne"
Burton, Joseph, Jr.
Bodine, John
Martino, Stephen (by mark)
Martino, Stephen
Beaty, John
Martino, Abraham
Smith, Christian
Peprall, Isack (by mark)
Neill, Anthony
Luke, Joseph
Mitchell, Lew^s (by mark)
Fountain, Vincent (by mark)
Roome, Andriss (by mark)
Lake, Richard
Symonson, Johannes
Lakerman, Richard
Griffin, John (by mark)
Baker, Joseph (by mark)
Garrison, John
Baker, Jeremiah (?) (by mark)
Crips, William
White, Gilbert (by mark)
Van Wagenen, Johan
Lake, Wm.
Wood, Timothy

Du Bois, Lewis
Wood, John
Grondain, Lewis
Granger, W^m (by mark)
Wood, Jacob
Inyard, Nicholas
Wood, Joseph
Swaim, Martines
Swaim, Simon
Ryersz, Aris
Cryps, Lawrence
Ward, Samuel
Symonson, Frederick

Poillon, James
Dubois, Augustus
Griffes, Arthor (by mark)
Keteltas, Abraham
Mitchell, Lewe (by mark)
Simonson, Henry (by mark)
Lake, Daniel
Mersereau, Paul
Venpelt, Anthony (by mark)
Johnson, James (by mark)
Thomas, Ab^m (by mark)
Jennes, Lambert

The following took the oath before David La Tourrette:

Perine, Henry
Decker, Isaac
Poillon, James
Decker, Matthew
Winant, Abraham
Decker, Abraham
Wood, Joseph
Mersereau, Joshua, Jr.
Taylor, Oliver
Simonson, John
Dubois, Lewis, Jr.
Guyon, Peter
Britten, Nathanil
Winants, Winant
Decker, Matthew, Jr.
Bogart, Isaac
Martino, Cornelius
Elliss, Bastan
McDaniel, Joseph
Androvet, John
Laforge, David
Journeay, John, Jr.
Journeeay, Albert
Stillwell, Nicholas
Androvet, John
Mannee, Abraham (by mark)
Marshal, John
Wrightman, Peter
Hooper, Daniel
Barnes, Rog^r
Winant, Daniel, Jr.
Bedell, Joseph

Butler, Thomas (by mark)
Tyson, John
Winant, Peter, Sr.
Cole, Cornelius
Merrell, Lambert
Cubberley, Joseph
Stouttenborough, John
Butler, Henry (by mark)
Perine, Edward
Poillon, Peter
Segine, James
Guyon, Joseph
Cole, Jacob
Stover, John
Guyon, James
Winant, Peter (ma? by mark?)
Van Clefe, Daniel
DuBois, Charles
Lake, Joseph
Poillon, John
Marshall, Abraham
Winants, Jacob
Doty, Moses
Vandeventer, Abraham
Prall, Isaac
Martino, Beniamen
Holmes, Samuel
Britten, Samuel
Burger, Minnah
Garretson, Har^s
Stoutenboughrow, Anthony

The following took the oath before Daniel Lake:

Van Wagenen, Cornelius
Bedell, Joseph
Seaman, Richard
Lake, Daniel, Jr.

Lake, William
Mersereau, Stephen
Hillyer, Lawrence
Simonson, Jeremiah

Scobey, William
Mersereau, Paul
Cole, Stephen
BarBanck, Abraham
Cook, Jacob
Beatty, John
Walton, W^m
Simonson, Gozen
Yates, Joseph
Latourrette, John
Dubois, Lewis
Cortelyou, Peter
Colon, James
Grondain, Peter
Lake, Daniel
Parkes, Abner
Yates, Joseph, Jr.
Stilwill, Abraham
Perine, Daniel
Vapelt, John
Vanpelt, John (by mark)
Simonson, Isaac
Egberts, John
Mersereau, John
Vanpelt, John
Mersereau, Richard
Bedell, Paul
Beatty, Edward
Rezeau, Peter
Ryersz, Adriaen
Britten, Necolas (by mark)
Menamee, Charles
Vanpelt, Joseph
Colon, Peter
Vanpelt, Anthony
Colon, George
Egbert, James
Johnson, John (by mark)
Egberts, Edward
Crips, Richard
Dubois, John
Barbank, Thomas
Barbank, John
Vanderbilt, John

Martino, John
Lake, Daniel
Vanderbilt, John
Barbank, James
Vreeland, Jacob
Guyon, John
Cubberley, Thomas
Barbank, Joseph
Egbert, Abraham
Barbanck, John (by mark)
Cortelyou, Cornelius
Swam, Matthias, Jr.
Britten, Nathaniel
Mersereau, John
Arosmith, Barnt
Johnson, George (by mark)
Cole, Isaac
Lewis, James, Jr. (by mark)
Lewis, James
Akrley (?), Nathanael
Scarrot, William (by mark)
Scarrot, Richard (by mark)
Vanpelt, Willm (by mark)
Webb, John
Egberts, Moses
Day, John
Simonson, Isaac
Morgan, William
Totten, Zebedee
Holmes, Samuel (by mark)
Poillon, John
Mersereau, Daniel
Mersereau, Stephen
Mersereau, John
Thirstan, Samuel
Garrison, Peter
Degroot, Peter
Seaman, Thomas
Butlar, James (by mark)
Ryersz, Lewis
Degroat, Garret (by mark)
Jones, Abraham (by mark)
McViking (?), John
Mersereau, Peter

The following took the oath before Richard Conner:

Seaman, Benjamin
Billopp, Christopher
Cortelyou, Aaron
Lawrence, Richard
Mersereau, John
Jones, Abraham
Spier, Abraham
Bedell, Stephen

Corson, Cornelies
Turk, Cornelius
Quin, Jon (?)
Haughwout, Peter
Totton, James
Jenner, John
Wood, John
Decker, Charles

Corsen, Daniel
Marling, Abraham (by mark)
Decker, John
Bisoph (?), Abraham
Keirstead, James
Garrison, Abraham
Brested, Peter
Egbert, Abraham
Laroza, Peter
Jenner, Lambert
Jenner, William
Stilwel, Joseph
Jones, David
Bedell, John
Arow, Jerimy
Vantuyl, Denice
Decker, Charles
Kandel, Micah (by mark)
Burnes, George
Parker, Benj^a
Simonson, John
Ward, William
Britten, Abraham
Crocheron, John
Krosen (?), Christian (by mark)
Mackswane (?), Daniel (by mark)
Lawrence, Leggett
Corsen, Daniel
Dawson, George
Decker, Moses
Decker, Richard
Merrell, Richard
Jones, Abraham
Cozine, Wilhelmos
Morrell (or Merrell?), Thomas
Fountain, Anthony
Elless, Garret
Wandel, John
Barcklow, Cornelious
Housman, Abraham
Christopher, Cornelus
Blake, Edward
Jannass, John (by mark)
George, Joseph
Decker, Matthew
Totten, James
Kingston, William
Miaer (?), Richard (by mark)
Vancese, Josephus
Merserea, John
Pritchert, Thomas
Vanpelt, William (by mark)
O'Dannil, John

Merrell, Jyon (?)
Depeu, Barnt (by mark)
Decker, Johanes (by mark)
Crocheron, Abr^m
Van Nam, Aron
Salter, Daniel
Perine, James
Clendenny, John
Lakerman, Nathanel
Bush, Garrit (by mark)
Christopher, Joseph
Cozine, Jacobus
Vanpelt, Peter (by mark)
Wood, Aren (by mark)
Fountain, Charles
Seloof, Jacob (by mark)
Merrell, John
Barger, Jacob
Micheau, Paul
Van Name, Simon
Durand, Peter
Wood, Richard
Wandel, John
Crusc...?, Cornlies
Crocheron, Abraham
Decker, John
Sagin, Elishe (by mark)
Butler, Daniel
Egberts, Peter
Christopher, Edmen
Christopher, Richard
Kingston, Thos
Decker, Joseph (by mark)
Lisk, James
Rolph, Jo^s
Dongan, Rich^d
Housman, John
Mackey, John
Housman, John
Marling, Peter (by mark)
Housman, Peter
Cosyne, Garret
Van Name, Aron, Jr.
Housman, Richard
Vansise, Chareles (by mark)
Keen, John
Krouse, Henry
Speer, John
Corson, Dowie (by mark)
Norylan (?), Samuel
Duffey, James
Merceriau, Jacob
Jones, W^m (by mark)

Stilwill, John
Vansise, Charles (by mark)
Krusen, Cornelius
Varick, Rey[s] (?)

Lynch, Tho.
Amerman, Jan
Amerman, Jan, Jr.
Ryersz, Gozen

The following took the oath before John Bedell:

Corsen, Daniel
Corsen, Richard
Dupuy, Moses
Barbank, Peter
Vanderbilt, John
Michel, John (by mark)
Decker, Jacob
Van Cef't (?), Cornelius
Seguin, John
Merel, Simon (by mark)
Van Pelt, John
Baker, Nicholas
Barcklow, Garret
Winants, John
Prall, Peter
Lakerr, Thomas
Melchet, Abraham (by mark)
Pritchet, James (by mark)
Gerbrantz, Christian
Cole, Beniamen
Butler, Henry (by mark)
Decker, Matthias (by mark)
Dupuy, Nicholus (by mark)
Simonson, Abraham (by mark)
Mucklane, Charles
Dupuy, John
Barrager, Hendrick
Prall, Benjamin (by mark)
McIntyre, John
Price, Benjamin
Dupuy, Barnt
Jones, Edward
Butler, John (by mark)
Pritchet, William
Prall, Benjamin
Deneyck, Andrew (by mark)
Breasted, John
Lisk, John
Vreland, Helmus
Simoson, John
Tysen, Barent
Selof, Peter (by mark)
Jones, Edward
Vaname, Peter
Lawrence, James
Fountain, Vincent (by mark)
Morgan, John
Simonson, John

Wood, Stephen
Merrell, William
Tysen, John
Haughwout, Nicholas
Speer, Abraham
Dupuy, John
La Tourrette, Paul
Bush, Edward
Crocheron, Daniel
Martino, Benjamin
Prall, Abraham
Wright, John (by mark)
Simonson, Barnt
Bell, Silas
Wade, Samuel
Moullony, Peter
Simonson, Daniel
Dupuy, Peter
Saunders, Richard
Van Name, Moses
Smith, Mattias (by mark)
Blake, William (by mark)
Silve, Joseph (by mark)
Salsby (?), William
Vanderbilt, Jacob
Crips, John (by mark)
Crocheron, Jacob
Simonson, Isaac
Simonson, Arthur
Decker, Mathias
Merel, Wilam[es], (by mark)
Webster, George
Wood, James
Decker, Samuel
Decker, Isaac
Bedell, Silas, Jr.
Dupuy, Ch.
Dupuy, Aron
Ridgway, Thomas
Cannon, David
Cannon, David, Jr.
Cannon, Isaac
Cannon, Jacob
Bessonett, Daniel
Decker, Matthew
Simonson, John
Crocheron, Henry
Simonson, John

Murshero, Paul (by mark)
Post, Peter
Post, Garret
Dehart, Samuel (by mark)
Dehart, Matthias
Post, Abraham (by mark)
Van Pelt, John
La Tourrette, John

Dehart, Edward
Gerbrantz, Daniel
Roome, Law^r
Keirstead, Samuel
Webb, Richard
Prall, Abraham
Bedell, Israel
Root, Robey

It is possible that the following "Names of Inhabitants of the Town of Hempstead 1673" are of persons taking the oath as prescribed by Governor Colve (DHNY 1:658):

John ....
John Smith Blew
Richard Geldersly, Sen
....
Vrolphert Jacobs
Jan Carman
John Symons , Jun
Robert Jackson
Symon Tory
John Smith
Peter Janse Schol
Richard Gildersly
Robbert Beedill
George Hallet
Samuel Allen
Richard Valentyn
Kaleb Carman
John Williams
Thomas Richmore
John Ellesson
Edward Spry
William Osborne
Edward Remsen
John Fossaker
John Sorram
James Payne
William Fixton
Samuel Denton
Robberd Hobbs
Thomas Sodderd
John Smith, Jun
Joseph Williams
Ralph Haal
Daniel Beedell
John Jackson
Johnathan Smith
John Champion
John Hobbs
John Langd
Jonathan Semmes
John Bordes
..... Comes

Robbard Marisseu
Mos Hemmery
John Beets, carpenter
Samuel Embry
Matthew Beedel
Thomas Ellison
Philip Davis
..... Hopkins
....
Adam View
Edward Titus
Richard Eliison
John Seavin
Thomas Teasay
Thomas Ireland
Thomas Ellison
Joseph Gem
Thomas Champion
Joseph Pettet
Richard Fotter
John Beddell
Thomas Southward
John Beates
Calvet Goullet
Christoffel Yeomans
John Woully
Edward Banbury
Thomas Gowes
John Mavein
Wm Thorne
Joshua Watske
Benjamin Symenson
Jan Roelossen
Elbert Hubssen
Lewis Niot
John Ellison, Jun
Thomas Seabrook
Samuel Jackson
John Pine
Peter Jansen
William Ware

Solomon Semmar
Teunis Smith
Richard Valentin, Jun
Joseph Wood
Herman Flouwer
William Dose
Symon Foster
Henry Mott
Wm. Fourmer
Joseph Small
Walter Pine
Josia Carman
John Peacock
John Quakerson

Thomas Daniels
John Napper
Richard Osborn
George Robbert
Charles Abram
Thomas Appelbe
Samuel Smith
..... Persell
Adam Mott, Jun
Samuel Jackson
Joseph Truax
Joseph Hoyt &
Nine others whose names are lost

INDEX OF PERSONS INCIDENTALLY MENTIONED AND IN
THE OATHS OF ALLEGIANCE

DALSEN, John Balthus 37
DAMEN, Jan 91
DANIEL, Pieter 92
  Thomas 100
DANIELSEN, Jacob 78
DANSWICK, William 87
DASCH/DAESCH,
  John Baltus/Balthus 26,
    29, 39, 41
DA SILVA, Miguel Pacheco 59
DATLIFF, Henry 42, 53
DAVID, Hayman viii
  James 78
  John 88
DAVIES, Willem 93
DAVIS, Philip 99
DAVITSEN, Jan 86
DAWSON, George 97
DAY, John 96
D'BEAUVOIS, Jacobus 91
DE ..., Manewel 86
DEBAENE, Joost 92
DEBELE, John 30, 56
DEBOYS, see DUBOIS
DE CAMP, Laurens Janse 92
DECKER, Abraham 95
  Charles 96, 97
  Gerritt Jansa 88
  Isaac 95, 98
  Jacob 88, 98
  Johanes 97
  John 97 (2)
  John Broerson 88
  Joseph 97
  Mathias 98 (2)
  Matthew 95, 97, 98
  Matthew, Jr. 95
  Moses 97
  Richard 97
  Samuel 98
DE CONSILIE, Jean 92
DE FORREST, Isaac 78
DEGROOT/DEGROAT, Garret 96
  Jacob Fredricksen 86
  Peter 96
  Staes 93
DE HAMAECKER, Basteiaen 86
DEHART/DE HAART, Balthazar 78
  Edward 99
  Matthias 99
  Samuel 99
DE HAYEN, Isaac 78
DEHOGOS, Johanas 89
DE HONDE, Coutrie Daniel 78

DE HONNEUR, Guillaume 78
DE HUBERT, Jeronimus 82
DEKEY, Jacobus/Jacob 67
DELA MONTAGNE/DE LAMONTANIJ,
  Johann[s] 78
  William 78, 87
DE LA PLAINE, Nicolas 78
DELLOE, George 87
DEMARR, Petter 89
DE MEYER, Nicolaus 78
DE MILT, Anthony 78
DE MONT, Wallraven, Jr. 88
  Wallraven, Sr. 89
DE MOTT, Maghell 89
DE MY[r]S, William 87
DENEYCK, Andrew 98
DENTON, Samuel 99
DE PEISTER, Johannes 78
DE ROMAGNAC, Catherine 30
DE RONDE, L. 32, 54
  Lambertus 16
DESBROSSES, Jacques/Jaque 43, 66
  Jas./James 15, 19, 47, 68
DESILLE, Lourens 78
DES MAIZEAUX, Lewis 23
  Magdaline 23
DES MAREST, David 84
  David, de Jonger 85
  Jean 84
  Samuel 85
DE VOOR/DU VOOR, Daniel 93
  Davit 86
DE VRIES, Jean 93
DE WEERHEM, Ambrosius 78
DE WINT, Elizabeth 23
DEWITT/DE WIIT, Andries 88
  Johannes 78
  John 88
  Pieter Janse 92
  Terrick Claes 89
D'HARRIETTE, Anna vii
  Benjamin vii
DIEFFENDORF, Jacob 33
DIETZ, Johan Willem 17, 71
DIRCKSE/DIRCKZEN, Lucas 78
  Meyer Jan 78
  Paulus 91
  Stoffel 92
  Volkert 92
DISLEAU, Mary Elizabeth 20
DITLOFF, Hinrich 73
DOECKLES (=Douglass?), William 78
DONGAN, Thomas/Governor vi, 87
  Rich[d] 97

VAN WICKELEN, Evert Janssen 92
VAN WIEN, Hendrick 88
VAN WYCK/VAN WIJCK
  Catharine 73
  Cornelis Barense 90
  Theodorus 90
VAN ZANDT, Wynant 16
VARETANGER, Jacob Hendrickzen 80
VARIAN, Isaac 53
VARICK, Rey[s] (?) 98
VARLETT, Abram 83
VEALE, Thomas, Junr. 84
VECHTEN, Claes Arense 90
  Hendrick 90
VERDON, Thomas 91
VERGEREAU, Peter 26,27
VERKERCK, Barent 92
  Roeloff 90
VERMLJE, Isaacq 85
VERMOON, Jacob 80
VERNOIJ, Cornelis 88
VERPLANK, Abraham 80
VERSCHUER/VERSCHIER, Hendrick 92
  Jochem 92
  Wouter Gysbert 92
VERVEEL/VERVEELEN, Daniel 80
  Johannes 85
VESEY, William 23, 54
VIDET, Jan 80
VIERVAN, Cornelis Adrianss 85
VIEW, Adam 99
VINCENT, Adrian 80
VING, Jan 80
VIS, Jacob 80
VISSCHER, Barent 55
VISSER, Theunis vii
VOS, Nicolaes 83
VRELAND/VREELAND, Helmus 98
  Jacob 96
VROOMAN, B. 45

WADE, Samuel 98
WALDRON, Daniel 92
  Resolveert 80, 84
WALLAFFISH, William 89
WALTER, Elizabeth 51
WALTON, W[m] 96
WANDEL, John 97 (2)
WANSHAER, Anthony 92
  Jan 80
WARD, Mathew 52
  Samuel 95
  William 97

WARE, William 99
WATERS, Edward 84
WATERSON, William 6
WATSKE, Joshua 99
WEAVER, Hendrick vii
WEBB, John 96
  Richard 99
WEBER, Johannes 62, 63
WEBSTER, George 98
WEESENER/WESNER, Johannes 71
WEILAND, Johan Leonhard 40
WEISS, G. M. 24, 29, 40, 58, 64
WELLS, Henry, Jr. 67
  James 21
WENTWORTH, Mary 13
WERTH, Johann Jacob 17, 24
WESSELS/WESSELLS/WESSELZEN/
  WESSELL
  David 80
  Francis 86
  Herman 80
  Warnar 80
WEST, John 56
WESTBROCK, Dirrick 88
  Johannas 88
WESTERLO, Catharine 71
WESTFALIN/WESTFALLIN, Abl 88
  Claes 88
  Johannas 88
  Symon 89
WEYGAND, John Albert/J.A.
  15, 16, 26, 29, 31, 34, 35,
  37, 39, 41, 42, 45, 47, 48,
  50, 51, 53, 54, 65, 70, 73
WHITE, Gilbert 94
WHITEFIELD, Justice 87
WHITEHEAD, Daniel 93
WHITEWAY, Samuel 87
WHITSON, John 67
WIDERWAX, Andrios 30
WIEDERSHYNE/WEATHERSHINE,
  Daniel 35
  Jane 73
WIEJNANTS, Pieter 91
WIJCKOFF, Claes Pieterse 92
  Gerrit Pieterse 92
  Hendrick Pieterse 92
  Jan Pieterse 92
  Pieter Claasen 92
WIJNHART, Cornelis 91
WILEMAN, Henry 72
WILL/WILLE, John viii
  John Michael 17, 35

Persons with no surname